Practical Theology Beyond the Empirical Turn

For Keith and for Maia

Practical Theology Beyond the Empirical Turn

Heather Walton

scm press

© Heather Walton 2025

Published in 2025 by SCM Press

Editorial office
3rd Floor, Invicta House,
110 Golden Lane,
London EC1Y 0TG, UK
www.scmpress.co.uk

SCM Press is an imprint of Hymns Ancient & Modern Ltd
(a registered charity)

Hymns Ancient & Modern® is a registered trademark of
Hymns Ancient & Modern Ltd
13A Hellesdon Park Road, Norwich,
Norfolk NR6 5DR, UK

All rights reserved. No part of this publication may be reproduced,
stored in a retrieval system, or transmitted,
in any form or by any means, electronic, mechanical,
photocopying or otherwise, without the prior permission of
the publisher, SCM Press.

The Author has asserted their right under the Copyright, Designs and
Patents Act 1988 to be identified as the Author of this Work

British Library Cataloguing in Publication data

A catalogue record for this book is available
from the British Library

ISBN: 978-0-334-05899-1

EU GPSR Authorised Representative
LOGOS EUROPE, 9 rue Nicolas Poussin, 17000, LA ROCHELLE, France
E-mail: Contact@logoseurope.eu

No part of this book may be used or reproduced in any manner for the
purpose of training artificial intelligence technologies or systems.

Typeset by Regent Typesetting

Contents

Acknowledgements	vii
Prologue: Beginning at the End of the World	ix

Part One: The Changed Climate of Practical Theological Research — 1

1 Research, Relationality and Relationships: New Ontologies in Critical Context — 3

2 Knowing, Knowing What We Don't Know and Being Mixed Up: Empiricism, Reflexivity and Representation — 18

3 Borrowing, Gifting and Growing Together: Relations between Theology and Social Research Practices — 37

Part Two: Practical Theology as Creative Work — 67

4 The Poetics and Politics of Practical Theology — 69

5 Reimagining Research as (Creative) Responsiveness — 95

6 Theology as Art in Our Troubles — 121

Part Three: Makings — 147

7 Making One: A Theopoetics of Practice — 149

8 Making Two: Heloise and Me, or, On Being a (Practical) Theologian — 168

9 Making Three: Writings in the Disaster — 183

Epilogue: Not a Conclusion but a Connection 190
Suggested Reading in Creative Research Methods 195
Bibliography 197
Index of Names and Subjects 213

Acknowledgements

This book is dedicated to the memory of my father and with love to my daughter; to both these beloved artists in my life.

It owes a great deal to a great many other people. I want especially to thank my partner Reinier for his loving support in what has been a *very* long process, and for all his practical help with preparing the typescript for submission. David Shervington has been patient, encouraging and kind throughout this project and it has been good to work with SCM Press again. I am grateful to Lou Davis for allowing me to use her art as a cover image and also for being the indomitable, first doctoral researcher on Glasgow University's PhD programme in theology through creative practice.

The diverse, international community of practical theologians has nourished and supported me for many years. My work on this text was helped by some members in particular. Grateful thanks go to Bonnie Miller-McLemore, Wren Radford, Pete Ward and Simon Hallonsten for their perspectives on drafts. Elaine Graham, Nicola Slee, Pam Couture, Stephen Pattison, Zoe Bennett, Doug Gay, Natalie Wigg-Stevenson, Tone Kaufman, Jonas Ideström, Callid Keefe Perry, Courtney Goto, Mark Johnston and Sayyidah Zaidi have all contributed through their generous friendship and their generative thinking. Beyond practical theology I am grateful to those who share my passion for bringing theology into dialogue with the creative arts and in particular my friends Alison Jasper, David Jasper, Debbie Lewer and Pádraig Ó Tuama.

Journeying with PhD candidates has undoubtedly been the most rewarding aspect of my academic career. I treasure the insights I have gained and all the friendships I have formed through this work. The ideas that are explored here are ones I have tested out with many of you in seminars and supervisions. Thank you for your curiosity, insight and astute critical comments.

Thank you to the Protestantse Theologische Universiteit of the Netherlands, and in particular to Henk de Roest, for hosting me as a visiting scholar during the very early days of this project.

Chapter 7 of this book is an edited version of my Presidential Address to the International Academy for Practical Theology. It was originally published in 2019 as 'A Theopoetics of Practice: Re-forming in Practical Theology', *International Journal of Practical Theology*, 23(1).

Heather Walton
Epiphany 2025

Prologue
Beginning at the End of the World

At the beginning I pray that this work might be acceptable:

To God who is mass, might, matter.
To God who is living, fragile, mortal flesh.
To God who is stable, enduring, resistant.
To God who is conceived and carried and cradled
To God who is strength and utter strangeness.
To God I have touched and felt.
To God who is solid and does not move.
To God who is tender and draws breath softly.

I offer it:

To God who is warmed by the sun and worn smooth by the waves.
To God who is sharp as a sword; piercing my heart also.
To God who is the cornerstone of the house, my dwelling place.
To God who refuses me refuge and offers no place to lay my head.
To God who shelters me as the small brown bird
who has made her nest in the temple courts.
*To God who tears down the sacred walls so not one stone is left
upon another. And the altar is bare. And it is broken.*

To God my Rock and my Redeemer.

Untimely times

If this book had been finished in the proper way and at the proper time it might have been quite a different text. Up to now my works have been long in the conception but the births have been easy and relatively painless. This time the idea was firmly implanted and it seemed very clear what needed to be done. There had to be a book that asked questions about the empirical turn in practical theology. It should explore whether in our adoption of some favoured approaches to research we had missed a number of important theoretical and methodological developments within the fields of anthropology and sociology. In particular, it should address the theological potential of arts-based and creative research methods that have long been integral to these research fields. Simple. Not a problem. The contract was signed. I was not expecting a difficult labour. However, the writing was interrupted and long delayed. Stuff happens …

The December 2019 UK election confirmed the exit of Britain from the European Union. This was a particularly painful outcome for my country, Scotland (which voted overwhelmingly to remain), and for my own household with close family ties across the Continent. The outcome came during a period of growing alarm concerning the devastating effects of climate change – as fires raged uncontrolled across the Australian bush. The international political context appeared equally combustible. Longstanding injustices smouldered into flame across the world and the fragile institutions built to secure cooperation on health, conflict avoidance and the support of refugees were increasingly being ignored or dismantled. When at the very end of that dismal year my university asked me to change my personal password I typed in WORLDS/END. The prompt came back to 'confirm' and I endorsed this grim prophecy by firmly typing the characters again.

Despite my pessimism I was not thinking then that the New Year would see the complete transformation of the life I had known. I did not expect it would open a chapter in which shared anxiety, grief and loss would be accompanied by a devastating confirmation of the consequences of social and racial inequality demonstrated in starkly different mortality statistics. I was not expecting such a casual unmooring from the assumed certainties of common life. Nevertheless, when rumours of a new virus circulating were confirmed in early January I could not help but think that I was somehow to blame. If only I had not chosen that particular phrase as the everyday portal into my academic and religious vocation. If only …

Everybody has their own story to tell of what life was like in the Covid years. Mine is a very mundane one. I struggled with anxiety – overwhelming at times. I spent a hard period away from my partner, living with and caring for my mother and, like most academics, faced the challenges of moving my teaching and supervision online. These events all

PROLOGUE: BEGINNING AT THE END OF THE WORLD

seem very distant now but something important changed for me during that period when the habitual rhythms of life were disrupted for a while. Perhaps because I had now experienced that normal life does not always 'carry on as normal', the reality of climate change moved from being a niggling worry to an urgent concern. I grasped, at long last, that the environmental crisis had to move to the centre of my life and work rather than being ritually mentioned in the final paragraph of an article or in the last section of the prayers I lead in worship.

At the same time, work on this book dwindled to nothing. I had entered a long period of 'hibernation' in which many aspects of my life appeared completely dormant but were beginning to take on new forms. During this time my partner and I rented a cottage on Scotland's Fife coast for a couple of weeks. I was teaching remotely at this point and there was a good internet connection. I rearranged my schedule so we could do a coastal walk each day. I was hoping that being by the sea would refresh me. Below are four extracts from the journal I kept during this time. They give some indication of the processes that have reshaped my work on this book and continue to reshape my theological vocation.

Journalling the not normal

Friday 6 November

I am not saying this out loud yet but coming here may have been a bad mistake. I was hoping that the change would renew me, gently, but when we walked out along the coast this afternoon I felt as if my inner territory of boulders and stony rubble had been inscribed on to the landscape also. The stretch of coast we scrambled over today was bleak and desolate. Long ribs of black rocks clawing out to sea which the locals call boat wreckers. Debris of ash vented from prehistoric volcanoes. Great fissures and cracks in the rocks. There is brokenness inside me and outside me also.

It's all such a wasteland. 60,000-plus Covid deaths now. Disaster of Brexit. Desperate migrants in wee boats risking the English Channel. Four dead in the last incident including two children. Small shoes and gloves washed up on the sands. The conspiracy theories are proliferating and shifting like shadows into public life. New forms of racist and extremist politics are rapidly mutating. Other viruses even more deadly than Covid spreading and spreading. And in my dream last night my mother carefully dressed in the lovely silk blouse I bought her, reaching for my hand and asking me, 'Where has my world gone?' I feel as if my familiar world is fast disappearing too. Ruin in the cities and sickness in the forests and fields and seas and everywhere and everywhere.

The discomfort of my neck and between my shoulder blades is continuous now and has crossed the boundary between ache and pain. It is not working at my laptop only. It is the weight of the trouble.

And I am supposed to go on writing my book, teaching my students and preparing my lectures. I am supposed to be creative. To think and speak something meaningful in the middle of all this. Not sure I can …

Tuesday 10 November

My friend Frankie sent me a present. It is a book called *Gift from the Sea*. The author, Anne Lindburgh, went to stay for a while by the sea – seeking to create and be productive. But, she writes, the beach confounds such intentions, it's not a place for flights of the spirit. 'No reading, no writing, no thoughts even. Or not at first.' You become, she says, elemental. 'Flattened by the sea, bare, open empty as the beach', 'Your yesterday's inscriptions all erased by today's tides.' Not action – but being open. 'Choiceless as a beach waiting for gifts from the sea.'

It is evocative writing but is there truth in it?

I do feel, as I walk this coast in all sorts of weathers, I'm being washed by the strong winds and am yielding little by little to the motion of the tides. This is a holy coast. There are caves where saints sheltered. The remains of chapels where pilgrims rested on their pilgrim way. I enter these roofless places half expecting to sense some presence but am calmed instead by the emptiness they offer. Not fullness, but space.

There is a rock we passed today known here as 'the castle'. It's huge, dark and grim but this afternoon it was suddenly bathed in late afternoon sunshine. All the massive bulk of it burnished into gold. An utter transformation. A vision of glory. Gone very soon but I saw it.

'All your waves and billows have gone over me and yet, O God, I remember you are my rock.' I touched the skin of the great stone all mottled with lichen and sensed its ancient heart beating.

Thursday 12 November

We have got used to spotting seals now. Learned how to distinguish between them and half-submerged rocks. We know the shape of their heads and how often it is simply the tip of the nose that is visible at first.

PROLOGUE: BEGINNING AT THE END OF THE WORLD

So now we see them most days but today was very special. This seal swam parallel to us as we walked along the beach. It was only metres away and was clearly as curious about us as we were about them. Their huge eyes watching us and the impossible curve of their spine as they ducked and dived between the waves.

We lost the seal at the Cormorant rocks. A whole line of the ancient birds stood silhouetted black against the white winter sky. They stand in 'cruciform' with their wings outstretched to dry. I found the sight of them almost unbearably painful. In the Bible cormorants along with owls and ravens inhabit wasted cities. They live among the ashes and their rasping calls sound where no human voices speak and where songbirds have stopped singing. Black crosses marking the burnt ruins.

But here they are dark and wild standing to face the wind. A living mark on this living landscape of rocks and sand and seals and people in fragile cruciform configurations. The silhouettes of the oil rigs beyond are also etched black upon the sky.

Saturday 14 November

When we packed to come here we made sure we had waterproof trousers as well as coats. We told ourselves we would walk sometime each day – whatever the weather. But to be honest I did not believe it. I thought if the weather was bad Reinier might stride out but I would more likely curl up with a book. Take a long bath. Stare into the fire. Sleep. But no. I'm out there and I love it. Perhaps even more when the weather is stormy. It does the raging for me. I can delegate ... which is a blessed relief.

Today is the second day of a deep fog. Walking the coast there's nowhere to rise above the mist. It's an element more like water than air – we move through it with the smooth motions of swimmers and it both supports and resists us.

The colours have faded and our world is only yards wide. No horizon. The offshore rocks have vanished and no line holds between earth and air, sea and sky. The sound of the waves is muffled – but somehow the cries of the small wading birds still carry. A poignant clear sound. Pitched at that perfect point between joy and sorrow.

Starting again

So all my writing deadlines were missed; work was picked up briefly and then abandoned for months and when I found the resources to write again I had developed a different perspective on my task. Had they been completed to schedule, these first pages would most likely have contained denunciations of the manifold faults and failings in practical theology; a catalogue of errors masquerading as the necessary academic background from which to propose other ways forward. I might have written about the ways in which 'we' as practical theologians had lacked vision, conformed to conservative agendas in research, not read widely enough, and generally failed to engage with theoretical and methodological developments in qualitative research crucial to our field. The word 'we' would not have been used to denote shared identity and common bonds *as I now intend it to signify*. I would have found a way to make it very clear that the writer – and a few select others – could be exempted from the dismal disappointments of the discipline.

I now ask myself, 'What was going on here?' Why was I so angry and so eager to apportion blame? What was at stake in my eagerness to defend certain research approaches and denigrate others? Who would my voice have been raised against but colleagues – many of whom are also dearly loved friends! Where we stand now, at this time and in this place, it feels more appropriate to acknowledge that we are all facing troubles. Familiar resources and patterns of thinking are being erased by the tides. We all wait, appropriately humbled and empty-handed, for gifts from the sea. We are all seeking a place and sign amid the ruins and the living wildness that endures. And it is very hard to see clearly here.

These realizations did not emerge from those two weeks of transformation as I walked a wet and windy coast – or even the months of social separation that preceded them. However, the reflexive mode they produced have enabled me to enter into this brokenness more deeply and acknowledge its presence 'in me' as well as 'out there'; it is not an 'other people problem'. The knowledge that we are broken people who live in a broken world is not, of course, new knowledge. Arguably it is the first theological premise. But what I am seeking to address here is something of the guilt-grief experienced at this particular historical moment, when the consequences of injustice and exploitation are so clearly written not only in media accounts but in the living world around us. In its travails.

And the Church does not stand as a safe shelter amid this turmoil. It too appears threatened by the flood tides. The little congregation I now belong to was once one of the strongest in Scotland. Our ragged community is still vibrant but we struggle to keep on going in buildings we can no longer well maintain. And it is not simply institutional religious life that is at breaking point in the UK. The beliefs we hold and the ways we worship increasingly lack resonance for many. A few years back at my father's funeral, friends and family joined to pronounce the words from the service book together. I was acutely aware that the hard, and sometimes ugly, old phrases hardly spoke to me, let alone to the majority of those gathered to affirm common bonds and express grief. I was gripped by a pain of loss. Not only bereaved of a parent but bereaved of a shared sacred space in which to place my deepest loves. We are living between ruins and wildness.

Reflections like the ones I am sharing here may reveal why I am drawn to creative writing and arts-based research methods in my academic and theological work. I am seeking ways to re-form, revision and renew; 'to make and make again/where such unmaking reigns' (Rich, 1978, p. 64). They might also shed some light on why I have been such a dialectical (disputatious) and judgemental thinker – and am perhaps not yet entirely transformed! This is partly personal temperament; an inheritance from the warm but gruff and highly combative Yorkshire working-class culture in which I was raised. But it has also been the result of my fear and anger. I know I am aggressively critical of the positions taken by others because I don't have secure solutions myself and often feel overwhelmed by the shambles of it all. The weary, broken, shambles of it all.

So now I have made a different start to my work. I deleted *everything* I had previously written and am attempting to construct a different kind of book. It is still located in the same conceptual terrain and remains fundamentally a book that explores the impact of developments in methodological approaches upon research undertaken in practical theology.[1] This is a sensitive sub-area of the discipline and I won't promise that what follows will be entirely unpolemical; I hardly know how to write any other way, but I will try and be kindlier. Norman Denzin, one of the most significant writers and thinkers in qualitative methodologies, designated as one of his criteria for excellent scholarship that

---

1 I should emphasize that this is a large but limited terrain. Practical theology is a diverse discipline and many different concerns and approaches are currently active and generative within it. Its work is by no means constrained to the areas I discuss in this book. It's not all about methodologies and nor should it be! See *The Wiley Blackwell Companion to Practical Theology* (Miller-McLemore, 2012b) for a much fuller picture.

it cares and is kind (2003, pp. 123–4). This seems good to me. It is an approach that I see modelled in the research I most admire and it sets an example I wish to follow here. In what I write I shall attempt to share in the best way I can what I have found interesting, challenging, or simply very useful in my engagement with contemporary theories, research methodologies and creative practices. I shall attempt to present clearly and critique constructively and my motivation throughout will be theological.

This book is in three parts. In Part One, 'The Changed Climate of Practical Theological Research', I will consider the changing terrain of qualitative research in the context of our current global crises. I will highlight key challenges and ask questions about the way relations between the social sciences (particularly anthropology and sociology) and practical theology are currently imaged and may be reimagined. Part Two is titled 'Practical Theology as Creative Work'. This explores the poetic conventions that *already* structure work in practical theology. It then describes how the use of arts-engaged methods enables responsiveness to contexts and issues that are difficult to address and invites responsiveness to these areas in new ways of writing. Finally, it explores what might happen if we took inspiration from art to develop modes for practical theological reflection in the climate disaster. Part Three of this book is rather different from the first two parts. I have titled it 'Makings' and within it I present three chapters that employ different creative modes to express my reflections upon practical theology and the vocation of the practical theologian.

PART ONE

The Changed Climate of Practical Theological Research

My concern in Part One of this book is to explore some of the methodological and theoretical developments that have taken place during practical theology's 'empirical turn' towards forms of qualitative research drawn, primarily, from anthropology and sociology. I will situate these developments not as internally generated progressions but as responses to the social and political challenges that have impacted upon these social science disciplines. In so doing I will be postulating an integral link between research practices in practical theology and our theological vocation in these challenging times.

Chapter 1 begins this task by presenting the hugely influential work of the anthropologist Anna Tsing as an example of ethnographic research in the climate emergency. Tsing's deeply engaged and committed approach has resonated widely and impacted profoundly. However, its way of proceeding contradicts many of the assumptions as to what constitutes good research practice that are currently held within practical theology. I will then go on to explore ethnography further and place its developing trajectory within the contemporary theoretical context of 'relational ontologies'. This has encouraged and enabled such moves as Tsing's in qualitative research to take place. The chapter concludes by asking what a focus on relationality might mean for relationships within our discipline.

Chapter 2 brings these concerns closer to home as I consider three big words that underpin practical theology's current approach to qualitative research. These are 'empirical', 'reflexivity' and 'representation'. This exercise enables me to argue that we need greater fluidity and openness in our research practices, although I shall continue to maintain that a collegial (if still argumentative) diversity should be regarded as a strength rather than a weakness in practical theology. Whatever methodology or approach is taken, the shared challenge to all practical theologians is to view their social research as both justice-oriented and sacramental. It must have the theological potential to draw us deeper into the divine economy.

Chapter 3 considers what modes of relation we might perceive as existing between practical theology and the disciplines from which some of our current methodological approaches were born. I shall present three 'stories' to illustrate three models of interdisciplinary encounter currently in circulation. These are simply models. None of them are exclusive and in reality they merge into one another. However, my own favoured approach will become clear. Just as an inclusive understanding now governs my approach to the community of scholarship that is practical theology, I long to see this community engaging more deeply with others – in scholarly, interdisciplinary ways and in solidarity as we respond to environmental and cultural challenges. It is my presupposition that in the (very) small world of research methodologies and the (even) smaller world of research methodologies in practical theology, the relations we form are not unconnected to the stances we take in response to the (enormously) bigger issues being played out on a planetary or even a cosmological level.

I

Research, Relationality and Relationships: New Ontologies in Critical Context

A spectre is haunting practical theology. It is the ghostly presence of the social scientist. However, it is a presence we have summoned and not one we have sought to exorcise. This fleshless figure has been extremely useful for us. It enables us to define our work in contrast to a spectral form from another world whose cold touch could petrify the theological life right out of us. At the beginning of the empirical turn in practical theology (see pp. 40–2), Johannes van der Ven made the self-evident hostility of the social scientist towards religion the reason why practical theologians themselves needed to adopt 'empirical' research methods in order to explore faith-based practice. Today we inhabit a very different disciplinary context yet often ritually evoke the same presence.

Frequently we add the preface 'secular' when referring to a shadowy persona who makes clinical judgements concerning validity, objectivity and evidence. The 'secular social scientist' hovering at the edge of our collective consciousness is sceptical concerning the ability of theologians to engage in proper research, and disputes any normative claims arising from their research projects. Their allegiances lie with the clear values of the academy rather than the messy world of a lived religious belonging which most practical theologians call home. In a complex process of identity negotiation, we *both* measure ourselves against *and* define our difference through referencing this figure.[1]

---

1 In her article 'You Don't Look Like a Baptist Minister' (2017), Natalie Wigg-Stevenson explores the boundary-marking processes through which we construct communal identities. She demonstrates how processes of 'othering' those we perceive as threatening is one of the mechanisms employed to generate a sense of belonging. She also shows how identity markers become intertwined in theological frame building. Assumptions of who and what we are, as well as who we are not, become intertwined with the way we form theological understandings. What is particularly important in Wigg-Stevenson's account is her description of how these conceptual frameworks may be shifted through grace-full encounters

My intention in this chapter is to present a rather different picture of the social scientist and, indeed, social research in the political and theoretical milieu we currently inhabit.

For, although we continually refer to social scientists and their 'research methods', this company is diverse and their methodologies are (highly) subject to ongoing change and development. Furthermore, practical theology itself has had a long engagement with the social sciences and there have been diverse emphases and different epochs within this.[2] This hinterland is hugely important but my focus is upon what I am designating the 'empirical turn' in practical theology. This began some 40 years ago when both quantitative and qualitative research methods practised within sociology were embraced as a means of elucidating theological reflection on religious practice. As this movement developed, anthropological approaches to the study of communities (particularly congregations) became deeply influential and ethnography, in particular, has emerged as our favoured research approach.

So this is where this chapter begins. With ethnography in our current context and with a brief case study of work by the celebrated contemporary anthropologist and ethnographer Anna Tsing. I choose this not only because of the challenges it delivers to our preconceptions of 'the secular social scientist' but also because of the transformative impact Tsing's work has produced. My focus then expands to include a wider discussion of ethnography in the current context, drawing upon the contribution of another significant anthropologist, Tim Ingold. This, in turn, leads to a consideration of the emergent theoretical landscape against which qualitative research methods are mutating and taking on new forms.

---

with those we have erected protective barriers against. It is such encounters that I am seeking to enable in this chapter.

2 In North America, in particular, there has been a long engagement with psychology that goes back at least a century. In my own context, economics and sociology have been drawn upon in formulating Christian approaches to public policy for a similar period. Liberation theology and other justice-seeking and contextual theological movements have also drawn heavily upon social theory (e.g. Marxism, feminist and decolonial theory) in developing their critical perspectives.

Ethnography at the end of the world

Anna Tsing is a living, breathing, 'bodied' qualitative researcher whose ethnographic work has made a profound contribution to contemporary understandings of human relationships: with one another, with other beings and with the living planet. Her best-known book, *The Mushroom at the End of the World* (2015), does not detail how to ameliorate apocalyptic anxiety through the use of hallucinogenic substances – although there have been many times recently when I would have gladly turned to such relief! The subtitle of her work is *On the Possibility of Life in Capitalist Ruins* and it interrogates and reflects upon the devastation of both ecological and social structures in the all-pervasive system we inhabit.

'We have the problem of living in that ugly ruin ... impossible as it is,' Tsing writes (2015, p. 212). And yet despite the impossibility, all the waste and loss, the central symbol of the book is the resilient ability of a particular type of highly prized mushroom to thrive in landscapes despoiled and scarred by human activity. They survive alongside communities of people diverse, transient, and who are sometimes considered waste – or wasted themselves. In her ethnographic work, Tsing travels these landscapes attending to the many facets of intertwined life she encounters within them. She notes how people form fragile relationships with the natural world as they tend broken forest habitats in order to harvest the valuable mushrooms. They cannot heal or restore – too late, too much lost – but they are part of a revitalizing web as heterogeneous and diverse as fungal life itself. 'Rather than redemption', she writes, they pick 'through the heap of alienation ...[and] acquire patience to mix with multi-species others without knowing where the world in process is going' (2015, p. 264).

Tsing's ethnographic work is a project of deep spiritual attentiveness, alert political listening, that takes place amid 'the wholesale, interconnected, and seemingly unstoppable ruination' in which it is 'not easy to know how to make a life, much less avert planetary destruction' (2015, p. 282). What is attended to are the ruins in their desolation but also those delicate, fragile entanglements and boundary confusions that mark the emergence of a *latent commons* on the 'overgrown verges of our blasted landscapes' (2015, p. 282). Tsing is careful not to romanticize these latent commons. While maintaining that they are ubiquitous (to be found in many sites of ruination) they are also fragile and ephemeral. Furthermore, they are not places of reclamation and regeneration offering sure signs of hope for the future. Instead, latent commons are convivial places of encounter experienced in the present moment where 'mutualist and nonantagonistic entanglements [are] found within the play of this confusion' (2015, p. 55). While their presence is testimony to the comforts of 'company, human and not human' (2015, p. 282) they cannot redeem us. Nor are they places to escape to. Rather, they exist 'here and now, amidst the trouble' (2015, p. 255) as testimony to the myriad ties that combine together into a form of life which is stubborn but inglorious; a '[m]uddling through with others … always in the midst of things' (2015, p. 278).

The insights emerging from Tsing's anthropological study have been deeply influential in discussions of entangled life in the climate emergency. For example, they inform Donna Haraway's *Staying with the Trouble* (2016), a book exploring the resilience required to make meaningful shared lives on/with a damaged planet. It is through disassociating themselves from the living networks Tsing identifies (which are essential to mortal creatures) that humans have brought planetary existence to this point of crisis. Therefore the first thing to learn is the significance of the connections that sustain us. A 'staying with' rather than going beyond is required. Haraway writes:

> In urgent times, many of us are tempted to address trouble in terms of making an imagined future safe, of stopping something from happening … Staying with the trouble does not require such a relationship to times called the future. In fact, staying with the trouble requires learning to be truly present, not as a vanishing pivot between awful or Edenic pasts and apocalyptic or salvific futures, but as mortal[s] … entwined in myriad unfinished configurations of places, times, matters. (Haraway, 2016, p. 1)

Characteristically, Haraway does not present our present state as tragic, but ambivalent. Trouble, she states, derives from a thirteenth-century French verb meaning to stir up, make cloudy or disturb. And learning to live 'in disturbing times, mixed-up times, troubling and turbid times' (2016, p. 1) entails stirring up trouble ourselves in response to devastating political and ecological events, but also calming troubled waters as we seek to live as best we can in a period overflowing with pain – but still shot through with joy. As Tsing's work reminds us, even in our damaged landscapes, we can still smell the glorious living/dying scent of autumn in the air: 'The smell evokes sadness and loss', but it also alerts all the senses to seek with the 'sharp intensity and heightened sensibilities of Autumn ... [paths] into a common life without guarantees' (Tsing, 2015, p. 2).

I have chosen to focus on Tsing's work at this point because it presents a profound example of how social inquiry is increasingly construed in the current landscape of qualitative research. For this is not a marginal text. It has won major prizes for ethnographic writing awarded by learned societies in anthropology.[3] But it is very different in approach to the cautious and methodologically guarded ethnographic work that predominates within practical theology. It is an intervention rather than a representation and there is no pretence at neutrality, objectivity or academic 'distance' here. Instead there is a passionate presentation of the precarious nature of life in the Anthropocene and Tsing's decision to cast her lot with those most at risk in the midst of climate uncertainty. She is deeply present in the text and her own self-narrative is integrally woven into her writing. We are made to feel her anxiety and terror at the 'world's climate going haywire' (2015, p. 1) and her bodily responses to the landscapes, plants and people she meets with on her research journey. Her 'method' is principally to be open and responsive to these myriad encounters and their insistent claims for witnessing:

> To listen and to tell a rush of stories is a *method*. And why not make a strong claim and call it a science, an addition to knowledge. Its research object is contaminated diversity and its unit of analysis is the indeterminate encounter ... A rush of stories cannot be neatly summed up. Its scales do not rest neatly; they draw attention to interrupting geographies and tempos. These interruptions elicit more stories. This is the rush of stories' power as a science. (2015, p. 37)

Ethnographers, as witnesses to 'a history of ruin ... need to follow the broken bits of many stories' (2015, p. 212) and their data, Tsing maintains, will inevitably be as 'contaminated' as the contexts they research. Just as fungal bodies emerge from cosmopolitan identity confusion and 'historical mergings – with trees, with other living and nonliving things' (2015, p. 238), so might new knowledge be the miscegenated outcomes

---

[3] Tsing's *The Mushroom at the End of the World* was awarded the 2016 Victor Turner Prize in Ethnographic Writing from the Society for Humanistic Anthropology and the 2016 Gregory Bateson Book Prize from the Society for Cultural Anthropology.

of illicit mergings with 'research subjects, living and nonliving, and with itself in other forms' (2015, p. 239). Of indeterminate substance, this knowledge is not of the kind it will be possible to codify neatly or analyse definitively – but that is not of utmost importance. Tsing's intention is neither to conceptually categorize her findings nor build a theory from them. It is to incite us to imagine the world differently; in other words, her ends are 'artistic' in the service of the most serious and creative 'science'. She claims that an open-ended approach such as this is required to work in a world which

> is recalcitrant to the kind of 'summing up' that has become the hallmark of modern knowledge ... If a rush of troubled stories is the best way to tell about contaminated diversity then it's time to make that rush a part of our knowledge practices. It is in listening to that cacophony of troubled stories that we might encounter our best hope for precarious survival. (2015, pp. 33–4)

Truth telling in the troubles

What Tsing has created through her ethnographic writing is a work of poetic, prophetic witness that inspires others with its transformative insights. Tim Ingold describes this form of anthropological writing 'a coming together of experience and imagination in a world that is alive and is alive to us' (2018, p. 7). Ingold, who is also an anthropologist of immense distinction, has demonstrated in his own work how many of the conventions we theologians might still assume to be operative within the social sciences are increasingly being challenged from within. He particularly critiques practices of ethnographic research that appropriate living contexts for the purposes of resource extraction and protests against the resulting academic constructions that claim to be built from 'knowledge of' others. He contrasts this (white/colonial) approach[4] with what he believes is a deeper anthropological impulse towards intense noticing *in company with* those who are different from ourselves.[5] This 'is not a means of data gathering but an ontological commitment' to

---

4 For further discussion of how ethnographic research is deeply bound up with the colonial project, see pp. 22–9.

5 Ingold makes here a polemical and heuristic distinction between ethnography and participant observation. In contrast to the former, the latter is imaged positively as the characteristic gesture of anthropology. See Ingold, 2017.

'study with people not to make studies out of them' (2017, p. 21). As stated, such study is not a process of data procurement but a commitment, undertaken today in the context of climate catastrophe, to shared 'inquiry into the conditions and possibilities of human life in the world' (2017, p. 21).

So in Ingold's frame, research is a conversation 'with' in which correspondence happens (see Ingold, 2020) – that is, an exchange of messages as well as a discovery of affinities – and it results in a change in perception not about an object of study but about our common existence in the world; it is 'to make a conversation of human life itself' (2017, p. 22). The 'results' are changed understandings. First, and necessarily, in the researcher themselves and subsequently through the creation of works manifesting correspondences that can be shared and provoke wonder beyond the immediate encounter. So there is an affinity here, Ingold argues, between artistic practice and the traditional anthropological discipline of attentive abiding in 'that they are not about understanding actions and works by embedding them in context – not about accounting for them, ticking them off, and laying them to rest – but about bringing them into presence so that we can address them, and answer to them, directly' (2017, pp. 24–5).

The work of both Tsing and Ingold demonstrate how some world-leading, 'real-life' social scientists are construing their work today. There is a rapidly changing climate of social research and this is having an impact at both macro and micro levels. In terms of the big picture, planetary and justice issues are foregrounded and critical attention is given to the modes of connection (being-with-others) that research entails. At micro level, questions arise about methodological issues such as reflexivity, validity, the nature of 'data', relations between research methods and, indeed, between researchers themselves. I will return to some of these issues later. However, I will first seek to describe the wider theoretical landscape upon which these larger and smaller changes are being played out. This theoretical 'diversion' is necessary because it is through understanding the perspectives being articulated in contemporary theory that we will gain a better sense of the emerging worldviews that are influencing developments in qualitative research.

Being as 'being with': relational ontologies

In referring to a 'theoretical landscape' I am talking about a terrain in which understandings continually shift, mutate and creatively coalesce across disciplines *as they tackle similar challenges* even when they appear to be engaged in very different knowledge projects. This is a diverse yet borderless epistemological habitat in which very different groups both contest territories and contribute resources, shaping the shared environment as they do so. So surveying the theoretical landscape enables us to identify how deeply felt concerns are evolving into new patterns of academic practice that are not confined to one particular discipline alone but make an impact upon a wide range of subjects in an interrelated ecology.

Before engaging with theory, however, I have to acknowledge that some practical theologians might regard this move as entering hostile territory. While there has been much greater openness to spiritual insights within theoretical discourse in recent years (see p. 51), it is a cacophonous realm and one in which religion has often been severely critiqued in modern times – albeit that it is also a sphere from which we draw some of our most significant insights (see Williams, 2000, pp. xiv–xv). Many researchers in practical theology also experience a nervousness about theory itself (Tveitereid, 2018, p. 42). This derives from a sense that theoretical discourse is likely to be complex and intimidating and also that it might obscure and compromise the theological understanding they seek when engaging in research from a faith perspective.

There is also some understandable uncertainty about what exactly theory is and does, for there is not a consensus on this point and differing definitions exist with differing implications for the concerns I am exploring in this chapter. I have found it helpful to distinguish between three significant understandings of the term in general use:

1 Theory is seen as abstracted knowledge. Its purpose is to clarify and communicate, through the process of abstraction from the concrete and the particular, in order that a wider critical perspective can be gained and customary practices assessed.
2 Theory is viewed as critical, political intervention. It shifts perception by developing new and different ways of naming phenomena *not only* in order that they can be more clearly seen, *but also* so they can be changed.
3 Theory is understood as the articulation and expression of emerging collective sentiments. It creatively responds to wider shifts in the

social/cultural/religious imaginary and plays a significant role in the way we comprehend the world. It finds expression in shared narratives, images, metaphors, cultural symbols and artistic practice.

While these understandings are very different, they are not antagonistic and each one of them can be conceptually and strategically helpful. However, in practical theology we have tended to focus upon the first two understandings of theory to the neglect of the third – and it is this third understanding that I want to include and highlight here. This presents theory as a shared symbolic system. Theoretical developments, in this frame, take place not simply as a result of changes in academic fashion – in the endless cycles and recycles of the knowledge industry – but rather as responses to the challenges encountered in the way we live now. As Elizabeth St. Pierre and colleagues state, '[theoretical] turns become necessary when our encounters with the world can no longer be explained or justified by orthodox thinking, when new problems overtake us' (St. Pierre, Jackson and Mazzei, 2016, p. 100).

As I have maintained, the problems threatening to overtake us are evident. They confront us in the environmental catastrophes and global injustices we increasingly realize will require a massive shift in the way we conceive and organize our collective lives if they are not to prove ultimately tragic. In this context, contemporary scholarship in many/most disciplines has begun to employ 'relational ontologies' as theoretical resources that provide a means of imaging and engaging with various aspects of these challenges. That is: *they are using relational terms and categories to explore the nature of our being in the world.* While relationality is at the heart of this theoretical turn there are, once again, diverse understandings of what relationality means and how it can become operative as a mode of understanding. Drawing on the important work of Jessica Smartt Gullion on the social sciences and relational ontologies (2018), I shall employ three images through which to illustrate this diversity.

The fold

The first of these images is the fold. This image is one that is particularly significant in the work of Gilles Deleuze who elaborates upon the legacy of Leibniz to develop a form of monadological thinking. A monad is unitary and indivisible so in this perspective multiplicity and difference (while important) are conceived of within a frame of connection not as separations, tears or cuts in the textile of existence but as folds. So Deleuze quotes Leibniz as saying, 'The division of the continuous must not be taken as of sand dividing into grains, but as that of a sheet of paper or of a tunic in folds, in such a way that an infinite number of folds can be produced, some smaller than others, but without the body ever dissolving into points' (1993, p. 6). This is a way of perceiving the universe that emphasizes how continuity and relation are maintained while allowing for infinite variations represented to our imaginations as foldings, unfoldings and refoldings. It is an origami philosophy of being. As Elizabeth de Freitas writes:

> Distinctiveness is no longer what cuts off one individual or object from another, but refers rather to a particular fold or twist in the undulating fabric of the universe. Processes of individuation, by which identities and subjects and institutions come into being, are not acts of disconnection or separation, whereby the one is cut off from the rest, but are continuous topological folds of the whole ... This process describes all being, whether it be the birth of an idea or concept, or the making of a bowl. If we were able to see monads, we would see how bowls and concepts were simply folds of the one simple substance. This is a ... theory of contiguous relationality, a way of studying life as it contracts and expands across a continuum of mind-matter. The smallest unit of matter or life, thus, is not the atom or any other particle, but is rather the fold. (2016, p. 225)

Entanglement

The second image is that of entanglement and this can be illustrated with reference to the hugely influential work of philosopher/science writer Karen Barad. Barad's thinking explores the implications of our growing awareness of weird quantum indeterminacy and entanglement at micro level. Contemporary science challenges us to acknowledge that matter matters itself differentially in relation to the means in which it is observed and measured and also that particles once related retain relational responses to one another despite distancing. Relationality, in this frame, is the very stuff of the universe and what physics reveals to be the case at micro level, Barad maintains, holds true at every level – we live in a quantum universe all the way up as well as all the way down. She writes, 'Boundaries don't hold, times, places, beings bleed through one another' (2014, p. 179). This being the case, what constitutes all things is not their distinctness *but their emergence through relational intra-action*. Furthermore, we are entangled – not simply with other people but with objects, histories, cultural formations. As stated, this entanglement is not to be understood as the encounters of discrete entities but rather individuality is what is constituted in the intra-action itself. She writes:

> 'Phenomena,' ... are the entanglement – the ontological inseparability – of intra-acting agencies ... It is through specific agential intra-actions that the boundaries and properties of 'individuals' within the phenomenon become determinate and particular material articulations of the world become meaningful ... The notion of intra-action marks an important shift in many foundational philosophical notions such as causality, agency, space, time, matter, meaning, knowing, being, responsibility, accountability, and justice. (Barad, in Kleinman, 2012, p. 77)

Such quantum thinking prompts us to radically challenge the distinctions between knowing and being (observer and observed). The instrument of observation has to be recognized as entangled in what it seeks to comprehend. Furthermore, knowing-being and ethics are also deeply interconnected as we are responsible and responsive at all levels. Barad's thinking thus generates an ethico-onto-epistemology – an ugly but functional term implying that a *moral responsibility for inextricably entangled being must inform our knowledge practices*. This understanding is currently being explored widely in politics, philosophy, poetics and even theology as a means of 'mattering' intra-active responses to climate crisis and neoliberal economic systems and, in the case of theologians like Catherine Keller, constructing images of human and divine being as interconnected and in mutual processes of becoming (Keller, 2014).

Network

The last image is that of the Network. Here I draw on the foundational work of Bruno Latour and his development of Actor Network Theory (ANT) as it has been elaborated by materialist thinkers such as Jane Bennett. Latour calls those engaged in attending to human behaviour through social science methods to shift their focus from isolating and abstracting meaning from social contexts and producing generalizable categories and theoretical structures, to *exploring connections between entities that in collaborative relations produce outcomes*. Assemblage[6] is agency and agency is not a purely human category at all. The distinction between things and beings with consciousness and what we describe as life is traversed in this image as actants are identified in networks that include things traditionally regarded as inanimate. Together these actants produce outcomes, whether these be in terms of gaming cultures, weather systems or political alliances, that are constituted from relationships between materials, living beings and the terrain on which their interactions take place. As Jane Bennett states, 'humans are always in composition with nonhumanity, never outside of a sticky web of connections or an *ecology*' (Bennett, 2004, p. 365). To give a crude example, the poet Richard Lovelace penned the famous words 'Stone Walls do not a Prison make,/Nor Iron bars a Cage' (1642). However, to misquote and misuse him, 'Stone walls do a prison make and iron bars a cage.' Or, at least, they contribute to the confining system that is a material assemblage of stone and iron, warder and prison uniform, bad coffee and smells of sweat and boiled vegetables, all inextricably joined to a legislative assemblage that incarcerates large numbers of people. Together these are indeed what 'a prison make'. In an ecclesial context pews, hymnbooks, sexual codes, gospel stories, coffee cups and choir gowns might be the lively stuff out of which a communal life is generated that includes *embodied* humans (not just their thoughts and beliefs) but also vibrant, vital matter.

Image, truth and resonance

I have used three images to represent significant and influential discourses operative in the contemporary theoretical landscape. They'll do, I think, perhaps better than many more words. Theoretical discourses can appear obtuse and yet they are also fascinating and compelling (if you like that kind of thing), but at the heart of every significant theoretical paradigm is a vivid image. Big ideas are also (essentially) simple ideas once you have some notion of what context or challenge they are addressing. But before moving on it is important to point out that these images are not commensurate with each other – although they may be folded and entangled and networked. Deleuze and Barad don't share

---

6 Assemblage is a term also associated with the work of Gilles Deleuze and Félix Guattari (1987) and it has a rather different emphasis in their work.

the same understandings of the universe although they may on occasion employ similar symbolic language, and similarly Latour's charting of the connectivity of the social is not the same as Barad's quantum ethics.

This might appear to pose a problem. Which if any of these images mirrors the 'truth'? Which offers the sturdiest epistemological frame?

If theory is understood as a collective, creative response that resonates with and responds to our changing encounters with the world, this is not a particularly disturbing question for us – either as social researchers or as theologians. All three images reveal the overriding significance of relationality and I approach them by drawing upon the theological trajectory of correlation articulated by Paul Tillich and developed further by David Tracey, and our own forebears in practical theology, Seward Hiltner and Don Browning (see Graham, Walton and Ward, 2019, pp. 151–83). Theology is envisaged here as a vitally engaged response to the questions articulated in cultural forms – a reading of the signs of the times. Each epoch has its own particular challenges. Informed by an understanding of these gained from many differing sources, the theologian identifies specific resources from their tradition (as the urgent needs of the day direct) and employs these to generate both credible apologetics and faithful responses in care and action.

Tillich saw many differing cultural forms as articulating in their own distinct ways the signs from the sacred depths of being that theology must continually attune to. Science itself is seismically sensitive to 'earthquakes' originating in the depths that shake established cultural assumptions – such as when 'Einstein questioned whether there is an absolute point from which an observer can look at the motions of things' (Tillich, 1966, p. 61). The social sciences can similarly serve as sensitive cultural registers of emerging ontologies. Significantly for this work, creative art is distinctly capable of plunging into the depths and sensing and expressing emerging cultural fissures and new alignments as yet invisible at surface level. Speaking of art during the rise of fascism, Tillich wrote: 'Painters expressed their feeling of the coming catastrophe by disrupting the surface of man [sic] and nature in their pictures. Poets used strange, offensive words and rhythms' (1966, p. 65) in order to shed light on the approaching disaster. I find Tillich's description of the prophetic role of art here both helpful and challenging.[7] It prompts me to seek theological forms that artistically probe beneath surface understandings even if this entails speaking in strange ways and rhythms and risking the dangers of offence.

---

7 For an informative perspective on Tillich on art, see Manning, 2005.

But to return to the discussion of theory and the relational ontologies represented by my three images. If we engage with these in a 'Tillichean' mode we will understand them as presenting both theological challenges and also generating a matrix of symbols and metaphors through which to offer theological responses to contemporary issues. In other words, as theologians, we will seek the points where insights concerning relationality creatively return us to our faith tradition to seek within it places of resonance. There are many of these in Scripture, doctrine and the classic texts of spiritual writing. They offer visions of the whole created order as implicated in divine incarnation and the reconciliation of all things in God. But it is not only a matter of seeking common ground. There will also be transformative elements to the encounter with contemporary theory – challenging previously held theological assumptions. For example, relational ontologies may cause us to re-examine understandings of transcendence and interrogate their meaning anew – perhaps reconceiving transcendence not as distance and separation, but rather as what is beyond yet not apart from us (see Rivera, 2007). Finally, there may be ways in which theologians wish to contribute their own voices to theoretical debate – providing insights that shape the trajectory of thought as well as veering with it. This is already a major agenda within constructive theology and theopoetics where, as Catherine Keller and Laurel Schneider state, relational thinking has become a crucible for theological reflection and 'Divinity understood in terms of multiplicity, open-endedness, and relationality now forms a matrix of revelation rather than ... evidence of its lack' (2011, p. 1).

Rewilding research

I now return from this exploration of the broader terrain of theoretical debate to explore the implications of this relational turn within the field of qualitative research.[8] Researchers who are undertaking social inquiry in the light of this theoretical turn employ an epistemological framework within which they:

1 Acknowledge the intraconnections out of which phenomena, agencies and persons (all stuff) are constituted.

---

8 Smartt Gullion (2018) presents a fuller discussion of the impact of the relational turn in ontology on qualitative research. I am very much indebted to her work in this part of the book.

2 Recognize and respect diversity and difference. However, these would be understood as constituted through relational interactions (including those predicated upon systemic injustices) rather than through essential division.[9]
3 Are aware of relationality 'all the way up and all the way down' and maintain a respectful curiosity about connections at all levels of inquiry that in itself constitutes an ethical stance.
4 Decentre the human. This would not entail the end of committed enquiry into human life and flourishing. Rather, it means placing humanity within a connected matrix; viewing humans 'with' rather than 'over against' planetary others.

In the rather narrower frame of their practical inquiries, relational researchers:

1 Eschew binary distinctions including those often regarded as constituting the essence of research such as distinctions between researcher and researched, data and interpretation, values and validity.
2 Attend to embodiment and affect as important sites for developing relational understanding.
3 Become radically interdisciplinary and breach traditional borders – even those that formerly appeared unbreachable, such as those between art and science and, more locally, quantitative and qualitative inquiry.

If we were to envisage a serious encounter within these transformed parameters of qualitative research it is clear that some of practical theology's most cherished perspectives and practices might be subject to revision. It is also evident that new and productive pathways towards conviviality (co-living) and cooperation might emerge. If, as I am arguing, observation/representation are being rethought, if data is now viewed not as a static substance to be mined or harvested but as lively, unpredictable resources we make with, if ethnography is being intensely critiqued and becoming weirdly wild, diffractive and creative, then we have some challenges, perturbing and exciting in equal measure, to contend with. These are the issues I shall consider in Chapter 2.

---

[9] One of the most significant problems identified in relational ontologies is whether they can allow for alterity. This is both an epistemological and a political issue.

2

Knowing, Knowing What We Don't Know and Being Mixed Up: Empiricism, Reflexivity and Representation

In the last chapter I offered an example and an overview of some of the shifts that are taking place in qualitative research. In this chapter I attempt to bring these changes much closer to home. I shall explore some of the familiar, 'taken for granted' assumptions that predominate in practical theology's current research practice – focusing first upon empiricism and, second, on reflexivity. I shall then go on to argue that practical theology needs to undertake its own, long-delayed, radical reckoning with the crisis of representation that transformed the landscape of qualitative research over 30 years ago now. Finally, I shall ask how relational paradigms might help us envisage convivial terms of encounter between different methods and methodological projects – all of which have contributions to make as we seek to respond to the enormous challenges that confront us.

Empiricism

I turn first to the term 'empirical' and here I must make a personal confession – I do not like this word. Part of my problem is simply local, cultural usage. Although I recognize that the word 'empirical' functions somewhat differently within the international context of practical theology, I cannot quite free myself from the nuances the term bears in the UK. The connotations that 'empirical' carries in my home context are those of 'common sense' understandings, no-nonsense thinking, a rigid determination to rule out of court anything considered fanciful or flighty – that is, anything 'arty'. In other words, I receive 'empirical' as a term of boundaries and power; of privileged perspectives and silencing that might be summed up in the phrase 'Only that which I can evidence will

I take seriously.' While my own context does influence my response the deep association between empiricism and 'evidence-based' approaches to knowledge does extend beyond this. For example, Bernard Meland was one of the leaders of the original empirical theology movement[1] in the USA which came into being many years before Johannes van der Ven and his colleagues at Nijmegan reclaimed this title to describe their revisioned form of practical theology. Meland found that as his theological understanding developed he had to make a decisive break with the movement because of its restricted vision:

> Once one is seized by the disturbing idea that reason and observation give only truncated accounts of existence one is no longer able to remain complacently empirical, nor content to remain inhospitable to imaginative efforts to comprehend the human problem is its vaster context. (Meland, in Wyman, 2017, p. 16)

Meland turned to literature and the arts as means to comprehend the mystery and tragedy of life which he doubted could be revealed in empirical terms.

I share Meland's concerns about empiricism. However, I do understand that when my colleagues use the term 'empirical' they are not advocating the restricted, one-dimensional worldview that he rejected as hostile to creative thinking. Rather, they are advocating that we take this world of vitality and suffering, of meaning-making and faith practice, seriously and on its own terms. They wish to look closely and reverently at its patterns and processes. This is something I deeply respect and would also view as vital for any responsible form of theological reflection. But in the light of the relational turn in qualitative research we are challenged to reassess critically the manner in which we do so.

According to Elizabeth St. Pierre (2016), empiricism is commonly expressed in two forms; both of these present challenges for the qualitative social researcher and, I would add, the practical theologian. The first is formed from the inheritance of logical empiricism which, even in chastened post-positivist forms, imports selected 'scientific' paradigms (arguably ones that are now entirely outmoded in their own sphere) into qualitative research. These may cause us to misrepresent the nature of work we are engaged in – for example, if we maintain discourses of academic impartiality, employ the language of statistical discourses

---

1 For an account of empirical theology and Meland's journey, see Wyman, 2017, pp. 14–16.

to claim 'validity', or reify data as if they were discrete entities standing somewhat apart from the researcher and participants who together 'make it up'. Power relationships and the politics of representation (see below) can be rendered invisible by such practices because they obscure the complex relationality of the research process.

A second, phenomenological, form of empiricism is also widely practised in practical theology. It is attractive because of its holistic and respectful emphasis upon life worlds, lived experience, and its sincere efforts to comprehend the ecology that research participants both construct and inhabit. However, the difficulties entailed in engaging with the life worlds and lived experience of others are acknowledged but not resolved by the emphasis that interpretative phenomenology places upon transparent and accountable research processes and profound reflexivity. There is also a danger that lived experience may be presented as primordial; existing before its communication in language. There is, however, no space, place or way behind discursive activity in which primal experience can be located. Indeed, what we call 'experience' may be the taken-for-granted discursive expression of 'common sense' and common sense can function as a way of dealing with the many unresolved challenges of existence by actively occluding them in apparently innocent accounts of 'what-actually-happened-to-me'. Careful attention to presenting data in the exact terms in which they were articulated by participants does not resolve such difficulties. When researchers base their epistemological claims on 'preserving the phenomenon exactly as described by participants in careful word-for-word transcriptions of interviews, when they "let the data speak for itself" and refuse to theorize in analysis' (St. Pierre, 2016, p. 116), they are insisting on the descriptive validity of their research as if description were not itself interpretation already ... which it definitely is.

These problems have been recognized and debated for decades in qualitative research. Empiricism has been modified and reimagined through developments such as standpoint epistemology[2] (with its insistence on the inherent value of multiple partial and located perspectives) but the relational turn presents further fundamental challenges to both the forms of empiricism named above (which are usually all mixed up in our practice). To recap: the separation between observer, instrument of observation and that which is observed is difficult to sustain in a context in which we recognize their deep relations and intra-actions. Clearly, we must not cease to be challenged by serious attentiveness to what is

---

[2] See Haraway, 1988; and Harding, 1991.

happening in the world. However, we will lose innocence concerning our own role in shaping and forming what is presented as pre-existent and observable. This leads naturally to a reconsideration of reflexivity in research processes.

Reflexivity

Once again, a confession is necessary. While I have never warmed to empiricism, quite the opposite is true of reflexivity. Indeed, a great deal of my academic energy over the years has been spent on developing and promoting processes of reflexivity in research and theological reflection. It has been a way of proceeding that, somewhat ironically, has been very slow to gain credence in practical theology despite the great store we place on reflecting on practice. As Courtney Goto states, in a work that exposes the ingrained racialized biases and structures of white power that continue to impact our discipline, 'reflexivity is practiced inconsistently in practical theological writing' (2018, p. 216). I think we would be correct in reading 'inconsistently' as 'highly selectively' here!

But although we have been slow to engage with reflexivity in any great depth some signs are encouraging. Katherine Turpin's recent work (2025) that demonstrates how whiteness has shaped every aspect of her practical theological vocation is an excellent example of how revelatory a reflexive approach can be. So why is it now, when we are just beginning to take the challenges of reflexivity seriously, that I am calling for a fundamental reappraisal of its efficacy and value?

The first reason is that the processes of reflexivity can (and often do) present a 'façade' of serious attention to the location, perspectives, limitations and blind spots of the researcher and the power differentials operative in all research relations. However, what often happens is that researchers from dominant groups, having ritually confessed their limited vision and privileged social position ('I am white, middle class, educated, cis gendered, implicated in institutionally racist structures', etc.), and consequently believing themselves to be absolved, then carry on with the old processes of categorization and representation of others as if nothing had happened. As Wanda Pillow states:

> Prominent in much qualitative research is the idea the researcher through reflexivity can transcend her own subjectivity and cultural context in a way that releases her/him from the weight of misrep-

resentation. Self-reflexivity can perform a modernist seduction – promising release from your tension, voyeurism, ethnocentrism – a release from your discomfort with representation. (2003, p. 186)

Second, and related to this, is the fact that resorting to discourses of reflexivity often serves not to display the possible contingency and unreliability of a researcher's judgements, but instead defend their work against challenges to its validity. Reflexivity becomes the false performance of vulnerability intended to enable recourse to positivist forms of validation: 'I have shown you where I am coming from and how I got here. It is all transparent. You can see how I have identified and accounted for my blurred vision and my work is therefore valid.'

Third, reflexivity is often presented as ethics in and of itself: 'I am reflexive therefore I must be ethical.' As demonstrated above, this is clearly not the case.

Once again these critiques of reflexivity have been made for many years but what the relational turn forces upon us is the disturbing challenge that not only might reflexivity be self-serving (certainly it has been in the case of white researchers from dominant social locations) it may also be, like empirical objectivity, a chimera, a mirage, unsustainable within relational thinking. So Donna Haraway and others argue that reflexivity, while gesturing towards relationality, still presents the illusion of a unitary, relatively discrete, fixed and stable, identity for the reflective researcher.[3] They are assumed able to stand apart from the webs in which they are woven and to assess these critically. However, what they are seeing is reflective of their own positionality. As Barad has also argued, reflexivity is often poorly attuned to the numerous entanglements through which the researcher is constituted (see Smartt Gullion, 2018, p. 89).

Finally, reflexive accounts are, alongside other aspects of ethnographic writing, textual 'fictions' (a topic I explore further in Chapter 4). I don't mean that they are not productive of understanding or lacking insight. However, I am a life writer as well as a practical theologian and life-writing lesson one is that you cannot *write* a life. It consists of myriad, complex interactions and therefore (strategic/aesthetic) selection happens and we *create* a life. In a similar 'fictive' process we choose how we perform reflexivity by creating boundaries around what appears significant, aesthetically productive or, very often, simply in our

---

3 For a more detailed exploration of reflexivity in practical theology, see Bennett et al., 2018, pp. 34–57.

best interest to confess. More attentive and nuanced forms of reflexivity that we currently engage in are certainly possible to imagine (again, the work of Turpin is instructive here). However, a comprehensively reflexive approach would need to be attuned not only to the researcher's position but to the myriad connections they form in the research process. Practical questions begin to emerge here. If you were really to undertake 'deep forms' of reflexivity seriously, where would you draw the line? Would you have time to do anything else in your research and would anybody else be at all interested in what you have achieved?

So where does this leave us? Is reflexivity to be completely abandoned? No – certainly not. It can help us become more aware of the complex web of power relations out of which research is always born. Furthermore, in an imperfect world it is the best resource we have for *discerning and acknowledging* the ambiguities, limitations and damaging potential inherent in our work. When it achieves these things it is helpful. When it performs the opposite function it is not.

Representation

Consideration of the fictive nature of ethnographic work brings me to one of the biggest challenges facing practical theological research today. This is the need to come to our own terms with what is referred to as the 'crisis in representation' – one of the most significant moments in the development of qualitative research to date. This 'crisis', which developed way back in the mid-1980s, was precipitated by a growing postcolonial awareness that ethnography had been deeply linked to the racist machinery of colonization from its inception and that the white/colonial gaze continued to be operative in many aspects of the discipline. This recognition generated grave concerns about the project of interpreting and representing the lives of others through ethnographic means. In other words, the 'crisis' was a shattering of confidence in research relationships.

This 'crisis' was refracted through the theoretical lens of poststructuralism which drew attention to the ways in which discursive practices (including those that structure academic life) are fundamental to the construction of both subjectivity and social identity. Employing this framework, questions were raised as to whether ethnographic discourses were functioning as a means of oppressive 'othering'. Despite humanistic claims that such studies further cultural understanding by generating knowledge and acknowledging diversity, it was recognized that ethnographic accounts are also powerful fables; constructing social imaginaries that support racist, binary and hierarchical models of human relations by the very analytical categories they employ.[4]

The publication of the key text *Writing Culture* (Clifford and Marcus, eds, 1986) is often taken as heralding the representational crisis within anthropology – and indeed far beyond it as its critiques were acknowledged in other disciplinary fields. As the contributors to this volume interrogate the processes through which accounts of others are generated, writing itself emerges as key. As any postgraduate student in practical theology quickly becomes very aware, there are conventions that constrain the ways in which we are encouraged to write research accounts. These are not only operative to secure the integrity and reliability of the work but to exclude those messy and uncategorizable elements that destabilize texts. These conventions also serve to occlude the deep ambivalence always present in research relationships as a result of the inherent power dynamics through which they are structured. *Writing Culture* is subtitled *The Poetics and Politics of Ethnography* and its various authors also highlight how ethnography employs a poetics that sustains its politics through maintaining genre conventions and employing particular tropes, symbols and devices to achieve its goals (a topic I explore further in Chapter 4).

Here I must acknowledge the deep irony that *Writing Culture* significantly excludes women's contributions. This is despite the fact that significant texts by radical women of colour, and white feminist authors, articulated many of its key concerns in works that both preceded (e.g. Moraga and Anzaldúa, eds, 1981) and postdated (e.g. Behar and Gordon, eds, 1995) the publication of this key text. These women-written works exemplify the radical heritage of women's cultural writing and challenge the white, male-centred conventions, language and discursive scripts of traditional ethnographic accounts. Their authors actively sought to write the body, emotions, personal and social lives of women into their research. By using the first person and making themselves visible within their ethnographic narratives they rejected the privileged status of impartial, expert observer. Anna Tsing, whose work I refer-

---

4 Initially these categories were clear – for example, primitive/civilized, magical/rational, bricoleur/engineer. Today the terms are less clear-cut but still evident as we implicitly continue to position research participants as actors, and researchers as knowers. For a critique of how such categories function, see Latour, 1993.

enced in the last chapter, was one of the emerging women scholars who contributed to this deconstructive work (Tsing and Ebron, 1995).

To be sure, highlighting the colonial origins, patriarchal conventions and the creative and literary character of ethnographic work does not necessarily invalidate its contribution. *The vast majority of academic discourses share these characteristics!* Rather, it means that we read it through a different lens. Furthermore, as we recognize that culture is 'written' we begin to perceive that it can be 'written differently' – allowing for diverse contributions and destabilizing taken-for-granted assumptions. The text box below places the crisis of representation within the historical trajectory of social research paradigms and indicates just how generative, methodologically speaking, it proved to be.

Denzin and Lincoln's 'moments' in the development of qualitative research

The changes that ensued from the crisis of representation took qualitative research into many new areas and arenas. The influential editors of the multi-editioned *Sage Handbook of Qualitative Research*, Norman Denzin and Yvonna Lincoln, have charted significant 'moments' in the developing trajectory of qualitative inquiry – see below. Their work illustrates how the impact of 'moment 4' (the crisis of representation) prompted a radical reassessment that enabled new research forms to flourish from the 1990s to the present.

The moments:

1 **Traditional/colonial** (1900). Aligned to positivist values and seeks objectivity in ethnographic fieldwork and reporting.
2 **Modernist phase** (1950). Methodological rigour and formal procedures still predominate in the research process, but challenges to positivism are emerging via movements such as symbolic interactionism.
3 **Blurred genres phase** (1970). Many alternative approaches are active – for example, hermeneutics, structuralism, phenomenology and feminism. Researchers borrow from other disciplines and engage in bricolage.

4 **Crisis of representation** (1986). Recognition that ethnographic texts are written constructions bearing the marks of power, race, gender, class and academic privilege. Traditional notions of validity and neutrality are fundamentally reassessed. There is a productive turn to various forms of reflexive writing.
5 **Postmodern experimentation** (1990). After the crisis of representation, responses to issues of legitimacy and practice are foregrounded in research. Activist, justice-seeking and participatory modes of research are developed and the 'forms' through which research is constructed are expanded. Creative and interpretative writing are employed and the perspectives of the writer are foregrounded.
6 **Post-experimental phase** (1995). At this stage the boundaries of qualitative research have expanded to include artistic and aesthetic resources. Creative non-fiction, autobiography and poetic forms are now regularly employed.
7 **Contestation phase** (2000). Political challenges impact upon social research and questions arise as to what ways research strategies (within the academy and the wider social, cultural and medical fields) sustain or transform oppressive economic systems. At the same time, diversity is now increasingly acknowledged in methodology and methods.
8 **Sacred textualities and moral visions** (2008). The secular orientation of social research is reimagined. Influenced by people of colour, indigenous people, and others in liminal and/or marginal contexts, research methodologies that acknowledge relationality, embodiment and spiritual connections are pursued. 'We may also be entering an age of greater spirituality within research efforts. The emphasis is on inquiry that reflects ecological values, on inquiry that respects communal forms of living that are not Western, on inquiry involving intense reflexivity [on] our own historical and gendered locations ... may yet reintegrate the sacred with the secular in ways that promote freedom and self-determination' (Lincoln, Linham and Guba, 2018, p. 145).

Beyond 'moment 8',[5] issues such as the development of big data render former accepted distinctions between qualitative and

> quantitative research increasingly unstable. The worsening of the climate crisis and the intensification of inequality evidence the need to develop solidarity across methodological terrains. Denzin and Lincoln name the space of 'social change issues' as one in which those committed to traditional methodologies and those who favour radical methods can unite to undertake forms of 'ground-level social justice inquiry ... that is indigenous, collaborative and community based' (2018, p. 889).

Courtney Goto has given the fullest voice, to date, to the challenges that the crisis of representation poses for practical theology. In her book *Taking on Practical Theology* (2018), she questions whether research should be assumed to be a benign and innocent process even (or especially) when it is conducted by people of faith who seek to approach their work with a benevolent concern for their participants, the health of Christian communities, and an awareness of academic protocols. In a critique of Mary McClintock Fulkerson's *Places of Redemption* (2007), one of the most highly regarded ethnographic works in our discipline and a classic text in congregational studies, she points out that the text frequently employs a poetics of seeing, viewing and displaying that 'unwittingly invites a colonizing gaze' (2018, p. 156) upon a multi-ethnic and socially disadvantaged congregation. Goto argues that although 'seeing is a common, poetic metaphor ... it takes on problematic nuances when used in relation to minoritized people ... [as it] takes for granted who is made available to be seen, who has the privilege of seeing, and who has the power to exhibit' (2018, p. 156). In the light of this critique she outlines four principles that practical theologians should 'take on' when approaching their ethnographic work. These are so important that I quote them fully below:

> A practical theologian using ethnography ... [first] might ask whether there are questions that should not be pursued with ethnography, particularly when a community has suffered historical, communal injury. Just because research tools are effective in producing answers does not justify their use. If researchers receive permission from a community

---

5 Other moments and accompanying methodological developments have been suggested by Denzin and Lincoln and their interpreters, yet (arguably) without the hermeneutical clarity achieved in the eight moments described in the text box.

to do the research, it does not give them a free pass to proceed with a clear conscience. Contrary to a history of academic imperialism, academics are not entitled to know. Second, rather than focusing the work primarily on the subjects, a less colonizing approach might be to document more consistently the constant negotiation between the researcher and the subjects across the boundaries of their respective assumptive worlds. It would be helpful if the theorist never let the reader lose sight of herself as a witness, consistently challenging her default frame of reference. Third, a theorist might incorporate representations of the community that resist interrogation, creating space and relationships that allow the other to be seen and known in a variety of ways. Artistic forms such as poetry, visual art, and performance art can defy concretization and domestication, especially if the theorist is sensitive to this. Finally, a researcher is obligated to ask whom the research benefits and to meet a higher standard if the community being researched mostly benefits indirectly. Practical theologians strive to be of service to faith communities, yet their research often falls short, tending primarily to benefit the academy. (2018, pp. 156–7)

Within this important statement of principles, Goto draws attention to the potential that artistic forms possess to communicate in ways that subvert the 'colonial gaze' by attending to communal forms of self-expression that defy reification and domination. In her own pedagogical practice, particularly with students from historically oppressed communities, she cultivates awareness of the *epistemic advantage* that is enjoyed by those who have experienced and resisted dominating social power.[6] She seeks to nurture in those she mentors creative writing practices that embody marginalized understandings, and display what she terms 'hyper-self-reflexivity'. Goto stresses that these self-disclosive reflexive writing practices differ from the forms of reflexivity that predominate within practical theology and which, as I have maintained, are generally framed in terms of transparency and validity. In contrast,

> hyper-self-reflexivity is employed not for the sake of allowing the reader to evaluate what is being discussed, which replicates a hierarchical subject–object relationship ... [It rather] invites readers to engage in a parallel process of examining the assumptions with which they

---

6 Locating the 'epistemic advantage' with the person who is simultaneously subject to and resistant to oppression represents a politically generative way of reconceiving epistemological privilege.

engage the text, which have also been shaped by patterns of prejudice, privilege, and violence. (2018, p. 216)

In other words, Goto is seeking to generate forms of relational writing that provoke an empathetic and self-interrogating response in readers who are thus provoked to begin their own reflexive journeys. Rejecting the notion that deeply personal forms of address are academically questionable or indulgent 'navel gazing', she insists instead that they are epistemologically significant and that fostering them is not only empowering but also necessary for 'the health and wellbeing of the field' (2018, p. 215).

The importance of an accountable 'personal voice' is powerfully illustrated in Turpin's indictment of dominating whiteness and racism in practical theology. As she struggled to make sense of her own inheritance, Turpin learned that it was necessary not to make abstract claims about racism or indulge in ritual expressions of shame and guilt. Rather, her task was to make clear the important but often unacknowledged links between personal life, academic practice, and the wider social and religious systems in which all these are set. To do so she needed to become concrete, located and present in her text; moving continually between fields and drawing out the important connections between them. This enables the awful damage that racism causes to become strikingly present in her work – exposing this wound in a way that is absolutely necessary to the health of the field.

Conviviality in the changed climate

I began this book by evoking the spectre of the social scientist within practical theology and, after travelling with me to this point, I do expect some of my readers might be thinking along the lines below:

> I know living and breathing social scientists, they work down the hall from me. They are not wandering round the woods looking for mushrooms and worrying about the end of the world. They do not attend creative writing classes to develop techniques of hyper-reflexivity. They are conducting sensible evidence-based inquiry into significant issues such as 'mental health interventions through gaming' or 'kinship patterns in migration'. It is the mystically inclined, self-disclosive relational social researcher being evoked in this chapter who is a phantasmagorical creature.

Clearly, qualitative research continues to be practised in many contexts by researchers less concerned with ontologies (folded, tangled or otherwise) than with significant outcomes that generate helpful evidence-based suggestions for improved practice. They are supported by funding bodies and answerable to academic councils who are interested in demonstrable conclusions, ethics and compliance with agreed protocol rather than empathy and communal self-expression. I understand this!

One of the dangers of offering interpretative models like Denzin and Lincoln's 'moments' (above) is that they tend to imply an evolution in research practice from 'primitive' forms towards more enlightened and progressive ways of proceeding. It is always more complicated than this. What actually happens is that diverse practices coexist (and sometimes contest and sometimes cooperate) across a shared terrain. I am certainly not advocating a wholesale shift away from methods shaped by the legacy of positivism and towards an uncritical adoption of arts-based research and practice – although this might once have been the case! But now I am advocating a more nuanced and relational position which concedes that aggressive debates concerning research methods have often contributed to unhelpful divides while the actual concerns behind the disagreements remained insufficiently examined.

My own interests now lie less in the methods being used, whether some are inherently better than others, but rather what political and theological potential a research project generates and whose interests it serves. I note that those whose worlds continue to be marginalized by conventional academic practices (e.g. women, people of colour, gay, lesbian and trans people, and members of indigenous communities) have been leading and guiding the development of new research methodologies, but I also note that injustices can emerge as issues of concern through painstaking work done by established researchers in the field using techniques that are widely accepted and legitimized within the academy. For all of us the world has changed. The oppositional categories that I and others have used to categorize research approaches in the past are changing also.

Beyond old divides

The relational ontologies I imaged earlier support such a 'moment' of communal rethinking. Alongside them, developments are now taking place within the field of social research that make reconnecting differing approaches appear a more feasible objective than it once appeared to be. To cite an important example, because of the increased prevalence of 'big data', generated through our contemporary, interactive, digital existence, quantitative research can no longer simply be understood as a process of extracting samples from a larger set, claiming them to be representative and categorizing them to generate evidence to support particular hypotheses. It has all become a lot more complicated than that. We recognize that big data itself is produced in networks of association (assemblages) by 'thinking' machines operating according to their own hidden architectures, algorithms, etc. This production of meaning through differential relations (Derrida must be smiling somewhere) implies that the stability of categories becomes uncertain and quantitative researchers need to address many of the same questions relating to the connections between ontology and epistemology and the quirkiness of lively data that qualitative researchers also face. In this context, qualitative researchers also have reason to reassess their outmoded, stereotyping of scientific approaches and realize that maybe science has always been much more exploratory, creative and imaginative than they have acknowledged. Perhaps science-based practices could even teach us something if we stopped saying 'I really don't like the word empirical' and attended to them.

But more than this. The insight is dawning on many radical qualitative researchers that their more traditional colleagues across the corridor are not their political enemies but very often their allies; as concerned as themselves with similar questions relating to power, social participation and environmental justice – although addressing them through other mediums and other means. As Denzin and Lincoln themselves argue when facing the threats of populist neoliberal politics and planetary disaster, researchers employing *all* modes of critical inquiry have the obligation to make connections and admit their relatedness. As I have noted, in the later versions of their typology a communal realignment is portrayed as one of the most important emerging characteristics of the field.

In this context I have come to question some of my own cherished preconceptions about research practice. I have to admit that a number of the new paradigms and methods I have encountered with great enthusiasm are complicated, difficult to implement on the ground and, crucially, not guaranteed by their novelty to deliver outcomes that are any more liberatory than traditional forms of research. For example, as a methods geek, I have very much enjoyed encountering 'post qualitative research' in the work of Elizabeth St. Pierre and others. However, even I find the refusal to provide guidelines to novice researchers (apart from 'go away, read poststructuralist theory and then do what you like'[7]) frustrating and elitist. In contrast, I have developed increasing sympathy for less rarefied approaches such as those advocated by Laura Ellingson, one of the leading practitioners of embodied research. In placing her priority upon the body and bodily knowledge she is flexibly strategic in her choice of research instruments and rejects 'the thick lines drawn between paradigms', arguing that, 'Authentic, emotional voices can ring through autoethnographic narratives *and* through grounded theory analyses. Rigorous analyses can be conducted by (post)positivist, interpretivist, *and* artistic methods' (Ellingson, 2017, p. 191).

Convinced that insight can be gained through the various methods situated on the continuum between positivist and arts-based research, Ellingson continues:

> Yes, live performances invigorate through their embodied manifestation of emotion and movement, and narratives illuminate bodies engaged in dialogue, relationships, and action. But interpretive, critical, and structured analyses offer vital insights into bodies and power, common threads that connect bodies, cultural constructions (and negations) of bodily value, and people's sense making about their bodily experiences of suffering, striving, and thriving. (2017, p. 192)

In other words, all points on the line of contemporary qualitative research from the positivist end, interpretative middle to the artistic edge may produce valuable outcomes, and in the world to come the line may be a wave, or even a circle maybe? Who knows? Ellingson calls her mixed methods approach irredeemably pragmatist. What determines methodological choices now becomes relational. Not a matter of picking sides but a political, emotional embodied act taken in consideration of what might be the most generative way forward in particular circumstances,

---

7 St. Pierre writes:

> First of all, you *must* study poststructuralism – that's required – and I guarantee that poststructural scholars will send you to many other theorists who will help you think. Remember that no one can read for you and people who read a lot can always tell when others don't. If you read hard you'll likely find concepts that can help reorient your thinking so that you can think differently about whatever you want to think about. (2020, p. 18)

producing the best results for the various stakeholders involved and always with awareness of the need for solidarity. Others have gone beyond pragmatism in describing their mingling of methods and disregard for methodological territorialism. Describing her own processes as promiscuous, Sara Childers states: 'Taking a cue from the world itself, messy, entangled, [my approach is] ... wily and analytically unrestrained yet responsive and committed to the vibrancy of the world and participants [and] other ways of thinking and doing' (2014, p. 820).

From fault lines to lines of flight

In this new mood of engagement across former frontiers some critical qualitative researchers are also acknowledging the cost to themselves of a continued combative approach to their colleagues. In an important article about research after the 'relational turn', Patti Lather explores the implications of this theoretical shift in terms of relationships between people and urges her colleagues to 'engage with what is abject about our work'. Acknowledging the abject means recognizing occasions when researchers have sought to 'ruin other people's knowledge', and wounding themselves and others in the process. Lather articulates a sense of weariness and fatigue at battles played out again and again without fruitful results. Rather than continuing this acrimony, Lather advocates 'embracing our discomforts, and mourning our losses', including the loss 'of our certainties in all their exhaustions and tired repetitions?' (2016, p. 127).

Differences within practical theology have not been either so visible or so bitterly fought out as those within the field of qualitative research. However, they have been present as a subterranean force influencing the way the discipline has developed over time. Conflicts regarding worldviews between empirical and feminist practical theologians were the source of considerable acrimony and bitterness when I first entered the discipline (see Walton, 2014b). These disputes were not only concerned with how best to proceed in research – although the now familiar fault lines were emerging here as quantitative methods were favoured by empirical researchers at that time and feminist researchers were beginning to experiment with narrative methods and life writing. Beneath the surface of academic debates gendered power relations were at play and, as is always the case, these were linked to issues related to representation, access to research funding, employment prospects and the recognition of merit. We should always 'follow the money' when we look at issues like this![8]

Today, things appear, *and I believe are*, more harmonious within the discipline. But it is clearly evident that theological allegiances still contribute to the type of social research practices practical theologians choose to employ. Those who favour dogmatic/doctrinal emphases in theology or 'magisterial' Catholic approaches are still more likely to favour research methods that appear to generate 'reliable' knowledge that can be trusted as a foundation for building evidence-based practice. Those who approach theology constructively are more likely to experiment with new research methods that entail active and participatory research processes, deliver vivid insights, but are less likely to generate categorizable, 'useful' data. And of course *all generalizations are false*, including this one!

Recent debates about normativity and whether theological understandings should be 'rescripted' (see Ideström and Kaufman, 2018c, p. 174) on the basis of insights that emerge from 'empirical' practical theological research unfold across a similar theological terrain. Those who espouse dogmatic/magisterial theology emphasize the hierarchical priority of the theological tradition and, while very open to changed forms of practice, are more resistant to conforming what is sacred to the wisdom of the world. Those who espouse a more constructive approach are more willing to contemplate theology being continually challenged and remade.

While such debates reveal real differences between us, I have increasingly come to believe that when it comes to our everyday practice, what we actually do when we engage with congregations and communities, study values and practice, and even when we write theology, are much less different than we might suppose from these crude positionings. In his work on constructive theology, Jason Wyman talks about the theologian's work in responding to a contemporary challenge or crisis. They seek to identify 'the doctrine that most clearly speaks to that insight or crisis ... Analyze the history of that doctrine, identifying its fissures and shortcomings' and offer 'reconstructions of that doctrine that are creatively faithful to both the doctrine and the matter at hand' (2017, p. 168). Katherine Tanner presents theology as emerging organically from messy and complex contexts that compel theologians, of all kinds, to rummage around among the resources from tradition and past prac-

---

8 For a discussion of the politics of practical theology as played out in the International Academy of Practical Theology, see Miller-McLemore, 2017.

tices; engaging with a 'disordered heap of already existing materials, pulling them apart and putting them back together again, tinkering with their shapes, twisting them this way and that' (Tanner, 1997, p. 166). I think this image represents the work of practical theologians from many different theological perspectives – that is, what we actually do. We may use differing discourses to characterize our work but all of us are seeking to form living relationships between our contexts, with their urgent questions, and the precious but unwieldy 'stuff' tradition has generated – in other words, the 'stuff' we work and make with.

In this chapter I have argued that in the changed climate of qualitative research we need to interrogate some key concepts routinely employed in practical theological research. I have also argued that conflictual approaches to methodology and method may hinder us from focusing upon issues of major concern to us all. Instead of marking out 'fault lines' that separate us from one another we might now embrace what Deleuze and Guattari term 'lines of flight' (1987): a term signalling the possibility of escape from landscapes that have become imprisoning. A flight line represents 'the elusive moment when change happens as … when a threshold between two paradigms is crossed' (Fournier, 2014, p. 121). This can happen when conviviality enables us to imagine new ways of co-living. But does conviviality mean that we cease to (loudly and persistently) advocate for positions that matter to us within the discipline? That would be a loss.

I believe that the challenge to rethink representational practices is one that is increasingly being addressed by practical theologians from all theological perspectives and at last (though very belatedly) by those who belong to dominant/white groups as well as by theologians of colour. Change in this area must and will come. This move, in and of itself, must entail a recognition of the political concerns that impelled the development of new research methods and thus open up creative space to experiment with them more freely. Does it mean that we will all shift our research practice to embrace such new approaches? No. But some of us will and others who have already made this journey will become more confident as we demonstrate their value and worth through our own practice. Once again, I draw on insights from the literature of qualitative research as I contemplate this issue. Patti Lather (drawing on the work of Jeffrey Nealon) places her hope in changes that

> … are immanent rather than vanguard and practice-based accretions rather than the 'big bang' of some new paradigm … Motored by

practice, the new emerges out of infiltrating/embedding/infusing, not killing. Intensifying, multiplying, and extending ... It is not about individual but collective procedure, a very social enterprise where we start where we are. (Lather, 2016, p. 127)

This means not everything proceeding exactly as it has done before but a shift in relational fields. And part of that shift will entail those of us who approach practical theological research differently, doing it differently, putting it out there, as our contribution to a shared and collegial project. Being the change we long for as the phrase goes. Not in an oppositional mode but respectfully and with the resilience that comes from a sense of solidarity with others. With people who, though working from differing premises and in different ways, share in faith's longing for justice and transformation.

3

Borrowing, Gifting and Growing Together: Relations between Theology and Social Research Practices

The very first words of this work were words of prayer. I offered them to the God who connects contraries, spans differences and is manifest in the impossible in-between where stone and flesh meet; the God who is both eternal rock and incarnate redeemer.

I went on to discuss how vibrant relational worldviews had emerged within contemporary scientific, philosophical and cultural discourses. I argued that these diverse 'relational ontologies' are also predicated upon connectivity between spheres and represent significant theoretical/political responses to the environmental and political crises experienced in the way we live now. The emergence of these relational perspectives has made a profound impact upon the way we perceive and apprehend the world. Specifically, they have contributed to a transformed climate within qualitative research. This, I maintained, should be interpreted as both a methodological and theological challenge to the established conventions of practical theology.

In the previous chapter I identified ways in which some of our most taken-for-granted concepts, and their corresponding ways of proceeding in practical theological research, demanded reassessment in the current context. I expressed the hope that this might be undertaken in a spirit of respect; with a recognition of mutual concerns and commitments. In this chapter, I journey further in exploring the challenges that relational perspectives pose to practical theology by engaging with a question that has preoccupied the discipline for many years. *How do we understand 'proper' relationships between theology and the resources generated by the social sciences?*

Before I attend to this a proviso is necessary. My concern here is to offer perspectives that specifically relate to practical theology's adoption of research methods drawn from sociology and anthropology from the 1980s onwards in 'the empirical turn'. This means that what I am offering is related to this relatively recent development and so does not constitute anything like a comprehensive analysis of the interdisciplinary conversations that have been taking place between theologians and social scientists for more than a century across a range of fields. For, as previously stated, there is a long backstory to our current context. This includes, for example, ongoing conversations concerning psychology and religion (particularly in the USA), debates about religion, economics and social policy that fed into the development of contemporary public theology and the turn towards critical social theory within liberation theologies.[1] I am not attempting to tell the whole story here and what I do recount will be from my own vantage point.

Within these defined limits I will present three narratives of encounters between different disciplinary worlds. These are presented as 'case studies' but they are also functioning here in a similar way to models or typologies;[2] that is, they are intended to enable comparative, critical reflection. The first represents an historical overview of the way in which practical theologians have engaged with social research methods during the past four decades. Much of the content of this section will be familiar to readers but I re-narrate it here in order to enable comparative assessment. The second case study is based upon the lively discussions currently ongoing between anthropology and (systematic) theology. This dialogue is being conducted in significant forums within both disciplines and important issues are being raised. Although, to date, this

---

1 I am grateful to Bonnie Miller-McLemore for emphasizing to me that in the USA conversations about the relation between theology and the social sciences that began at the turn of the twentieth century led to intense and lively debates between the 1930s to the 1950s stimulated by the work of theologians such as Reinhold Niebuhr and Paul Tillich. These impacted upon practical theology through the significant contributions of Anton Boisen and Seward Hiltner. Many of these conversations were focused upon psychology and religion but they provided a bridge to current 'empirical' work through the influential work of Don Browning and others whose contributions are less well-known and remembered. My friendship with Elaine Graham has similarly alerted me to the long prehistory of public theology and the long tradition (in the UK and elsewhere) of engagement with sociology and social theory in the context of seeking Christian interventions in public policy for the common good – a legacy that Graham's reflections re-enliven in today's context (2013a, 2017a). Liberation theology and feminist theologies have also drawn upon the social sciences in a variety of significant ways long before the evolution of the empirical turn I am concerned with here.

2 A common technique used to discern appropriate forms of engaging between the spiritual and social worlds. See Niebuhr, 1951; and Dulles, 1974.

conversation appears to have been conducted without significant input from practical theology,³ it is appropriate to give attention to what is taking place so close to home. Finally, I shall consider an alternative way of conceiving future interdisciplinary encounters. This emerging model is necessarily more tentatively drawn – but is placed alongside the other two; again, as an aid to comparative reflections.

I am very aware that modelling is political work. When models are presented it is not only to enable clarity in thinking but also to advocate implicitly for particular ways of going forward. In theological writing, as elsewhere, the author generally presents their own favoured perspective last – as I will do here.⁴ To make it abundantly clear, therefore, that my models are pretty fanciful constructions designed to serve (my own) strategic ends, I am employing a literary device to introduce them. I am going to tell some fairy tales.

Tools for the job

I ask you to enter imaginatively into one of the many stories in which a struggling hero receives new tools that transform their work.

So the central character may be a shoemaker, or a carpenter or a lacemaker (for example). They are established in their craft and make things in the way they were trained to do for 7 (or maybe 14 or 21) long years of apprenticeship. They ply their trade in their little shop in a small town somewhere in central Europe. It has cobbled streets and lies next to a forest. But it seems that people are not very interested in buying what is being offered for sale. It is sad. The little brass bell above the door does not ring very often. Cobwebs hang over the shelves of carefully crafted goods. But one day a mysterious parcel arrives containing a shiny set of strange new tools. The skilled maker does not know how to use them at first but they seem full of mysterious potential. They persevere and once they get the hang of things, the tools seem easy to manipulate and enable them to make things they could not make before. People peer in through the dusty windows and they even come in to buy. Some young

---

3 Some involved speak respectfully of the contribution of a very few practical theologians. Others are less respectful in relation to our ethnographic efforts. However, profound disinterest is the dominant response overall.

4 Furthermore, as the last model I introduce is future orientated, it neatly escapes some of the criticisms that can always be made concerning how an ideal type actually functions in practice.

assistants are hired to help with the work. The shop is cleaned. It is busy and cheerful and bright. But after some time has passed the shopkeeper becomes a little worried. What is all my own hard-gained craft knowledge worth now? Is what these new tools help me make really useful and truly beautiful? Is it sound and sturdy? Is it good and true?

Two streams converge

In the first days of the empirical turn in practical theology, the talk was everywhere of 'tools' – *social science research tools* as we, rather quaintly, still often call them. There was great excitement about what could be achieved when practical theologians began to use them. There were two main focal points for this new enthusiasm.

The first was the emergence in the 1980s of empirical theology in Europe through the work of Johannes van der Ven and his colleagues in Nijmegen – in conversation with international colleagues including Leslie Francis and Peter Kay in the UK. The influence of this movement quickly spread to other countries and contexts. I use van der Ven's approach as my template in describing this movement because it is so well expounded and proved so compelling.

It was his conviction that the model for theological reflection, adopted within his university department, was not working. Through the 1970s, the Catholic pastoral theologians of Nijmegen had been basing their research upon a two-stage process that had influenced Karl Rahner's approach to pastoral theology. This advocated the study of a significant issue as a first stage and this investigation was generally imagined as being undertaken by social scientists with social science methods. The theologians came along at stage two to consider the matter from a theological perspective and in the light of the normative values of their tradition. However, van der Ven argued, this model was based upon a number of flawed assumptions. First, because of a deep antipathy towards religion, very few social scientists were interested in researching matters related to faith practices that pastoral theologians wished to reflect upon – a conclusion that was probably well founded at that time. Second, the model was a conversational one based upon notions of collaborative dialogue between theologians and social scientists, but this conversation, van der Ven argued, was heuristically conceived and dialogues never actually happened.[5] Finally, in this way of proceeding

---

5 In fact, most academic conversations between disciplines are textual rather

theologians would never be able to set the research agenda or introduce theological concerns at the start of the research process where they might shape the project and achieve the serious consideration they deserved.

Van der Ven's solution to this impasse was, and this has become a famous phrase, that 'theology itself becomes empirical' (1993, p. 101).[6] To do so it was necessary to 'expand its range of instruments' (1993, p. 101). Just as the methods of textual criticism were used in biblical studies or philosophical approaches adopted within systematic theology, so must pastoral theology gain command of necessary and appropriate tools. These would then be used in an *intra-disciplinary* way; that is, among ourselves, rather than with people from other disciplines. We would employ them to engage in a critical, theological interrogation of religious practice and practices of religious significance. This rigorous approach was envisaged as a four-stage process that began with intense theological study of a significant faith issue, proceeded to operationalize theological concepts in a manner amenable to social research, undertook research through appropriate research methods, and returned to intense theological study of the data to produce new theological insight. This theologically centred agenda required 'borrowed tools', but removed the requirement to engage with 'actual' social scientists – although, as I have maintained, their spectres would continue to haunt the field.

Synchronous to this European development, the field of congregational studies was growing and developing in the USA with the support of religious bodies and endowments from sources such as the Lily Foundation. Approaches and techniques developed in sociology, psychology, anthropology and cultural studies were brought to bear upon the dynamics of congregational life. As an early shaper of this field, Don Browning drew upon his experience to write the discipline-transforming intervention, *A Fundamental Practical Theology* (1991).[7] This positioned the every-

---

than 'face-to-face'. It is likely that van der Ven's objections here are based on the disparaging approach of social scientists to theology that he considered endemic in the field at that time.

6 Van der Ven was of course aware that empirical theology had had an earlier incarnation as a movement centred in the USA and concerned with framing theology as an empirical discipline. He discusses this in his essay 'Practical Theology: From Applied to Empirical Theology' (1988).

7 Browning was one of the original researchers in the pioneering research project that generated *Building Effective Ministry* (Dudley, 1983). However, because he is one of the best-known practical theologians, and because *A Fundamental Practical Theology* has become such a landmark text, it is easy to overstate his contribution. The developments I am exploring were not based on his work alone.

day life of faith-based communities as a site of productive theological reflection manifest in their value-laden practices. To better understand this form of theological agency, he declared that a phase of empirical research was necessary to generate 'thick descriptions' (following the approach of the anthropologist Clifford Geertz) of congregations and their guiding commitments (for a discussing of Browning's approach, see Graham, Walton and Ward, 2019, pp. 134–7).

Clearly there were overlaps of interest between these two movements and a lively international conversation between related 'empirical' projects was very soon underway. Although from diverse backgrounds, participants shared confidence that faith practices were purposeful and intelligible when appropriate tools were used to bring them to view. Quantitative methods were enthusiastically employed by the first European empirical theologians[8] but ethnography (loosely defined) later began to predominate across the board. Theological traditions were similarly regarded as clear, reliable and amenable to delivering their normative values in proper proportions to the research process as occasion demanded.

There can be no doubt that practical theology was reinvigorated by its empirical turn. It revived academic potency, attracted funding, research posts and graduate students. More than this, a clear sense of identity and purpose emerged among those committed to this trajectory.[9] They held that practical theology could now claim its own defined sphere of concerns and distinct methods of approach. Still better, these were now easily communicable within the academy and of evident usefulness to faith-based communities. While not all practical theologians enthusiastically welcomed these developments – both methodological and political concerns were raised by feminist scholars in particular (see Walton, 2014b; and Miller-McLemore, 2017) – their impact was profound and transformative. Furthermore, significant new currents were developing in theological thinking that were to further intensify the interest that had been awakened in the constitution, practice and witness of ecclesial communities.

---

8 Although van der Ven argued from the beginning that both modes of research could make important contributions.

9 For an account of the formation of the International Academy of Practical Theology, and van der Ven's bid to use the term 'empirical theology' as the new name of the discipline, see Riet Bons-Storm's 'The birth of the IAPT, a personal impression', https://www.ia-practicaltheology.org/history (accessed 02.04.2025).

An ecclesial turn

It is beyond the scope of this work to discuss in detail the elements that have contributed to a renewed theological focus on ecclesial life.[10] However, it will be helpful to point towards some elements of its varied genealogy. It drew inspiration from reinterpretations of the work of Karl Barth, who is now interpreted as being a narrative and performative theologian. The work of the philosopher Alasdair MacIntyre (1981) provided insights into the ways in which narrative traditions shaped the distinctive values embodied in communal life. The postliberal analyses of Yale theologians, notably Hans Frei and George Lindbeck, were employed to explore ways in which Christian communities possessed their own distinctive idioms/culture/language and identity. Interestingly, Lindbeck in particular had also drawn heavily upon the work of Clifford Geertz to establish this, albeit in a rather different theological milieu (e.g. Lindbeck, 1984, pp. 37, 115). In the 'postmodern' context such cultural distinctiveness, postliberal theologians maintained, was not to be regarded as problematic, preventing faith groups from fully engaging with a wider culture. Instead of maintaining the grand narratives of 'Christendom', attention should be given to the ways in which groups possessed their own essential charisms and intracommunal sources of wisdom. This concern with Christian distinctiveness resonated with Stanley Hauerwas's influential theological vision of the Church as a story-formed community whose members inhabited its narrative and continually performed its truth in their lives (1978, 1981). In this frame, churches constitute 'virtuous' communities shaping members in faithful ways of living that offered a countercultural witness to the countercultural gospel. The practices of ecclesial communities were thus not merely palely illustrative of certain doctrines and beliefs – they incarnated them. There was an unbreakable link between revelation and performance, which implies that interrogating the life of congregations was vital theological work.[11] As Pete Ward maintained, 'to understand the church we should view it as being simultaneously theological and social/cultural' (2012b, p. 2).

Recognition of the importance of performative practice in Christian communities contributed to an increasingly ecclesial focus to 'empirical' work in practical theology – although wider perspectives were main-

---

10 For a fuller discussion, see Graham, Walton and Ward, 2019, pp. 102–18.

11 However, this does not mean that Hauerwas and others were necessarily enthusiastic about social scientific approaches being applied to ecclesial life.

tained in areas of the discipline where qualitative research methods enjoyed a less hegemonic role.[12] Whereas van der Ven and his colleagues had pursued research interests in matters of theological importance *both within and beyond the household of faith* (perhaps reflecting their Catholic ethos and traditions), the identity and practice of Christian groups was now becoming a central focus. Attention turned towards how use of qualitative research tools might inform both doctrinal theology and missional engagement. New research networks emerged. A gathering at Yale led to the formation of what was to become an international 'Ecclesiology and Ethnography Network'[13] and later the establishment of the Ecclesial Practices Unit of the American Academy of Religion.[14] The Theological Action Research Network (TARN) developed in the UK out of similar missional concerns.[15] Receiving insights from a range of ecclesial traditions, it focused on relations between espoused, operative, formal and normative beliefs embodied in the everyday practices of Christians living out their faith in particular cultures and contexts (see Cameron et al., 2010).

As these movements have gained in influence, the agenda of those engaged in using qualitative research in ecclesial contexts has also expanded and has lately become decidedly more inclusive. Practical theologians from a wide range of theological and denominational traditions, and many geographical locations, are now actively and collegially engaged in research in the field. The participation of women scholars has increased exponentially – the early empirical theology movement was decidedly male-centred – and their contributions are now mainstream. In *The Wiley Blackwell Companion to Theology and Qualitative Research* (Ward and Tveitereid, 2022) women's work plays a central role. This important text also contains contributions from theologians of colour and queer perspectives on practical theological research. Furthermore, challenges to the boundaries in which qualitative research, and indeed

---

12 *The Wiley Blackwell Companion to Practical Theology* (Miller-McLemore, 2012b) and *The International Handbook of Practical Theology* (Weyel et al., 2022) demonstrate the wide scope of the discipline, exploring a huge range of pastoral, political and practice concerns pursued through various scholarly means.

13 See Ward, 2018, p. 173, for a discussion of the theological genesis of the network.

14 The Brill journal *Ecclesial Practices* has also become an important forum for work undertaken in these contexts.

15 TARN draws inspiration and leadership from a wide range of Christian denominations. However, the approach to reflection employed assumes precedence of established tradition viewed as normative.

theology, have been positioned are now being made by those who have been closely involved in these academic networks. Natalie Wigg-Stevenson, for example, has been particularly active in her efforts to expand the horizons of research methods employed to study ecclesial contexts (Wigg-Stevenson, 2018a, 2018b, 2022). Nicola Slee has also persistently advocated for and exemplified poetic approaches to qualitative research on spirituality and faith issues (e.g. Slee, 2017). Helen Cameron has played a leading role in the development of Project Violet (on women's ministry in the Baptist Union of Great Britain) which is a creative and participatory initiative that is path-breaking in terms of ecclesial research.[16] This is an active, lively and rapidly evolving scholarly area but although it is one of increased diversity in terms of participants there is still much less diversity in approaches to research or to engagement with contemporary theoretical thinking.

Making with borrowed tools

So this is, in many ways, a success story. Yet despite, or because of, the generative productivity qualitative research methods have enabled within practical theology, strong currents of unease do surface periodically concerning the status of the research tools now so routinely employed. Concern has been expressed about the alien values that may be imported when tools from a secular discipline are accorded such a central place within the theological domain – a particular concern to those holding a postliberal or Hauerwasian theological stance. John Swinton is one of those who has repeatedly raised this as an area of concern. He has pointed out, entirely correctly, that research methods have genealogical characteristics, particular histories and form perspectives that may not only enable wider vision but also occlude certain ways of apprehending the world (Swinton, 2012, p. 77). His characteristic gesture in response to this has been to warn of the danger that practical theologians might encounter if their own distinctive values are compromised (2012, p. 90). At the same time he advocates maintaining the position of a hospitable householder who welcomes guests warmly, but cherishes the sacrality of the theological domain and seeks to sanctify the secular tools that are now being routinely employed for sacred use.

---

16 For details of this important project, see: https://www.baptist.org.uk/Groups/363283/What_is_Project.aspx (accessed 24.04.2025).

A second concern, and one I particularly resonate with, has been raised consistently by Pete Ward. It was the cherished hope of van der Ven, Browning and other pioneering practical theologians that the espousal of 'empirical methods' would facilitate deeper theological thinking. But perhaps our borrowed tools really do have a disturbing power of their own to shift attention away from theological reflection, for there has been a decided lack of creative vitality in this domain. I believe that practical theology's agenda should take us far beyond the production of small-scale, scattered studies on aspects of church life and, like Ward, I am deeply dismayed by the lack of theological agency I discern within the discipline.[17] When I survey the field in journals, monographs, doctoral theses and conference contributions, I observe a striking theological reticence in what is being presented. Often those who have conducted empirical research present their results and then express the hope that others (who are these others?) will perceive its significance for further theological thinking. It is as if we were humbly resigned to serve as lab technicians preparing fine slices of religious life for the real scientists to examine and draw conclusions from. As Ward maintains:

> Theology is ... seen as [an] ... enterprise ... that is somewhat disconnected from [our concern] practice ...[it] is dealt with by systematic theologians and they have their conversations ... but those of us who are engaged in empirical research ... when it comes to practice we have a better way of looking at things. The fact that this kind of social scientific enquiry [we do] is generally regarded as practical theology ... serves to disguise what is effectively a move away from theology. (2018, pp. 159–60)

Third, the status of what we make – what takes shape when we employ our 'tools' – remains a topic of debate. A 'Chalcedonian' paradigm[18] is sometimes employed to manifest a necessary order in relations between the 'disciplines' of doctrinal theology and qualitative research. This combines indissoluble differentiation; inseparable unity; indestructible order and *logical priority*. John Swinton writes honestly and sensitively

---

17 See Miller-McLemore's presidential address to IAPT, Miller-McLemore, 2012a, for another perspective on this concern.

18 Developed from the work of Deborah van Deusen Hunsinger (1995) who was an active interlocuter in earlier debates among pastoral theologians seeking to interpret and assess the relationship between psychology and theology. I am grateful to Bonnie Miller-McLemore for her recollections of these conversations.

about the challenges this question poses and, while receptive to differing approaches, names his anxiety concerning those 'who have fallen in love with the social sciences and want to grant them too much authority over theology' (2012, p. 92). When other practical theologians have focused upon the dilemmas posed when our research reveals ecclesial communities haphazardly and happily, or indeed consciously and purposefully, embodying divergent beliefs, values and practices from those assumed to possess normative status, what do we make of our results? But if we identify emergent theologies in their practice that may be different to/critical of those legitimated by the historical tradition, what judgements do we make concerning these? Where does authority lie? For some there is an obvious answer to this question. In such a frame, Clare Watkins stresses that 'there remains an intractable asymmetry [here] ... given that the authority of the normative (notably magisterial) voices are already legitimated readings [of] ... tradition' (2015, p. 147).

In contrast to this position, however, other colleagues are now reassessing the notion of normativity itself. The term is being reconceived and used less to imply the essential precedence of established norms and more to express commitment to an outworking of values (which may be mutable) in contextual practice.[19] Natalie Wigg-Stevenson, for example, suggests that establishing normativity is constructive work and 'ethnographic theologians can use the ethnographic research question to shape the normative weight of sources in the field and what types of normative claims can be made out of that fieldwork in the theological text' (2015, p. 1) In this frame, being justly concerned about normativity involves being open to change and also, in many contexts, discerning (sometimes painfully) how faith can be embodied with authenticity in ambiguous circumstances.[20]

Finally, when assessing relations between practical theology and qualitative research, there are pragmatic methodological concerns to consider. These are important but rarely addressed. I am particularly anxious that if we 'borrow' tools (or perhaps a better metaphor for this distanced transaction would be 'buy them online') rather than engage with and participate in the community that constructs, regulates and trains people in their use, and from time to time retires and replaces

---

19 Both interpretations of normativity can justly be seen as representing classical interpretations of the term, but have very different implications for theological thinking.

20 For further reflections on this theme, see Kaufman, 2016; and Ideström and Kaufman, 2018b.

them, then we will become increasingly out of touch with 'health and safety' considerations as well as new developments in technique and practice.

Being out of touch also means that our 'tool set' can become far too restricted, rendering us unable to seize the new opportunities that now exist to craft and create far beyond our restricted repertoire. There is a danger that we undertake our work in a practical theology 'echo-chamber' and do not look beyond this for inspiration and challenge. This is a real threat to scholarship in our discipline. While welcoming the important achievement that *The Wiley Blackwell Companion to Theology and Qualitative Research* (Ward and Tveitereid, 2022) represents, I was dismayed to note how many of the authors did not reference secular literature on research methodology in their contributions, and how those that did tended to draw from a very restricted range of sources. Theoretical encounters are similarly limited, with the same (usually male and white[21]) scholars being repeatedly referenced. As Wigg-Stevenson has noted, our default mode of qualitative research and ethnography is often perceived in very limited terms.[22] She states:

> When we talk about ethnography, we are talking about practical methods, and very few practical methods at that: interviews, participant observation, surveys and sometimes action research. The proliferation of creative, literary, artistic, or performance-based approaches with which anthropologists have experimented have not, by and large, found their way into the array of methodological options for theologians. (2017, p. 5)

Gifts for the journey

I now turn to explore a different way of imaging the relationship between theology and qualitative research and to do so I offer another fairy tale scenario.

Let us imagine a hero who has set out on their hero's quest. A few hours of questing makes them hungry. Just as they are thinking it is time to sit down beneath a tree to eat their vegan cheese sandwich (wrapped

---

21 There are a great many male and white theorists in this book as well ... but different ones ...

22 This is in spite of the fact that ethnography has been relentlessly critiqued, reflected upon and revisioned by qualitative researchers. See Smartt Gullion, 2018.

in a red and white spotted handkerchief) they encounter a wise old woman, or a mysterious little man, or maybe even an eloquent, talking beast. This (very strange) stranger gives the hero a special gift to help them on their way. It is a gift that they could in no way have made themselves, but which is incredibly useful. A tablecloth that spreads itself with delicious food whenever the hero lays it out, seven league boots, a golden thread to guide them through the dark forest, a smartphone with Google maps ... whatever.

Beyond borrowing

I began this chapter by discussing various encounters between qualitative research and practical theology that have decisively impacted upon our discipline. While both the first and second wave of 'empirical' engagements have been internally transformative, their impact has not resonated as far beyond our particular academic community as might have been hoped. A largely separate debate, however, is currently taking place between anthropology and 'impractical' theology (systematic/dogmatic theology and moral theology/theological ethics). This has engaged major figures from both fields.[23] While the focus of this book remains upon practical theology, it is very useful to consider the rather different terms on which this cognate conversation is predicated because of the useful comparisons this generates with our own project.

An interesting thing to note at the beginning is that a dialogue is envisaged that goes beyond employing the tools of one discipline to pursue aims already established within another. The theologian Michael Banner states, 'It is not a matter here then, of anthropology simply providing tools ready to hand for a moral theology which already knows very well what it is doing. I suggest that the encounter is more dynamic' (2016, p. 29). The anthropologist Joel Robbins similarly states he is seeking a relationship that goes beyond one in which (practical[24]) theologians become enthusiastic about 'borrowing anthropology's method

---

23 See Lemons, 2018a, for an excellent overview. See also *The Journal of the Royal Anthropological Institute*, 28 (2022), in which religious thinkers from differing faith perspectives engage in thought-provoking conversations with anthropologists.

24 Robbins names Scharen and Vigen and Wigg-Stevenson as examples of such 'borrowing' here.

of ethnography' (2020, p. 5).²⁵ I will return to explore the contribution of these two interlocuters below, but their hopeful expectation of mutually enriching encounters demonstrates why I have employed the shared anthropological/theological motif of 'gift giving' as a symbolics through which to characterize their dialogue. It is being undertaken in a spirit of curious optimism that mutually transformative 'new insights and theories are waiting to be discovered in the largely unexplored territories between the disciplines' (Lemons, 2018b, p. 119). Such positive statements about the potential of conversations between anthropology and theology contrast strikingly with the view of van der Ven (see page xx) that social scientists, representing the vanguard of secularization, were likely to be hostile to – or disinterested in – theological thinking. Clearly, some at least have moved far beyond this position in recent decades. Developments within both disciplines have led scholars to seek new forms of reciprocity between them.

Anthropologists engaging with theology

In terms of anthropology a number of reasons for engaging with theology are clearly identifiable within the literature. First, some scholars have sought to highlight the contributions Christian anthropologists have made to the development of the discipline (for example, Larson, 2014; and Merz and Merz, 2015, p. 2). E. E. Evans-Pritchard, Mary Douglas and Victor and Edith Turner are among the acknowledged pioneers of anthropological methods. But if genealogies are being drawn, I believe the more ambiguous religious identities of Michel de Certeau and Bruno Latour should also be acknowledged here.²⁶ There is a danger, however, as Derrick Lemons points out, in looking back towards lineages when the aim of current conversations should be to move forward into new futures. Nevertheless, as he concedes, such genealogical reclamations may have the helpful effect of stimulating 'a new conversation about the role of Christian faith commitments in anthropology' (2016, p. 143).

A second major trigger for dialogue has been a 'religious' turn in theory, one that has been underway since the 1990s, generating impacts

---

25 Robbins is also very scathing about the ways in which practical theologians, in particular, have used ethnographic techniques to prove things they already knew. He regards the approaches to anthropology made on the basis of what can be gained by using its tools as akin to marrying for money!

26 Both of these radical heroes of mine retained deep connections with Catholicism while pursuing their path-making social and cultural analyses.

within many disciplinary contexts. This movement can be understood as part of a wider quest to employ cultural resources not exhausted by their conscription to traditional modes of philosophical and political thinking in order to deconstruct and revision reflection on human futures.[27] Philip Fountain and Sin Wen Lau describe, *perhaps a little too extravagantly*, some of the parameters of this turn:[28]

> While theology was widely occluded as a meaningful conversation partner in the decades up to the 1990s, theological concerns are now being discussed by leading social theorists. From the widespread resurgent interest in Schmitt's ... analysis of 'political theology' ... via the surprising critical reappraisal of Saint Paul as a radical political and philosophical revolutionary (Badiou, 2003; Žižek, 2003; Agamben, 2005; Milbank et al., 2010), to the growing recognition of the pertinence that particular strands of contemporary theological enquiry have for philosophy (De Vries, 1999), and to renewed reflections on the implications of living in a post-secular (or never secular) world ... theology is now back at the centre of progressive and critical theoretical analysis. (2013, p. 229)

Yet another 'turn' has been a third significant motivating factor. The so-called ontological turn challenged anthropological (and other) researchers to consider their apprehension of the ontologies (worldviews, and indeed the 'divergent worlds' and 'worlding' activities) of the populations they were engaged with. What position should they assume in relation to these 'ontologies'? Were they measuring what was perceived as 'different' against an uninterrogated cultural norm? Might a deep engagement with the thoughtforms of unfamiliar worlds, *on their own terms*, be potentially generative of important new theoretical insights? Particularly as these might possess the potential to 'shatter our own familiar ways of analysing the world' (Robbins, 2020, p. 19). Some proponents of the ontological turn pressed even further than this. They

---

27 For a persuasive account of how theoretical developments rely on the continual 'colonization' of fresh territories (such as the feminine, the body and religion), see Alice Jardine's classic analysis of the place of the feminine in post-structuralist theory (Jardine, 1985).

28 Personally I think this is rather an over-statement of the significance of a religious turn in theory. I am not sure my colleagues in the university system in the UK would have noticed this new enthusiasm for theology! However, in terms of publications, conferences, academic debates and interdisciplinary research projects, there is certainly much more curiosity and openness than previously.

asked on what basis research participants' perspectives concerning the nature of being and the agency of beings were automatically deemed less 'true' than modern Western perspectives. Was it really possible to comprehend the ontologies of people when this was the default position? In other words, they countenanced taking 'leaps of faith' that would shift the anthropologist far from their traditional observational role and propel them into other spheres and dimensions entirely (see Bialecki, 2018).

There is not the space here to explore this movement further. However, it has clearly helped to create a climate in which Christianity (as one faith-based ontology among many) could be interrogated on its own terms and not as an unacknowledged norm that generates categories through which to assess the religion of others.[29] It also furthered recognition that the lived beliefs of Christians are entitled to the same sort of deeply curious respect that would be given to those generated from other traditions. Supported by such developments, there has been a growing recognition that Christianity is not only an imperialist imposition upon oppressed peoples but is also an 'indigenous' religion of the global South, and can make an emancipatory contribution in our challenging contemporary circumstances. James Bielo, for example, writes positively of the gifts that traditions of prophetic critique within Christianity offer. These inspire him to hope that 'meaningful collaboration with theology is possible and the broader project of human flourishing could advance as a result (Bielo, 2018a, p. 34).[30] Significantly, for the issues being explored in this text, all these developments functioning together mean that not only the rituals and practices of Christians, but also their theological inheritance, could be re-evaluated as worthy of sustained anthropological attention and potentially able to offer their particular contributions to the discipline.

---

29 It is a persistent anxiety within anthropology, as in Religious Studies, that a 'Protestant' model of interior assent to a set of beliefs has functioned as an unacknowledged norm in exploring traditions that do not conform to this template.

30 Bielo is far more interested in practical collaboration between anthropologists and people of faith than he is about comparing theoretical discourses. He hopes that this will stimulate a more daring and strategic exploration of those precious existing resources within traditions rather than smoothing out differences. He writes, 'Theologians have a tradition of prophetic critique that anthropologists equally interested in human flourishing might support. If a relationship between anthropology and theology is to blossom, each would do well to think less about dialoguing and more about collaborating' (2018a, p. 34).

Theologians receiving from anthropology

The motivating factors encouraging theologians to engage in conversation with anthropologists are rather more diffuse and diverse. This may be because theology is already so deeply implicated in relations with many other disciplines – although there are very different ways of understanding the nature of these relations. We might see theology as a queen of sciences whose royal 'gene code' has been irradicably passed on to disciplinary daughters in other fields of study (e.g. Milbank, 1993). Alternatively, we could see theology as a nomadic discipline which is forever forging its peculiar identity from transforming resources it receives from outside itself (e.g. Tanner, 1994). It should be said that this latter perspective does not imply a negative view of this process. Engaging theology with the resources of diverse cultural movements might be understood as faithfully responding to the revelatory signs of the times. Similarly, positing a 'weak' status for theological discourse could be viewed as integral to witnessing a kenotic divine becoming flesh and dwelling among us. Yet whatever our understanding of theology among the disciplines, it is undeniable that it perpetually trespasses beyond its own defined territories. Even postliberal theologians, keen to affirm the distinctiveness and particularity of Christian identity, have freely drawn upon anthropological resources, from the work of Geertz in particular – and without the appearance of any undue anxiety. However, a (re)turn to anthropology at this moment in time seems to have become particularly appealing.

In her concluding responses to the significant essays in *Theologically Engaged Anthropology* (Lemons, 2018a), Sarah Coakley identifies three reasons that theology should welcome productive encounters with anthropology and the enrichment these can bring. First she observes that anthropology's concern with lived religion, as opposed to institutional representations of ideal forms, draws attention to the 'everyday embodied practices of believers' – for example, 'in personal prayer, ritual enactment, acts of charity' (2018a, p. 373). These practices have been too long occluded in theological reflection and demand renewed attention.[31] Second, she maintains, anthropology can call Christianity to account for the 'distortions' and 'manipulations' of doctrinal teaching that generate abusive and oppressive practices – particularly in relation

---

31 It is very sad that the communications barrier that has long existed between practical theology and systematic/constructive theology means that Coakley does not engage with the work practical theologians have undertaken in this sphere for many years.

to gender, race and sexuality. 'It is not uncommon ... for a veneer of orthodox theological observance ... to hide a "multitude of sins" in terms of behaviours, practices, and prejudices: anything from child abuse to rampant sexism and racism' (2018, p. 374). Finally, she argues that anthropology offers rich, strange, startling insights and wisdom from the 'left field' of everyday religious practice that provokes new theological thinking.

> [These] would never be garnered simply from the classic sources of Scripture, reason, and tradition. Here are insights that often demand the most searing new reflection on those classic sources, since almost always they creatively entangle *with* them. In short, when doctrine and theological ethics are 'earthed' in 'lived religion', one has the opportunity to realign the kaleidoscope vision of 'systematic' theology in ever-creative and novel ways. (Coakley and Robbins, 2018, p. 374)

Although Coakley is at pains to stress that she is speaking as a systematic theologian, the concerns she outlines above are *very similar indeed* to those that have motivated practical theologians to study religious practice for the past half-century. It is perturbing how little impact scholarship in practical theology has made beyond our circumscribed disciplinary arena during this time. I wonder whether conceptualizing our work as an intradisciplinary project may have contributed to this isolation. I ponder this but realize that the boundaries between intra- and interdisciplinary approaches are probably more heuristic than actual in 'real-life' contexts. Whatever the case, Coakley's points are well made, but their tone now feels a little too pre-pandemic, too climate-crisis-blind, to express the urgency with which all theological subdisciplines are being challenged to discover new ways of embodying our concerns. It is a compelling challenge to find ways of communicating hope, articulating faith and proclaiming justice in forms that can be heard and understood in the midst of troubles. Clearly, anthropological resources might be helpful in discovering different modes in which to speak. And our own need to respond to troubled times finds a profound echo within anthropological circles. The sense that a new ethical posture, a new outlook on cultural change and crisis, is required is also being loudly articulated within this discipline (see Fassin, 2012, 2014). The giving and receiving of insights from one another appears to be both timely and potentially productive for both parties. Yet when we consider how this process functions in practice we become aware of unconsidered dangers that might be encountered on the hero's quest.

On looking gift horses in the mouth

As may be evident, I find metaphors of reciprocal 'gift giving' a more appealing way of picturing the relationship between disciplines than 'borrowing tools'. I like the conviviality, mutual enrichment and the openness to change that is implied. However, this does not mean that *actual* interdisciplinary encounters are straightforward or that the gifts each party imagines the other might provide are actually what they can offer. To illustrate some of the problems that can be encountered I now briefly turn to examine two key texts in this interdisciplinary exchange – first, Michael Banner's *The Ethics of Everyday Life* (2016) and then Joel Robbins's *Theology and the Anthropology of Christian Life* (2020).

Banner's book was enthusiastically received. His plea that moral theology might reconsider its previous reliance upon philosophical thinking when forming its ethical judgements struck a chord with many. He argued that this has created a tendency to: treat human dilemmas in abstract terms, focus upon consideration of 'difficult cases' removed from their context, and leave the theologian without the resources to understand why people make significant decisions in the way they do. In other words, why they act in ways that can seem simply unaccountable when employing the conventional resources of moral theology. It is Banner's conviction that if theologians turn to anthropological studies that shed light on deeply held cultural understandings, then what now appears unaccountable would be rendered comprehensible within its own terms. For 'what appears unfathomable ... [is] only unfathomable from where we may currently stand, with our particular limitations of experience and knowledge and failures of imagination and insight' (2016, p. 16). The 'psychologically and socio-culturally realistic' (2016, p. 24)[32] accounts that he believes anthropologists construct could enable moral theology to expand its limited understanding. It would then be able to respond to contemporary cultural values and practice 'therapeutically and evangelically' (2016, p. 202)[33] rather than with puzzlement or unconsidered condemnation.

---

32 Banner draws here from Robbins when assessing what the 'best' of social anthropology can contribute. For a discussion of realism as a genre in ethnography, see pp. 86–91.

33 Banner adds that theology might also learn from these countervisions (2016, p. 202), but it is not clear which of these would be instructive or how and in what way this might happen.

I welcome the motivations behind Banner's project. Welcome too are some thought-provoking reflections on identity and agency in the context of dementia, and the unexpected and sometimes beautiful artistic and spiritual reflections on the humanity of Christ that punctuate the text. However, there are troubling features to the work. I encounter these aspects as one of the people to whom Banner wishes to speak a therapeutic and evangelical word. I experienced many years of infertility and my daughter was conceived through IVF. To understand the perplexing conundrum of why I (and others) decided to undertake this harrowing and burdensome procedure, Banner has turned to certain ethnographic studies for guidance. He draws from these sources the clear conviction that contemporary cultural framings of childlessness point towards the persistence of notions of kinship that emphasize biological parenthood and lineage. So those women like myself who choose IVF are to be understood as 'chasing the blood tie' (2016, p. 50) – a very strange phrase[34] used repeatedly in Banner's text. It is this prevailing bloodline ideology, he argues, that presents childlessness as a desperate ill only to be remedied by the commodified attainment of a child of one's own. This ideology, supported by the medical establishment, a sexist culture and the many other dark forces that prey upon our grief must be challenged by an alternative vision that does not 'chase the blood tie', but instead celebrates the 'troubling' of kinship and formation of different relationship ties within the Church:

> Virginity, godparenthood, and baptism ... propose a therapeutic and evangelical word in relation to the subject of infertility ... The task for Christian ethics here, then, is to try to come to terms with and narrate the difference which the reality of Christian troubling of kinship should make to our understanding. (2016, p. 55)

There are some elements I would not contest within Banner's position: of course, powerful ideologies are at play across the terrain of women's bodies; and, of course, childlessness is not an inevitably tragic condition. Yes, all sorts of queer kin ties (even with virgins and godparents) are good in forming bonds beyond the blood relations; and it is clearly a horrible idea to think you can 'possess' a child. However, I wrestle with Banner's self-assured diagnosis of a many-angled-knees-and-elbows-

---

34 Banner borrows the phrase 'blood tie' from the work of M. C. Inhorn and D. Birenbaum-Carmeli, 2008. They in turn borrowed it from Helena Ragoné who was writing about surrogacy way back in 1996.

sharp-edged issue. His representation of infertility is simply too simple. Although Banner rejects the cerebral offerings of philosophy he appears to be seeking similar forms of 'sure knowledge' concerning the nature of things from his new anthropological conversation partner. To achieve his confident perspective on infertility and the blood tie it has been necessary to single out a particular 'realist' genre of anthropological research from the diverse approaches in the field,[35] and then to combine some selected resources he finds within it. He does this without justification for selecting these and ignoring others, until a picture emerges that has all the appearances of reality and can be addressed as such. The debates that have shaped anthropology in recent years (only some of which I have discussed above) are ignored as Banner unselfconsciously explains to women like me where our problems really lie – that is, in misconceptions, or wrong thinking, that could be remedied by better understanding.

Theologians need to discover 'ways to tell the truth from people's lives that refuse to be "violently simple or demonically final"' (Wigg-Stevenson, 2018b, p. 199, quoting Jordan, 2013, p. 5) as this. We need to enter contexts that are messy, conflictual and uncertain because they are inhabited by desiring, affective, embodied persons positioned within multiple complex networks that shape their choices and identities in troubled times. We will not be able to see clearly here, but anthropology may indeed help us to find our way. For there are alternative anthropological ways of proceeding that would enable theologians to sit down and listen to the 'rush of troubled stories' women have to tell about infertility and make such listening 'part of our knowledge practices' (Tsing, 2015, p. 33; see p. 7). In adopting such modes of approach we might come to recognize the painful ambiguities of *all* reproductive pathways (for there is no 'normal' as there is no 'other'). Alongside anthropologists we could

---

35 Bielo, for example, identifies at least three genres within contemporary anthropology: realist, confessional and impressionist (2018b, pp. 153–4). All of these are mainstream but have very different conventions and understandings of the anthropological task. The realist strand (which I think is what Banner is singling out when he talks of 'good anthropology') is only one voice and increasingly speaks in more circumspect tones. Bielo writes that realist ethnography assumes the voice 'of a third-party scribe reporting directly on the life of the observed ... Authority rests largely on the unexplicated experience of the author in the setting and the "feel" [he or she] has apparently developed for the time, place, and people.' Realist writing boasts a certain confidence that what is being reported and argued aligns closely with the way things really were and, through the rhetorical device of the ethnographic present, still are (2018b, p. 153).

share in the struggle to find ways of transcribing the body's longing into the scholarly lexicon and find our theological categories challenged and changed as a result. These concerns are ones I shall continue to reflect on as this work progresses.

But to turn back now to anthropology. I have argued that Banner is seeking from anthropology forms of 'sure knowledge', unobtainable from within theology itself, which appear useful for his project. Anthropologists are very unlikely to be seeking the forms of sure knowledge – that is, concerning the things of God – that theology might be expected to offer in return.[36] Indeed, anthropological approaches to theology imply neither interest in, or assent to, the existence of God at all. So on what terms might anthropologists hope profitable exchanges could take place?

Joel Robbins was one of the first anthropologists to seriously consider the discomforting potential theology might possess and to suggest that it might provoke and disturb anthropology through encounters with 'real otherness in the world' (2006, p. 292). In his recent work he explores the theological provocation to imagine otherwise and differently through bringing theological approaches to bear on a series of anthropological case studies. These enable him to: explore 'conversion' as a paradigm of positive, radical discontinuity in contrast to traditional anthropological perspectives that have framed cultural change in terms of loss; reflect on how differing theologies of atonement interact with cultural forms to construct very different understandings of personhood and agency in what might superficially be understood as similar religious settings; consider how modern eschatological theologies might help anthropologists comprehend the worlds and practices of those who live in ever-present millennial expectations of overwhelming change. He also examines ways in which Christian theologians have expressed criticisms of 'prosperity gospel' approaches to faith as a challenge to anthropologists seeking to discern ways to make ethical judgements in a manner that is appropriate to their discipline. In his reflections upon what these case studies have revealed, he concludes that theology pushes anthropology towards deep reflection upon such fundamental issues as time, continuity and change; the springs of hope and creative action; and the ethical wisdom needed

---

36 Individual anthropologists clearly have interests in this question and fascinating debates are taking place as to whether God can be regarded as possessing agency in cultural contexts even if God is not a person, as traditionally understood, but rather a conjunction of active material and social constructed forces that together produce outcomes.

to 'name and judge' in those dark places in which people are 'poor, suffering, ill and/or oppressed' (Robbins, 2020, p. 166).

Robbins's writing style is very different from that of Banner. As someone whose disciplinary training fosters self-reflexivity and openness he constructs his arguments in a less didactic mode – and it is always very interesting to read engaging narratives from unfamiliar contexts, and his book contains many of these. Yet despite these apparent differences there is a correspondence between the work of these two scholars. Like Banner, Robbins often appears to be looking for something firm and strong from theology that will deliver its potency to the anthropological project. His insightful reflections betray a fascination with issues of normativity and transcending perspectives which challenge through compelling otherness. Perhaps, as some of his interlocuters have suggested, Robbins's approach to theology has been shaped by his initial engagement with the work of John Milbank (see Fountain and Wen Lau, 2013; and Coakley and Robbins, 2018). This would certainly have fostered a perception of the peculiar status of theological discourse and a tendency to identify theology with 'the written practices of elites' (Coakley, in Coakley and Robbins, 2018, p. 371) as it is in this form that theology best assumes its normative guise. It is not that Robbins, actively engaged in conversations with theology for many years now, is unaware of the theological practice that takes place in a variety of contexts beyond the academic or magisterial domains (2018). Rather, it is simply that the resources he is most attracted to within theology tend to be those that appear to have a clarity and luminescence that improvised and performed local theologies do not possess. However, their radiance may be illusory. For, as Sarah Coakley wryly states, 'If theology *is* essentially normative or prescriptive, it is not a priori obvious *in what way*' (Coakley, in Coakley and Robbins, 2018, p. 370) and one of the most significant outcomes of the dialogue with anthropology might have been that this has now become abundantly clear.

Metamorphosis and mingling

Through engaging with the work of Banner and Robbins I have noted some of the issues that arise when we employ a symbolism of gifting to explore relations between theology and the social sciences. The 'gift' might be imagined to supply a lack and what is desired may be eagerly consumed without reference to the way in which the gift itself is subject to ongoing testing and tasting within its own context. I now turn to the more uncertain and challenging stories of form shifting and transitions to be found in many myths, legends and fairy stories.

Such a story could be told in this way. Once there was a (male) heir to a rich inheritance; a prince perhaps, or maybe even a whole band of royal brothers. Unfortunately, they foolishly transgressed a deep code or were cruelly bewitched by a wicked usurper. Either way, they were changed from their proud and manly forms into those of a beast, a frog, a fierce bear in the forest, or a flock of wild geese or swans. They had to live like this until their enchantment could be undone (by a pure love, of course) and what was rightfully theirs was restored to them. When they regained their true form deep changes endured. The youngest royal brother still has a white-feathered wing where his arm should be, the frog prince spends hours in the bath, the bear king has appallingly long toenails. All of them carry back to the heart of their kingdoms the wisdom of wild.

I should point out that there is a rather different story for girls. You, my dear, are beautiful beyond words. So beautiful indeed that everyone wishes either to possess you or destroy you. I am afraid there is only one way out for a woman in this position – and that is plant life. Just as your enemy seems to have you in their grasp, your legs grow into the ground, your arms become branches, and your beautiful tresses turn into soft green leaves. You are safe, but sadly there is no return from this verdant state. Fairy tales, as you know, dearest one, don't always favour our sex! However, although you have become organic, your personhood endures. You retain your voice. You can sing, you can weep and lament, and you can utter warnings. You can even wrap your strong arms around those in danger and rescue them from peril.

Latent commons

I enjoy stories such as these which point to changes that rend us apart and strangely remake us. They invite us to take a walk on the wild side and to find love where the wild things are. They anticipate the gains and the losses we may encounter there and teach us to listen very carefully to what the trees are saying. But, before I get too carried away, they also return me to some of the concerns I explored in Chapter 1 through the work of Anna Tsing (see pp. 5–8). Tsing asked how we might, in the midst of ruination and troubles, become part of a vital web and discover ways of life that entail mixing with 'multi-species others without knowing where the world-in-process is going' (2015, p. 264). Tsing's work is situated both literally and metaphorically in the devastated forests and wasted landscapes at the periphery of things. It is here she notes the potentiality of a *latent commons*[37] in which 'mutualist and non-antagonistic entanglements [are] found within the play of this confusion' (2015, p. 254). It is within this real-imagined terrain that I now wish to place theology and the social sciences and envision the sort of encounters between them that Tsing evokes as mergings (with trees and other living and non-living things), contaminations and conviviality. Such forms of mutual-and-mutating living, to follow Tsing's parabolic work further, are necessary because our fragile environment cannot support the territories of single life forms. It is not clear what such minglings will generate. The future is uncertain but our symbiotic interdependence represents a tenacious, if inglorious, muddling through, all mixed up together in the midst of things, which might be our best hope now.

Clearly, my reflections here are less related to 'developments in the field' than has been the case in my previous case studies. However, similar images of interdisciplinary encounters are emerging elsewhere as people seek to revision epistemologies emergent in our changed climate. The anthropologists Johannes Merz and Sharon Merz (2015), for example, argue that ethnography always takes place in a liminal sphere of meetings, 'where our whole beings are questioned and affected'. This space can be extended to form what they term 'the ontological penumbra'. This environment is one in which a mutated anthropology open to the sacred can flourish. Their vision is worth quoting at length:

> Anthropologists access the ontological penumbra by the means of a common humanity ... in order to expose ourselves both ethnographically and experientially to difference and change ... The ontological penumbra is an area where the self and the other, belief and disbelief, as well as the secular and the religious, meet, overlap and intermingle, sometimes even to the extent of conflation ... As a space of dialogue and encounter, it should be open to plural epistemologies ... this is also the area where other academic disciplines, such as theology, could

---

37 Although the concept of a 'latent commons' is a heuristic device, its resonance is such that it has been taken up and concretized across such diverse fields as environmental geography and performance art. See, for example, Callaghan, Marojevic and Kennedy, 2019; and Dawney, 2020.

make their contributions to anthropology. The ontological penumbra is a challenging position to occupy, since it is in constant flux and subject to paradoxes, ambiguity, uncertainty, tension and negotiation, presenting itself occasionally even as threatening, sometimes leading to acute anxiety. This is why anthropologists need to occupy the ontological penumbra consciously and engage with it reflexively, both emotionally and analytically ... This, in turn, leads to productivity and creativity. In a nutshell, we argue that the ontological penumbra is a suitable locus that lends itself to the development of postsecular anthropology. (2015, p. 9)

Entering the wild

Theologians are also beginning to venture into the commons of this shadowland. In several contributions, Leive Orye (2018) has challenged theologians to stray beyond what they consider to be safe anthropological sources and engage with the deeply relational work of Bruno Latour (see pp. 13–14) and Tim Ingold (see pp. 8–9) in particular. She believes we should respond to Ingold's vision of anthropology as a process of urgent, imaginative, creative explorations *with others* and his openness to theology as a means of 'imaginative participation in a more-than-human world' (2018, p. 331). Following the arguments of Elizabeth O'Donnell Gandolfo (2018), she argues for a recovery of a sense of the wildness of the space in which we dwell alongside others and do our work. For O'Donnell Gandolfo speaks of theological imagination developing situations that lack security, that are unpredictable, and in which we can experience 'A deep sense of relationship ... of knowing oneself to be a part of a larger whole – however wild and wounding that whole can be' (O'Donnell Gandolfo, 2018, p. 306). Real changes happen here: '... of learning, of transformation, of learning to see differently ... Of encountering the other as one's neighbor, engaging, risking ... allowing the other to be revelatory to oneself and allowing God to use oneself as revelatory for the other, in his or her way of being' (McFague, in O'Donnell Gandolfo, 2018).

And practical theologians seeking modes of interdisciplinary engagement beyond borrowing and gifting are also making our own trails towards the unregulated commons and leave helpful tracks and traces behind us for those who wish to enter there. I particularly value some of the path-making work contained in the edited collections *Ethnography* as *Christian Theology and Ethics* (Scharen and Vigen, 2011), *Qualitative Research in Theological Education* (Moschella and Willhauck, 2018) and *What Really Matters* (Ideström and Kaufman, 2018b). Elsewhere individual practical theologians are making their own forays into an emerging latent commons with transformative results (e.g. Wigg-Stevenson, 2022; Turpin, 2025; and Whitmore, 2019).

I should say that I do see these ventures into a common territory as being rather different from Ward's proposal that we come to view the 'methods associated with qualitative research as something distinct from any disciplinary location within the social sciences' (2022, p. 8) and therefore easily transposed and accommodated within practical theology. To view them as 'detachable' in this way and therefore capable of becoming integrated into the theological project comes close to the intradisciplinary perspective espoused by van der Ven (see p. 41). It is also, ironically, to hypostasize these methods and give them an enduring body and form that I do not believe they possess.

There are no such things as qualitative research methods per se in a timeless and decontextualized sense. There are simply ways of seeing and paying attention that have been developed in specific locations, drawing on specialized wisdoms and experience, and which we might engage with to transformative effect. These methods develop, mutate and change. They are also open to critique through which their limitations are recognized and addressed. As I have argued, practical theology has been slow to recognize these processes of change because we have maintained a posture of separation rather than relation. Although my appreciation of Ward's generative work is genuine and despite the fact that we share very many common concerns, there is an important difference in our perspectives here. I am imagining generative relational intimacy and he is advocating for a form of fruitful incorporation.

Of course, there are theological perspectives at play here. More and more I am of the opinion that the theological drivers that prompted emphases upon the distinctive identity of the Christian community *as a form of witness* may no longer speak to the situation in which we find ourselves today. As Latour has argued, new relational cosmologies are developing as significant responses to the climate disaster (2024, p. 8). The environmental crisis presses upon us the need to discover resources in the Christian tradition to witness within this entangled political/spiritual context. The forming of radical, ecclesial communities of difference does not testify in this time in the way it once might have. However, I do not understand relationality to imply an eradication of difference. Diversity is what constitutes a cosmopolitan commons. Nor do I believe entanglement implies an end to radical critique as we engage in the, sometimes wounding, efforts to find ways towards convivial living.

It has been a long journey for me but I am now drawn towards visions of practical theology that both reconceive ecclesial theology and also extend its concerns beyond the boundaries of the Church. In coming to this perspective I have been deeply influenced by the work and example of my friend Elaine Graham with her persistent insistence upon the need to discover creative ways of co-living and cooperation in the public square (e.g. Graham, 2017a, pp. 7–9). Academic work by, and interactions with, Muslim scholars have also been part of this development. I have been fortunate in my friendships with both Nevin Reda and Saiyyidah Zaidi – as well as benefiting from their significant work (e.g. Reda, 2018; and Zaidi, 2023). Such friendly encounters have been transformative for me – as I know they have been for others.[38]

I am coming to the end of this chapter and need to emphasize again that the models I have presented here are only models. My fairy stories are fairy stories. In the big, wild world, ways of thinking, doing and being bleed into one another, they overlap, and they are not neatly divisible into the categories I have framed. Sometimes we may borrow, sometimes gift, sometimes cohabit and mingle. While we like to debate our terms of engagement, often all these processes are happening at once. At other times it is necessary to seek to restrain certain encounters for very good reasons in order to allow difference itself to become regenerative for common life. Furthermore, while these small debates about disciplinary encounters appear to be of limited significance I am locating them in the wider political and theological context and seeking a bridge between these worlds. It is for this reason that I have pursued Tsing's image of the latent commons through this text. I treasure its stress upon mutuality in a context of uncertainty and its earthy, indeterminate, provisional nature. It speaks across diverse terrains, and even as an imagined space it gives me hope. The commons are the space where I wish to dwell.

So I close this chapter and this part of the book with some words by the Caribbean poet and visionary Édouard Glissant, who pointed towards creative (if sometimes chaotic) reconfigurations of territories

---

38 See Zaidi and Stoddart, 2024, for a moving and informative testimony to the impact of personal and collegial encounters between those engaged in practical theology from different faith traditions.

and belonging as co-habitations and celebrated 'creolizations' as a mode of resilient and resisting living:

> Our common places, even though today they are of no use, of absolutely no use against the concrete oppressions that stun the world, are nevertheless capable of changing the imagination of human communities: it is through the imagination that we will ultimately conquer these derelictions that attack us. (Glissant, 2020, p. 7)

PART TWO

Practical Theology as Creative Work

Part Two of this book wrestles with some of the methodological issues that I persist in seeing as linked to the bigger questions and challenges we currently face. It begins by exploring our current ethnographic practice as a mode of poetics before moving to advocate for the greater use of arts-engaged methods and artistic models in practical theological research.

I begin in Chapter 4 by exploring how contemporary research in practical theology has been shaped and formed by tropes and writing traditions that were inherent in the ambivalent, colonial formation of ethnography. I explore how our work has been intertwined with traditions that are spiritual and secular all-at-once and resist disentanglement. These traditions are also mythic, imaginative and artistic. The question, therefore, is not whether practical theology should employ creative resources in its work. The issue is how do we discern what elements from the diverse traditions we have adopted might be most productive for us in our current context.

Chapter 5 pursues this theme further by arguing that arts-engaged research projects and the employment of arts-based methods might enable us to engage with responsiveness to matters that are difficult to comprehend by other means. I also argue that this responsiveness has implications for our current understandings of academic rigour and prompts us to reconsider how we understand by excellence in research.

The final chapter in Part Two reconnects domestic discussions of research methodologies to the bigger challenges of living in troubled times. I explore some key ways in which artists, activists and cultural theorists have understood the role that art plays in times of crisis. I argue that these provide pointers towards the way that practical theologians might understand our vocation as theological 'creatives' – and I point towards ways in which we are already starting to do so.

4

The Poetics and Politics of Practical Theology

In the last chapter I imaged theology as borrowing and gifting resources and as located in a liminal space of intimate conviviality, mutual adaptiveness and transformation. In this chapter I continue this discussion of interdisciplinary interaction by exploring the inheritance practical theology has already received from anthropology and sociology (in particular from the ethnographic project) in greater depth. Moving away from fairy tales I take a critical approach to one aspect of this legacy in particular – our writing practices and the politics our poetics embody (for a broader discussion of poetics in practical theology, see Walton, 2012).

For while transformative encounters between disciplines are both inevitable and life-giving, this aspect of our bequest has not been sufficiently interrogated or examined. Much of our focus has been on the supposedly secular nature of social research and how this can be accommodated within a sacred frame. Questions of normativity have predominated but we have paid less attention to how the forms of writing that have been prominent in qualitative research are everywhere mirrored in the ways practical theology has come to be written.[1] I am keen to discern in what ways established styles, genres and figurative devices may be disciplining our work and, most particularly, our theological labours.

To achieve these ends it is necessary to trespass beyond 'common sense' discourses that present qualitative research as simply a beneficent means of hearing, seeing or disclosing things we were unable to hear, see or perceive as well before. In other words, to move beyond empirical tropes of knowledge formed through sense experience and to engage with qualitative research as a discursive form – that is, 'as writing'. In what follows there will be a particular focus upon ethnography within

---

1 'Correlation does not equal causation' as the saying goes. But ...

my wider discussion. This is the most widely utilized form of qualitative research within practical theology and one that frequently stands as a cipher representing the wider qualitative research tradition within our discipline. I shall explore the three dominant modes in which ethnography and contemporary practical theology have been written. In conclusion, I shall suggest that in the changed climate of social research other ways of constructing our research, other ways of attending and writing, might nourish new possibilities for theological making.

The ethnographer writes ...

It is hard to overestimate how much writing matters.

In her radical interrogation of dominant modes of inscription in ethnographic research, Penelope Papailias describes how the anthropologist Clifford Geertz '... famously closed the gap between research and writing, toward a decidedly literary conception of ethnography, when he posed the rhetorical question "What does the ethnographer do?" and responded "—he writes".' Papailias goes on to add that Geertz was assuming not only a white, male, academic writer but a particular 'kind of writing born of late late-nineteenth- and twentieth-century scholarly print culture' (2021, p. 181). In other words, the answer to the question 'What does the ethnographer do?' might more properly have been: 'they write out of a particular location, in a particular sort of way, in a restricted range of mediums, and they use an established range of devices to generate certain effects and achieve particular ends'.

The identification of the politics underlying ethnographic poetics was one of the key factors precipitating the crisis of representation in the latter years of the last century. As I have discussed (see pp. 23–9), significant questions were raised concerning which people's work (and which people's worldviews) found their ways into print as well as the (colonial/white) discursive mechanisms through which representations of 'others' and the figure of the researcher had been constructed in ethnographic texts. Both these issues continue to be of pressing concern and, alongside them, further writing challenges have emerged into prominence in the contemporary context. These include: finding modes of transcribing affect and embodiment (Ellingson, 2017), how research outputs can best serve as 'performative' political interventions (Denzin and Salvo, 2020), and the impact of the deconstruction of author/reader and viewer/creator binaries in contemporary digital culture (Papailias, 2021). A lively conversation concerning the assumed *forms and norms* of ethnographic outputs is currently underway that is both interrogating previous writing practices and inscribing new ones. And, in the midst of this, the impact of relational ontologies upon understandings of the generative process we describe as 'research' continues to unfold.

In the light of these developments qualitative research is now increasingly figured as emerging through multi-faceted constructive practices that are at play from the initial genesis of a research project, and which continue right through to the reception of findings – and beyond (see Mockler, 2011). In seeking to describe these, Ellingson and Sotirin (2020) paint an evocative picture of interlinked processes of *making, assembling and becoming,* all of which take place in an animate environment in which researcher, research object, research context and research process are constantly mobile and cannot be clearly separated out. In this context, an ethnographer does not work with discrete elements called 'data' gathered up and abstracted from their environment like pebbles collected on a beach. Rather, data form one lively part of a landscape in motion; of 'consistently shifting sands subject to an ever-changing landscape of rilling waves, sun, wind and human and non-human activity … in motion and in relation; they brim with possibilities for ongoing engagement' (Ellingson and Sotirin, 2020, p. 9).

From this vantage point, the writing (or indeed other modes of communicating, presenting or performing) of research accomplishes a great deal more than presenting for scholarly inspection material previously picked up, cleaned up, labelled and arranged in place. It forms an integral part of a vibrant ecology in which things assume form but also shift, shape and develop. In other words, writing is not a detached and differentiated activity – 'something we do after the research is done' (2020, p. 81). Rather, it appears as 'creative and dynamic … imperative to the whole research process' (2020, p. 81). This opens up liberating possibilities for writing practice. However, it also requires us to recognize the lines of descent that have produced our current literary stratagems and that constrain the forms in which we write. For we now know not only that the ethnographer writes, states Ruth Behar. We understand 'further, that what they write – a strange cross between the *realist novel, the travel account, the memoir and the scientific report* – [is] to be understood in terms of poetics and politics' (Behar, 1995, p. 3, my emphasis).

As I seek to enquire more deeply into the strange mixtures of genres through which the poetics and politics of practical theological research are currently constituted, I shall begin with the what is, arguably, the hegemonic form – the scientific report. I shall then turn to examine the other writing genres Behar has identified.

A critical and distanced 'scientific' style

Scare quotes, please

When using the term 'scientific' in this discussion I should note that I am not referring to the quirky, adventurous, imaginative, exploratory processes of scientists or the deeply mysterious mechanisms of the universe that scientific explorations enable us to contemplate. In other words, I am not referring to science properly at all. I also note that rigorous academic scholarship (in general) is frequently translated as 'science' in many European contexts – whereas the word typically has much narrower disciplinary connotations in English. There is room for much confusion here. So, to be clear, when I use the term 'scientific' below I am referring to a discursive style that has been described as 'scientism'.[2] This is a way of writing that employs the literary tropes that are commonly associated with scientific endeavour and that has come to enjoy a privileged place within the contemporary academy and in modern Western cultural contexts more widely.

Scientific writing is characterized by textual postures of unbiased observation: the assembling of evidence and categorically authoritative analyses of what this evidence implies. It is written in an impersonal narrative voice and addressed to an unidentified reader. The use of image, metaphor and symbol is restrained – although dominant tropes such as seeing and hearing are regularly employed. Emotion is rarely scripted, nor is the body given voice. In contrast, a rational and moderated tone of critical distance is contrived. This magisterially resolves

---

2 Pattison identifies scientism as 'a powerful and defining social and cultural myth/discourse against which all other myths, practices and discourses can be evaluated. The more a phenomena or activities ... can be deemed as "scientific" in a diffuse, undefined way, the more social and intellectual legitimacy they are likely to have' (2007, p. 264). He argues that scientism represents an exaltation

> of the general virtues of science and all that goes with it, often without understanding how it works, its limits or its methods. In particular we relate all our notions of the meaning and value of knowledge to their proximity to science ... Thus we are impressed with notions of statistics, objectivity, empiricism, etc. (2007, p. 265)

apparently discordant elements through the 'holism' of its synthesizing vision (Marcus, 1986, p. 192).

While these discursive conventions have been closely associated with the natural sciences,[3] they have had a massive impact upon writing styles across many fields of study – including those in which scientific techniques of statistical calculation and independent verification of evidence are either inappropriate or simply impossible. As the name implies, quantitative research in the social sciences seeks to adhere, as far as is possible, to the measuring and monitoring techniques established in natural scientific disciplines. Qualitative research, however, is well understood as functioning according to quite different rubrics. Yet this does not mean that the majority of qualitative researchers have abandoned deeply ingrained 'scientific' conventions that are widely held to represent the purest form of academic endeavour. We often continue (either consciously or unconsciously) to transpose these tropes and translate them into our work. As John Van Maanen maintains:

> We cultivate and teach a writing style of nonstyle that values limited metaphor, simplicity and a formal, if not mathematical, precision. Much of our writing is washed by a thick spray of claimed objectivity since artful delights and forms are seen by many if not most writers (and readers) in the field to interfere with the presentation of what is actually there in a given social world. (In Essén and Värlander, 2012, p. 405)

Reliability, responsibility and restraint

This is an enduring issue. The early anthropological researchers engaged in the (very messy) processes of birthing a discipline, unselfconsciously embraced and sought to adhere to many of the cautiously distanced principles of 'scientific' enquiry. They developed their own disciplinary conventions (such as the construction of detailed research journals, census-taking, and the visual imaging of ritual processes) to validate the reliability of their observations. In classic forms of ethnographic writing an impassionate, knowing – but unknowable – narrator presents their expert observations alongside their definitive interpretations of

---

[3] Although early scientific texts often did not conform to the divisions between scientific and creative styles we have come to regard as natural. See, for example, Hawkins, 2019.

what has taken place. As Marcus and Cushman state in their famous essay 'Ethnographies as Texts' (1982), the analyses written into early ethnographies were presented in such a way as 'to exhibit closure, consistency, and the formality of a systems framework – the marks of reliable, certain knowledge for the reader' (1982, p. 45).

For many qualitative researchers today the quest for knowledge and understanding relating to human behaviour continues to demand reverence for such reliable epistemic forms. This, in turn, means that political, artistic and subjective approaches to knowing must be treated with caution within the research sphere. Martyn Hammersley, for example, talks of the ethical responsibilities of the publicly funded researcher to maintain professional standards of objectivity and accountability. This does not place a total ban on engaging with the soft substances generated through creative methods:

> What is essential, though, is that these forms are used in ways that are appropriate to the task involved and must be subordinated to the purpose of developing arguments supported by evidence, that provide convincing answers to factual questions about the world. (Hammersley, 2010, p. 6)

In other words, a spirit of restraint must govern the writing of qualitative research if it is to be useful and deliver value for money. Assumed 'scientific' standards function as the guarantors of worth; questions must be clear, evidence trustworthy, and conclusions convincing. In their work *Method as Identity: Manufacturing Distance in the Academic Study of Religion* (2018), Christopher Driscoll and Monica Miller focus upon research into religious practice and maintain that this is a sphere that is particularly disciplined and regulated by the assumed conventions of a 'scientific' approach. Their contention is that (in this most affective, embodied and enchanted of terrains) a posture of self-disciplined asceticism is assumed to be the best stance for the researcher. They should divest themselves of all those things that might compromise an objective position:

> Throughout the study of religion today, there exists a widespread and prevailing assumption that certain (critically oriented) methodological approaches are best suited to stave off subjective/ideological dangers emanating from unbridled social interests and privatized experiential realities. In short, such a methodologically induced *posture of experi-*

ential abstinence works to conceal particular human interests impacting our analyses by manufacturing 'critical' distance through various theoretical and methodological techniques that seek to buffer the battle between academic duty and the encroaching demands of proximal subjective identity and experience-based interests. (2018, p. 2, my emphasis)

Maintaining a 'distance' in practical theology

The critical and distanced 'scientific' mode of address is one that has been prominent in practical theology in the empirical turn. It formed the 'natural' register for early published work in empirical theology – predicated, as it was, largely upon quantitative approaches (e.g. van der Ven, 1998). Yet, even as qualitative methods gradually became dominant throughout the discipline, the style of many published outputs maintained the posture of abstinence previously established.[4] The hegemony of this 'scientific' style means that justifications are not offered for its prevailing ethos, conventions and assumptions. Rather, it is the genre that all others feel the need to justify departure from. In many contexts it would be professionally disastrous to adopt any other voice.[5]

This predominant style is particularly evident today in practical theological writing focused upon health, education and social care (such as research on chaplaincy, for example). These are areas of professional practice in which evidence-based research is highly valued, and in

---

4 As so many works in practical theology are written in this style, it is difficult to know which to reference here. I had thought to include a list of recent references from leading journals in our fields as exemplary. However, I decided against it as it seemed as if this would be randomly singling out particular sources when this style predominates across the field.

5 For early doctoral candidates, early career researchers and those seeking tenure this is particularly so; although 'guerrilla scholarship' (Rawlins, 2007) might be practised whereby subversive insights are disguised and smuggled into mainstream contexts. Rawlins describes how his early work was structured according to 'the dominating ethos of quantitative social science ... aping its trappings, writing style, and subdivisions ... in order to *pass* as a serious researcher' (2007, p. 59). 'Passing' here is undertaken not simply to fit in but also to subvert. That is, to infiltrate ideas and insights, shaped as a result of interventions that would not be automatically ceded academic credibility, into the accepted channels of scholarly communication – such as journal articles and conference presentations. In other words, a scientific writing style is adopted for tactical reasons. Clearly, this is not an innocent process.

these contexts it is very common for researchers to employ techniques associated with qualitative approaches (e.g. open-ended questions, unstructured interviews, life narrative accounts and even artistic approaches such as photo-journalling) but to code, analyse and present their work in ways that are more usually associated with quantitative research.[6] It is easy to comprehend why 'scientific' discursive modes are employed for strategic reasons by practical theologians seeking to make an impact in these spheres. Research written according to 'scientific' conventions appears to offer clear and measurable outcomes of self-evident utility in developing evidence-based practice. Not only does it possess academic credibility, it is also appealing to the managers, budget holders and policy-makers of large secular institutions that practical theologians may be seeking to engage with and to influence.

However, within the areas of practical theological research that are explicitly confessional, where faith speaks to faith, critical and distanced writing modes are also often employed as 'scientism' exerts its hegemonic influence in these spheres also and is upheld by concerns to produce writing that will signal 'good sense' to stakeholders and policy-makers. But other factors are also at play. A distanced style secures the right to articulate authoritative interpretations of complex situations. So, for example, in early work produced by members of the Theological Action Research Network, TARN (Cameron et al., 2010),[7] the 'posture of experiential abstinence' (the writing out of association and affect) is employed to place the TARN research team in a position of critical distance from the people whose beliefs and practices are being presented to the reader. As Elaine Graham states, their positionality was kept resolutely 'off the page' in terms of any declaration or exploration of their own reflexivity (2013b, p. 164). As the professional researchers

---

6 A distanced critical tone is also the lingua franca of grant applications and funding bids. Projects promising clear and measurable outcomes of apparent utility are more likely to achieve support. Qualitative methods are welcomed but, in my experience of many years of work on funding panels, practical theologians are keen to display that these can achieve Hammersley's essential outcomes of 'arguments supported by evidence, that provide convincing answers to factual questions about the world' (2010, p. 6).

7 The critique of TARN's approach by Graham here relates primarily to the early work of those pioneering this approach. Contemporary initiatives, for example, Helen Cameron's research consultancy in the Baptist Union of Great Britain's 'Project Violet' (on women's leadership and ministry), adopt a more adventurous, creative and participatory approach to research. See https://www.baptist.org.uk/Groups/363245/Project_Violet.aspx (accessed 02.04.2025).

were implicitly functioning as 'consultants' advising 'clients' in faith-based communities on missional practice, the distanced and discerning posture of the writing implicitly conveys the discursive authority of the sense-making work that was being offered. It also secured a firm foundation for theological judgements within the locus of TARN's project as vernacular insights were sifted and sorted within the research team's wider frame.

So the tropes of 'scientific' writing are present and endure within the written narratives of research across a wide range of contexts within practical theology. They are useful, effective and serviceable. They pass without notice as the established conventions of academic work rather than as performative and symbolic means of world construction. However, as undeniably valuable insights are being communicated through their use, and as these undoubtedly make significant contributions to knowledge and practice, does it matter at all what style, tone and literary genres are at play?

Once, ideological positioning would have determined my answer to this question. I would have argued that some modes of writing in practical theology were inherently better (more honest, more reflexive, more impactful, etc.) than others. My position on this has changed. I would now say that a range of writing styles and possibilities are open to us and pragmatic and strategic concerns should govern their use. To use an economic trope (for the devil still has all the best tunes) it is a matter of 'opportunity cost'. The choices we make offer up certain benefits and opportunities. They close down other possibilities. A scientific style can be useful and strategically appropriate; but it can also become impoverished and confining.

In this pragmatic frame the reasons why a scientific style might be chosen are evident. It is widely accepted as the lingua franca of good scholarship. This is of strategic importance when a researcher is applying for funding, seeking professional advancement, claiming academic credibility or, importantly, seeking to make a transformative intervention that will lead to real change for the stakeholders involved in their research project. When seeking to revise current practices or generate resources for new initiatives it is often necessary to present 'evidence' in a manner that strongly indicates why a proposed way forward is likely to be beneficial or effective. However, it is important not to overstate the strategic gains that scientific rhetoric makes possible. An artistic intervention can testify to important concerns that are routinely abstracted out of austerely constructed research reports. Art also offers modes of address that possess the potential to communicate complex, ambiguous and challenging issues effectively, and to a wider audience, thus provoking affective as well as rational responses to situations of concern. Most significantly, they can also enable insights to emerge that are currently 'unthinkable' within established terms of reference and academic exchange.

These are matters for practical theologians to weigh up and consider. However, we must also contemplate issues specifically pertinent to our theological vocation. In his classic text *On Christian Theology* (2000), Rowan Williams reflects upon the dangers inherent in adopting what he terms a 'naïve scientific model' (2000, p. 13) as the discursive pattern for theological work. He argues that if theology is understood as being comparable to a science in common thinking then its role will be seen as to 'clarify, perhaps to explain, it will seek to establish procedures for arguing and criteria for conclusions' (2000, p. 13). In relation to the divine economy, Williams believes, such procedures are both limiting and hazardous. This is particularly so as one of the most identifiable features of 'scientific' writing (scare quotes are particularly important here as science does not proceed in this ordered way) is the trajectory it follows from muddle and uncertainty towards order; from a partial picture to a holistic understanding. It is a form that is inherently resistant to the disruption of discordant elements. As Williams states: 'For an empirically based science, the only interruptions that matter are those of new phenomena not catered for in previous schemata.' Rigour in theology, however, means watching out for and guarding against our tendency to claim the 'total perspective; it is a rigour directed against the naïve scientific model' (2000, p. 13). Williams maintains that if scientific discourse supplies the pattern and tropes for theological writing then it lies open to the dangers of appearing as a total system, whereas the health of theology lies in a direction entirely opposite to this. Theology must foster a constant sense of its own impossible vocation and endure the necessary provocation of being continually broken open by encounters with what lies beyond itself (in both the divine and human spheres).

A final point made by Williams is one I find particularly resonant. One of the greatest problems with transposing scientific discursive strategies into the theological realm, he argues, is that the tone of the writing conveys as much as the content of the text. 'One of the temptations of theology,' he states, 'has been – at least in the modern era – to suppose not so much that there is a normative content for theological utterance but there is a normative style' (2000, p. 31). This normative style he describes as being characterized by 'critical austerity'. This is very similar to the styles of abstinence or restraint that Driscoll and Miller identified above. It has been a major theme of this book so far that while current work in practical theology is undoubtedly generating insight this is rarely transubstantiated into the powerful forms of theological address that are required to meet the challenges of our times. Williams's perspective encourages me to reflect on how difficult it is within the customary forms of austere, restrained discourse that practical theology routinely generates to nurture and express a potent theological imagination. New wine bursts old wineskins and new visions may require new tropes, a different poetics.

Stories we tell of journeys taken

Having spent some time critiquing a 'scientific' discursive style, I must now admit that the literature of qualitative research, even in its more conservative and traditional incarnations, is very far from uniformly restrained or austere.[8] Ethnographic writing, in particular, is shot through with bright flashes of colour as authors offer vignettes of their research encounters and personal experiences during fieldwork. As Behar noted, the strange mixture that constitutes ethnographic work also displays traces of the *travelogue and memoir*; literary forms in which the presence of the narrator is vividly inscribed within the body of the text.

This mixing of the abstractly impersonal and the deeply impressionistic may appear unstable but is actually crucial to the successful functioning of ethnographic writing. For the ethnographer must persuade their reader to journey with them into worlds where what is familiar will be rendered strange and the unfamiliar accounted for. To do so they must not only present what they have discovered in precise, 'objective' terms

---

8 I recognize that my description of the plain, unadorned and restrained writing that characterizes much of the published research in practical theology might appear a caricature to many of my readers. It is true that in some locations it is now acceptable to work in deeply reflexive ways and employ methods, like autoethnography, which are gaining in academic credibility. It is also the case that a number of individuals are pursuing their own experimental modes of writing that are creative, original and push beyond traditional boundaries. In addition, the challenging subject matter of some of our research (e.g. on sexuality, trauma and loss) means that even the most conventionally structured work contains passionate and moving narratives evoking strong affective responses. The picture I am painting here is in very broad brushstrokes and omits a lot of the most interesting details.

but also establish themselves as an experienced voyager and trustworthy guide. The ethnographer must appear as someone who has explored the terrain themselves and undergone their own processes of discovery within it. This necessitates the use of personal-journey narratives and autobiographical markers of veracity to reassure the reader.

Ethnographers are not the first writers to have experienced the tension of what Stoller describes as tacking 'between the analytic and the sensible' (Stoller, in Whitmore, 2019, p. 146). In travel writing, in the accounts of explorers charting new territories and adventurous naturalists seeking to discover new species, similar tensions are present. A balance must be achieved between expertly informed explanations and engaging narratives that enables the reader to 'travel with'. (I shall later argue that this tradition has even older roots.) As Pratt explains:

> The practice of combining personal narrative and objectified description is hardly the invention of modern ethnography ... It has a long history ... By the early sixteenth century in Europe, it was conventional for travel accounts to consist of a combination of first-person narration, recounting one's trip, and description of the flora and fauna of regions passed through and the manners and customs of the inhabitants. (1986, p. 33)

In the early days of ethnographic writing the personal elements of the anthropologist's testimony tended to be located in introductory sections (in which the narrator's credentials are revealed), in short supplementary passages, epilogues or companion essays accompanying larger scholarly works (Pratt, 1986, p. 35). However, personal narratives are now accepted as prominent features of the genre. Furthermore, since the crisis of representation, 'mainstream' ethnographic accounts, while not radically transformed (sadly), have given greater and greater emphasis to 'the voice and subjectivity of the narrator ... guiding the reader' (Papailias, 2021, p. 181) and engaging them through the sharing of personal experience.

But such personal contributions, while often vivid, are far from artless or spontaneous. In his *Tales from the Field*, John van Maanen refers disparagingly to repeatedly rehearsed themes presented in highly patterned form: 'stories of infiltration, fables of fieldwork rapport, minimelodramas of hardships endured (and overcome), and accounts of what fieldwork did to the fieldworker' (1988, p. 73). Van Maanen is correct in noting that a predefined set of small human dramas, regularly restaged, have served to construct a widely recognized trope: that of the 'ethnographic quest' to be found throughout the research literature. This proceeds through certain recognized stages as researchers:

- Gain entry to an alternative world.
- Form relationships within it.
- Endure trials and temptations.
- Become transformed and gain the treasure sought.

The fact that this narrative form is so deeply embedded in ethnographic writing should generate awareness of the powerful literary conventions that are shaping our own work. However, it should not necessarily cause us to become dismissive of writing structured in these ways. The form of the ethnographic quest narrative endures not only because it has become so ubiquitous but also because of the deep resonances it calls forth.

Travellers' tales in practical theology

Within practical theology it is small personal stories that have been told alongside description and analysis that constitute some of the most evocative resources in our disciplinary lexicon. An early representative of these is Don Browning's narrative of his encounter with a vibrant black church, in his foundational work *A Fundamental Practical Theology* (1991, pp. 26–33). These passages, describing his experiences of welcome and challenge, bring his monumental text to life. They also artfully embody Browning's key concerns and his 'fundamental' fascination with the irrepressible theological dynamism that animates diverse modes of incarnating Church. In Mary McClintock Fulkerson's *Places of Redemption* (2007), the (actually quite terse and sparse) personal narratives naming her discomfort of whiteness and recognition of privilege in the presence of darker and disabled bodies have achieved iconic status in congregational studies. Once again, these vignettes incarnate her core theme – namely, the fleshly woundedness and yet grace-full nature of the body of Christ. It is important to note here that both Browning and McClintock Fulkerson are employing another common but highly problematic ethnographic trope – that of the initiation of the (white) outsider through encounter with the (black) other.[9]

---

9 Browning appears unselfconscious in conforming to this trope. McClintock Fulkerson's work explores themes of inequality, othering and racialized power in

While McClintock Fulkerson's work features the classic elements of the ethnographic quest, they are particularly well exemplified in Browning's tale-telling. He describes his *entry* into a 'remarkable' (1991, p. 30) world that was both very close (streets away) and yet fresh and challenging to him. In this context, surprising *relationships are formed* of a deeply spiritual nature with those he had assumed would simply serve as participants in his study. The text presents him as *undergoing the trials* as he confronts ignorance and self-doubt: coming to question many of his previous convictions and challenged to the core of his 'liberal, intellectual Christianity' (1991, p. 32). 'Would I, as a reasonably respected scholar from the University of Chicago have anything to contribute to this dialogue at all?' he asks (1991, p. 30). The ethnographic journey ultimately becomes one of transformation deeper than he could have imagined: 'What I found in the Apostolic Church of God far exceeded in interest and power anything I expected in my most expansive dreams' (1991, p. 32).[10]

These travellers' tales from within practical theology are simply well-known examples – representative of the myriad other small, personal stories that are embedded throughout our ethnographic works. Although I read them critically here, as displaying the white, colonial genealogy of the ethnographic project, I am not at all cynical about the use of personal testimonies per se. Stories of research encounters, research trials and revelations can be reflexively self-critical and greatly enliven their descriptive and analytic surroundings. But it is important to recognize their dual discursive function. On the one hand, they are genuine efforts to communicate important insights formed within a context. On the other, these personal accounts constitute literary tropes that 'are crafted not raw and unmediated experience' (Spry, 2011, p. 124). They are moments that form an integral part of an overall performance within an established tradition. This is a tradition in which we might feel particularly at home for the key moments in the ethnographic quest are in fact predicated upon much older traditions of the spiritual quest. This is archetypally narrated in Augustine's *Confessions*

---

some depth and so it is particularly significant that she fails to critique the impact of her own white narrative perspective. *Places of Redemption* is, to my (white) mind, simultaneously one of the most significant texts in congregational studies and one that mirrors some of the most problematic aspects of the white colonial ethnographic gaze. See my discussion of Goto's critique.

10 In the early 1990s I visited Don Browning in Chicago and accompanied him to a service at this church. There could be no doubting the deep feelings he had developed for this congregation and the great value he placed upon its witness.

and was imprinted upon the Western cultural imagination through the unprecedented influence of John Bunyan's *Pilgrim's Progress* – for many centuries the most widely read text alongside the Bible.[11] This quest is one that leads upwards: from chaos to coherence, from illusion to truth and from wayward selfhood to redemption life.

The pilgrim way

When I consider my own journeys as a researcher in practical theology, I find I can accommodate many elements of my own experiences within the familiar template of the spiritual quest. I find it useful to make reference to this framework in my teaching and supervision and I also encourage my own students to engage with the growing body of literature in practical theology that explicitly links processes of qualitative research to spiritual journeying and spiritual formation. This includes the work of Eileen Campbell-Reed and Christian Scharen on the refashioning ethnography as a theological and spiritual practice (2013), and Todd Whitmore's advocacy of ethnographic research as a spiritual discipline or askesis (2018).

I have been particularly indebted to the work of my friend Nicola Slee and her linking of the apprenticeship of deep attentiveness undertaken in qualitative research to prayer and the receptivity of the mystical tradition. Referring to the practice of feminist research among women and girls, she writes:

> It strikes me that the way we listen as women researchers is, itself, a form of spiritual practice that has many of the qualities of prayer

---

11 Quest narratives, stories of seekers dislocated into strange territories (deep forests, underworld caverns, tempestuous oceans and alien lands) facing temptations and trials as they seek to obtain a gift, blessing or reward, form one of the most ancient narrative forms. A key moment in their development occurred when Augustine took the elements of the hero stories told in Greek and Roman myths and transposed these into motifs in a pattern for the spiritual journey of the soul towards its home in God (Walton, 2015a; Staude, 2005, p. 257). His *Confessions* became the pattern for a journey that has been repeatedly recounted in spiritual material and literature. According to literary critic Linda Anderson (2004), it formed the basis for development of the modern autobiography and decisively stamped itself upon the Western cultural imagination through the publication of John Bunyan's *Pilgrim's Progress*. It is also widely recognized to have provided a template for a great body of Western fiction from the *Wizard of Oz* to *Harry Potter*.

understood as the most attentive listening to self, other and God we can manage ... It's shaped by our own hunger to be listened to, by positive experiences of what it is to be listened to well but also by the painful reality we all know of not being heard, of having our voices and lives silenced. We listen with our whole bodies, paying attention to feeling, memory, desire. We listen with emotional as well as intellectual intelligence, on the lookout for patterns, resonances, allusions. We listen to what is explicit in what we read or hear, to what is implicit but not directly said, and to what is null or absent – the inconceivable, unsayable, or not yet capable of being articulated. (2020, p. 210)

I resonate with this moving representation of research as a formative, embodied and deeply spiritual practice. I am, however, uneasy about the 'upward' trajectory that is implicit in the spiritual quest narratives we practical theologians employ so frequently in our ethnographic and theological work. To exemplify this I remain with Slee's writing a while longer. So, she maintains, we travel a journey in research and 'we do not return the same' (2020, p. 215). Humbled, challenged and growing in wisdom through processes of deep, attentive listening, we become transformed. This transformation entails recognizing 'our own risenness ... claiming an authentic, rightful authority to witness to what we have discovered' (2020, pp. 215–16). And this personal resurrection may become part of a wider social trajectory towards liberation 'as we move together into a world where women and girls, alongside boys and men, can be all that they have it in them to be, and where all can be free' (2020, p. 216).[12]

Slee is testifying here to the faith and hope that motivates and sustains many practical theologians in ethnographic research. Her vision is one I share and hold in common with many 'secular' ethnographers. Ruth Behar, whose work I also admire immensely, states that the vision that inspired her to become a researcher was to 'listen to other people's stories, especially to the stories of those whose voices often go unheard. We believe that by listening to these stories and then retelling them, displacing these stories to other places and audiences, we can help save the world' (Behar, 2003, p. 18).

---

12 It is important to note that, although sanguine concerning its redemptive value, Slee does not deny the 'messy, confusing, uncertain processes of research; labouring and struggling and suffering, as well as knowing elation, joy and excitement' (2020, p. 215).

However, I have to articulate another perspective which must be weighed alongside this hopeful, redemptive narrative.[13] In this unheimlich season it is appropriate to acknowledge that there is always a deep ambivalence and precariousness inherent in qualitative research. We are always in danger of toppling over into what Ingold describes as ethnography's awful colonial capacity to take people as objects of study and make objects out of them. As Behar herself reflects:

> Ethnography began as a method discovered, perfected and institutionalized in Western centers of power – for telling stories about the marginalized populations of the world. It has its origins in the flagrant colonial inequalities ... Knowing this history, how can ethnography still be practiced today ... What can be salvaged ... to make it a project of emancipation? (2003, p. 16)

This is a serious question. We must continually ask whether our research journeys 'elsewhere' really do form in us the wisdom and capacity to carry 'treasures' home again or whether we are bearing counterfeit, or worse, stolen or appropriated goods. Even if what we have brought is of true value, are we capable of – or indeed do we have the right and claim to – shaping it into our own products for our own purposes?

In this context I am drawn to a different image of research as pilgrimage that I want to hold together and in tension with the more familiar narratives of 'pilgrim's progress' that dominate the Western imaginary and have been widely employed within practical theology. In Celtic understandings, pilgrimage is not taking a path towards a particular sacred place and it is not undertaken in the hope of a return to home bearing gifts. To be a pilgrim is to be cast afloat in a small boat and to voyage with your comrades wherever the waves will carry you. It is to be carried by the deluge to an unknown place where witness is called for (Aist, 2017). This offers me an alternative trope for the work of qualitative research in practical theology which may be more appropriate for these troubled times. The researcher here is adrift, unmoored, and unsure where they are heading. Tsing speaks of entering deeply into challenging circumstances with others as fellow seekers – not to

---

13 I have long loved the poet William Blake's *Songs of Innocence and Experience* ([1794] 1970). This contains poems full of hope and joy paired with poems of darkness and despair. Neither perspective is true or false but both forms of song witness to aspects of existence that cannot be synthesized into one picture without sacrificing their truth.

construct visions of redemption but rather to discern what can be discovered in the midst of this confusion. Shelly Rambo transposes this motif into theological terms when she refers to the need for some theologians to stay with the undertow, to 'remain' in the chaos outwith their control and yet to keep improvising with and through the provisional and partial testimonies told here; to keep staging the performance of their 'tangled lines' (2017, p. 2). What I am arguing here is that the dominant trope of the spiritual quest in ethnographic writing can be brought into creative tension with an alternative trope that speaks both of the ambivalent nature of research and also testifies to the nature of spiritual life in our times.

Real fictions

Made-up worlds

The final literary form that Behar identifies as structuring ethnography is that of realist fiction. Scientific discourse, travel accounts and memoirs might be thought of as possibly imperfect but sincere efforts to communicate truthfully about the nature of things. However, to nominate a fictional mode of writing, that of the realist novel, as characterizing ethnographic texts might appear to cross all sorts of invisible lines. To further suggest that this literary form has deeply influenced theological thinking in our discipline will require me to address the manner in which the defining characteristics of this genre impact upon the scope and form of theological reflection.

To begin, it is important to note that realist literary writing emerged at a particular moment in cultural history. The great realist novels of the eighteenth and nineteenth century were inscribed during a period of industrialization, colonial expansion and cultural change. It became important to offer comprehensible pictures of a rapidly changing world in order to gain a sense of coherence within it and, indeed, achieve mastery over it. This is facilitated, in part, by the presence of a guiding narrator who describes, interprets and connects, thus opening up both the outer world of events and the inner world of actors to their readers.

Other devices and techniques in realist fiction serve to deepen the sense that the reader is being initiated into an understanding of a world that not only corresponds to 'real life' but allows us to enter this at peculiar depth. We are introduced to the context in which action takes place, a timeline is established, characters are presented with their distinct features and roles. The work often opens with a breach or crisis to be addressed and a plot develops that connects all of these elements, offering resolution within a unified whole. In the realist genre proximate features, markers of particularity, also play an important role. The small details of a way of life are described with apparent naturalness. We learn about modes of dress, forms of address, and there are references to objects, sights, smells and sensations that all contribute to the verisimilitude of the picture created.

When in the critical literature on ethnography the term 'realist' is used it is this range of poetic techniques and devices for world creation that are being referenced. As John Law argues, ethnographers, like fiction writers, employ the conventions of realism to provide the invisible scaffolding through which their narratives achieve mastery over 'a reality that was multiple, slippery and fuzzy. Indefinite' (Law, 2007, p. 603). They draw upon the common techniques of realist fiction as they establish context; create a range of characters (gatekeepers, informants, mentors, tricksters, saints and friends) with specific roles and idiosyncratic traits; and pursue a plot that moves from breach or crisis to its resolution. Small details interwoven throughout convey a sense of intimacy and veracity. For in realist literature what the philosopher Paul Ricoeur calls the rule of semblance must apply. Realist fiction under this rule must 'create the belief that this artifice *stands for* genuine testimony about reality and life'. But he adds the function of this literary genre is not one of faithful representation but of world creation and 'the artifice involved undermines from within the realist motivation' (1985, p. 158).

Fictions of faith

The manner in which the tropes of realist fiction have been activated in practical theology can be illustrated with reference to the very first pages of the very first congregational study.[14] In this, Alice Evans and Robert Evans present a narrative that they insist is extensively researched, objective, and offers 'a true account of a series of events in the life of a specific congregation' (1983, p. 4). It is naughty, I know, to take such

---

14 It is important to stress that this narrative is presented completely unselfconsciously as a case study which the team of researchers used as 'a common focus to model their distinctive approaches to the local church' (Evans and Evans, 1983, p. 4) and to form the basis for their analysis.

an early piece of research as an example. Our work is undoubtedly more sophisticated now; our semblances much more subtle. But it is such a good illustration I could not resist it ... and it's such a 'ripping yarn'. It begins:

> Alan Hyatt shook his head and smiled to himself as he hung up the phone. This was the second call he'd had tonight from other members of the administrative board of the Wiltshire Methodist Church. How naïve and eager he had been to accept one of the five annual openings on the fifteen-member church board. Now ... he was faced with voting for or against a building plan. Though the plan had initially seemed very straightforward Alan was aware that the vote was much more complex than he had ever imagined. Alan now saw a string of accumulated and unresolved problems. These ranged from housing for the senior pastor and staff conflicts to divisions among board members and grumbling about 'no spirituality' and 'too-weak lay leadership'. Most disturbing to Alan was the undercurrent of rumours that was tearing at the heart of the congregation.
>
> Alan opened his study door, called to his teenage son and daughter upstairs to turn down their competing stereo sets, went into the kitchen to pour another cup of hot coffee, then retreated again to his desk ... As he sought to put things into perspective Alan turned his thoughts to the town of Wiltshire. He had become increasingly intrigued with the idea that the history not only of the church but of the town of Wiltshire was relevant to the issues the church was now facing. (Evans and Evans, 1983, p. 5)

In two short paragraphs, we are initiated by the narrators into the exterior and interior worlds in which a drama will unfold. We are offered contextual details and the character of nice Alan to relate to as he considers his difficult dilemmas. The homely features (coffee, teenage children and the man-cave study) ensure verisimilitude. And, as we read further, we become aware of another significant feature of realist fictions. Both in their literary and ethnographic form realist narratives are presented as accounts of authentic, believable situations. But they are also intended to *convey wider meanings of more general application*. So there is a lively subtext operative beneath the surface of this 'genesis' chapter. In relating their narrative of the crisis in the Wiltshire church the authors insist that although it functions as a factual case study it also has 'universal elements' (1983, p. 5). And these can be drawn upon by other congregations to 'gain objectivity and insights about themselves' (1983, p. 4). In other words, what is being presented here is a moral fable – an allegory.

Allegorical imaginings

The allegorical nature of ethnographic writing has long been recognized. As Clifford maintains, ethnographic texts are 'inescapably allegorical, and a serious acceptance of this fact changes the ways they can be written and read' (Clifford and Marcus, 1986, p. 100). Many of the early 'discipline shaping' anthropologists had pedagogical and ethical ambitions and were well aware that their ethnographic descriptions of diverse cultures were functioning as counter-perspectives to assumed Western norms. Without fundamentally rupturing the framework of Western liberal humanism, their interrogation of difference was undertaken with the broader intent of provoking revisionings of human nature and the ordering of communal life. In other words, they were telling one story (about somewhere else) in order to provoke the unfolding of another (right here). This allegorical mechanism functions most effectively when the narrative is realistic and compelling. If it was *truly like this* (over there), then it *might be just possible* to reimagine what it could be like (back home).

While the allegorical nature of their work may not necessarily be signposted by ethnographers, very often such a reading is clearly anticipated (as in the work of Evans and Evans above). Similar processes are at work in the research undertaken by practical theologians into diverse ways of being church. Loving attention given to particular congregations/faith practices generates convincing narratives about specific contexts. The telling of stories of difference then leads researchers and their readers to imaginatively craft new scripts of faithful identity and life together in the body of Christ. There is much to celebrate in the allegorical imaginings that can be generated through this work. Yet, as ever, there are also more problematic aspects to consider.

I have extensively referenced the politics of representation but it is important to note again that research participants are often objectified (in racist or classist or other oppressive ways), and their beliefs and practices commoditized when these are shaped into narratives to engage audiences from dominant groups on issues of domestic concern. Furthermore, the allegorical imaginings provoked by ethnographic work are not always subtle or beautiful – and certainly not all are progressive.[15] For ethnographic allegories, as moral fables, not only provoke us to ask *whether what is should be* but to form judgements about right and wrong, good things and bad things. These can quickly become judgements about good and bad people and better or worse ways of life.

In practical theology, as Wigg-Stevenson notes, there has been a tendency to produce ethnographic work that not only represents diverse models of belief and practice, but judges which are authentic and which are faithless or inadequate embodiments of the Church.[16] 'When we write the Church,' she states, 'we all too often want to be able to say which parts are the redeemed ones and which ones still stand beyond the pale. Ethnographic theologians fall into this trap as much as any others' (2022, p. 120). Through proceeding in this way our research can generate allegorical imaginings that fail to engage with one of the most important aspects of the Church: its ambivalence or woundedness. Its calling to glory and its capacity for sin.

Despite the temptation to align ethnographic studies with normative visions of the Church there are significant works in practical theology that do take the ambivalence of the Church as their theological lens and employ allegorical subtext works that uphold this perspective. In James Hopewell's classic work *Congregation* (1988), his allegory evolves as he intertwines reflections concerning the nature of congregational life with accounts of his own terminal illness.[17] When he discusses how congregations construct differing worldviews he relates this to the varying positions on his mortality taken by visitors to his bedside. This braiding is both desperately poignant and highly evocative as we are shown, rather than told about, the fragile, corporeal nature of the Church and the grace of its flickering life.

And I return once more to McClintock Fulkerson's *Places of Redemption*, a work that meditates throughout on the woundedness and worldly nature of church. A congregation's story can be told, she argues, in terms that honour its spatial, flawed and fleshly incarnation and not only its spiritual life. She writes:

---

15 Tales of 'primitive' peoples and their uncivilized habits have been translated into the bloody allegories of colonialism and fascism.

16 A tendency already evident within *Building Effective Ministry* (Dudley, 1983).

17 Hopewell's text is not strictly speaking an ethnographic study, but rather a loose conglomeration of methodologies and approaches that his personal experiences permeate throughout.

Good Samaritan was a church characterized by gospel conviction and ambiguity, pain and joy ... It was a worldly church. To do theological justice to this community will be to write about its people, about its habits and idiosyncrasies, its mistakes and its blindness, as well as its moments of honesty and grace. That requires attention to the markers of difference, the role of bodies, and visceral responses. These are ... part of the ambiguity and grace – the 'worldliness' of this faith community. (2007, p. 6)

What is particularly pertinent (and almost unprecedented in practical theology) is that McClintock Fulkerson explicitly states that as she embodies the Church in these fleshly terms her work assumes the features of allegory (2007, p. 42). She knows exactly what she is doing here. By recounting the narrative of a congregation in worldly ways she is acutely aware of making far-reaching claims about church more generally and consequently about the nature of God's presence in human life. Her very terms of analysis have shifted attention away from the common identifiers of spiritual communities (corporate identity, beliefs and religious practices) to the messy sites where (she perceives) 'redemptive existence' is embodied:

In that sense, my portrayal of Good Samaritan ... can be seen as a form of testimony to that which indicates the reality of God ... this worldly way grace happens ... In all its fragility and ambiguity, redemptive existence did occur ... in the worldly church that was Good Samaritan. (2007, p. 254)

Realism and theology

Hopewell and McClintock Fulkerson both possess an acute awareness of the multivalent, 'literary' nature of realist writing and this enables them to take ownership of its allegorical potency and skilfully exercise this in their theological work. But realism is a capacious and generative genre and it has played another significant, if often overlooked, role in practical theology's development. This deserves a (very brief) mention here.

The postliberal 'Yale' approach to theology, with its renewed ecclesial focus, was deeply informed by representations of Scripture, doctrine and communal life as possessing many common features with the realist literary tradition.[18] This interpretative alignment enabled key thinkers (e.g. Hans Frei, George Lindbeck and Stanley Hauerwas) to image the Christian narrative as a holistic, coherent story unfolding over time in accordance with a meaningful plot. Not only, it was claimed, is this story entirely believable in common sense terms but it also possesses a *profounder realism* than secular imaginings; judging, inspiring and inviting the incorporation of believers within its frame through the story-formed community of the Church. As Hans Frei famously stated:

> In trying to work out the hermeneutical principles of this program of interpretation, I found that a certain kind of understanding is involved which is perhaps best exemplified by what goes on in the 19th-century realistic novel and the attempts to understand it (George Eliot's *Adam Bede* and *Middlemarch* come to mind). (Frei, 1993, p. 32)

The origins of the ecclesiology and ethnography network lies in initiatives that arose out of the vitality of postliberal thinking at Yale. The impetus to explore ways in which Christian congregations represent a real embodiment (in lived practice) of a realistic story owes a great deal to the continuing outworkings of this important theological inheritance. While postliberal theology has continued to develop, and is today much more receptive to diverse spiritual readings of Scripture and doctrine,

---

18 The Yale biblical scholar Hans Frei was deeply influenced by the work of literary critic Eric Auerbach, who (comparing the Bible to classical mythology) claimed that Scripture presents a world that is 'entirely real, average, identifiable' (1953, p. 42), and further that the 'world of scripture stories is not satisfied with claims to be a historically true reality – it insists that it is the only real world' (Auerbach, 1953, pp. 14–15). From this inheritance, Frei developed the perspective that the Bible could be studied not in textual 'fragments' but rather as a long unfolding story. George Lindbeck, Frei's colleague at Yale, extended this thinking into the doctrinal realm through arguing that specific historical and cultural communities, in this case Christian communities, are also communities of narration and that their doctrinal inheritance is the 'grammar' that regulates the way their stories are performed. Stanley Hauerwas developed even further the implications of this move into the ethical and communal realm, picturing church as a narrative community based upon an overarching story that forms the pattern for Christian living. It is evident why a renewed focus on ecclesial practice emerged as highly significant in this theological context. In the postliberal perspective, congregations become places where the biblical narrative conveys distinctive character, cultivates specific virtues and, above all, is performed as a countercultural witness to the dominant narratives of a secular age.

a tendency to interpret ecclesial life within a realistic narrative frame is persistent within practical theology and it endures.

When narratives fail

Practical theology is thus deeply indebted to realism as a genre as a result of a convergence of several significant streams in its identity formation. However, contemporary debates in literary and trauma studies raise questions about what can – and cannot – be articulated within realism as a genre – and these have implications for practical theological reflection in troubled times. Those engaged in Holocaust studies have long questioned whether literary realism is an appropriate way of conveying experiences so extreme that this 'normalizing' realistic frame cannot contain them. Similarly, we now recognize that many people and communities who have suffered the world-fracturing impact of trauma may become dispossessed of the means to turn their experiences into coherent stories. They struggle with the ever-recurring intrusions of an unassimilable past into the haunted present. Just as reality is fractured, so the conventions of realism become inaccessible as a means of self-narration. As the path-making trauma theorist Laurence Kirmayer bluntly states: 'There is no narrative of trauma' (1996, p. 175).[19]

This is a challenge that is particularly difficult to face, as Rambo points out, in religious traditions such as Christianity in which there is an overwhelming desire to establish coherence out of ruin. For trauma entails 'shattering of familiar frameworks by which persons and communities have orientated themselves in the world' (Rambo, 2010, p. 8). It is Rambo's conviction that testimony to trauma requires the strange tones of poetic speech. She insists that theology needs to develop new and unfamiliar registers to address those impacted by trauma, to represent the wounded community of the Church, and attend to the wounded Christ it serves. For trauma presses us towards the need 'for new language to express God's relation to the world' (2010, p. 14). As Rebecca Chopp (whose landmark essay on this theme should be compulsory reading for all practical theologians, in my opinion) maintains, trauma testimony

---

19 Quoting Greenspan, Kirmayer argues that such trauma narratives are attempts to make sense of what 'for the survivors live on as the negation of comprehensible and communicable form. Set against those memories all such accounts are attempts to "make a story" out of what is "not a story"' (Greenspan, in Kirmayer, 1996, p. 185).

requires speaking in strange ways, employing poetics that 'refigure, refashion and reshape the world' (2001, p. 61).

We have always been creative

In this chapter I addressed two related themes. First I have sought to examine how the ways in which practical theology is written mirrors the conventions of the ethnographic project. This tradition has a particular discursive style that we have emulated in our writing. It is one predicated upon certain established literary genres. We have always been 'creative' in that our work in the empirical turn has always been deeply imbued with the poetics of ethnography.

Second, I have sought to argue that the ethnographic poetics we practise is (in the broadest sense) a political discourse. It facilitates certain ways of seeing the world while occluding others. In particular, it encourages us towards a narrative stance that establishes coherence, stability and resolution rather than allowing for disruption, dislocation and trauma. This causes us to reflect upon ways in which practical theology might be written differently. Would a more expansive and adventurous repertoire enable us: to engage with those ways of knowing excluded by scientism; to offer visions of alternative modes of faithful research/ spiritual journeying; and to comprehend the shattering of familiar frameworks that accompany our troubles? Can our poetics, our creative making, be expanded beyond the bounds of textual poetics alone? And if so, could it generate resources to support a generous and inclusive revisioning of the poetics and politics of practical theology?

5

Reimagining Research as (Creative) Responsiveness

The last chapter ended on a note of challenge. I asked whether moving beyond our customary approaches in practical theology might enable us to better fulfil our theological vocation in these times. This chapter relates to that challenge very directly as I turn to examine what it might mean to incorporate ways of proceeding associated with the arts into our research practice. Expanding our research repertoire in this way would not entail simply adding a few new tools or techniques for decorative effect. It has the potential to change the way we currently work in radical ways and thus requires serious consideration of what these new resources might offer and what changes and challenges their use might entail. For if our empirical approach to scholarship is wedded to an understanding of research as the representation and interpretation of practice in as accurate and objective way as possible, then the introduction of artistic modes could be seen as a bane rather than a blessing; causing confusion and compromising the academic status of our labours. However, if we acknowledge that our empirical project has always incubated an implicit poetics, then we might be less cautious about expanding our range of creative epistemological resources further – particularly so if this expanded repertoire enables us to meet academic, political and theological challenges in some insightful and creative ways.

Although I am enthusiastic about the possibilities an engagement with art in research offers, it is important to register that this will not somehow miraculously 'fix' the problems that are implicit within all forms of research practice. Established power relationships endure whatever research methods are employed. As Radford maintains, arts-based research is just as capable as any other methodological approach of reinforcing power relations between the researcher and researched. But it may 'draw us closer to these problems of representation, interpretation and power' (Radford, 2024), rendering us less able to escape their challenges.

Radford's caution here is well founded and salutary. It reminds me that it is not some inherent quality of 'artiness' that is to be prized in and for itself. Advocating for creative research methods must be part of seeking a justice-orientated ethos[1] for all research practice. It should entail continually questioning whether the way we undertake research is congruent with the worldviews we espouse and our primary vocation as theologians.[2]

I have struggled to find words to express this ethos and eventually settled upon the word 'responsiveness' to convey the key features of the approach I am advocating. It is not a very sexy term and far from unproblematic![3] I am sorry I have not found a more appropriate one (yet), but it bears the burden for now. I desire that practical theology become more responsive at all the various levels of our activity. I believe that a 'creative turn' would facilitate this development, not because it would resolve all that is problematic or supersede other approaches, but because it might extend our 'research-imagination' into spheres that have been neglected thus far. I anticipate artistic engagement could enable responsiveness to challenging topics that lack definition, to people and worldviews that have not been listened to, and epistemological challenges that we should urgently consider. Particularly, I hope that it would encourage us in responsive processes of creative theological making that address our current context at both micro and macro level.

In the next chapter I will turn to address these 'bigger' challenges through an artistic lens. This chapter is more narrowly focused upon

---

[1] More specifically, I have argued throughout this book that the pursuit of new knowledge should be undertaken within the frameworks of deep relationality and in the context of our current pluracrises.

[2] In their path-making essay on the potential of arts-based research in practical theology Radford argues that, significant as the social research gains might be, it is the theological richness of creative approaches that might prove of paramount importance. They write, 'Creative methods in practical theology take us further into what is complex, contradictory, and uncertain in our attempts to trace the sacred in our practices of liturgy and learning, protest and peacemaking, and everyday life' (Radford, 2021, p. 62).

[3] In personal correspondence, Radford (2024) has remarked that responsiveness is a fuzzier, softer term than 'usefulness' and they have challenged me to consider whether I am not still seeking to improve the utility of practical theological research without fully engaging with the ambivalence of this quest. I see the force of this perspective and continue to reflect upon it. However, I remain hopeful that divergent ways of seeing and making in research might enable a genuine responsiveness to occluded insights.

the practices associated with academic research. In particular, I shall explore how artistic approaches might enable responsiveness to:

- Areas that are significant but difficult to comprehend. I shall focus upon embodiment.
- Fields that are unapproachable in conventional terms. Here I focus upon affect.
- People whose concerns are misrepresented or silenced within dominant paradigms.
- Cultural wisdom expressed through artistic mediums.
- Modes of knowing that resist traditional terms of validation.
- Alternative ways of writing and creating in research.

But before engaging with these issues I should briefly clarify some of the terms I will be employing.

Coming to terms

In what follows I will refer to 'arts-engaged research' when describing *research projects* that employ artistic resources at some point in the research cycle. There is a whole spectrum of ways in which art might be engaged with in research and a multitude of terms for describing this![4] These range from arts-informed research in which an artistic element is included within a research process (e.g. as a means of generating data or of communicating outcomes), to practice as research (PAR) in which an artistic making *itself* constitutes both the research process and outcome. Arts-engaged research is my way of referring to this entire spectrum of approaches in an inclusive way.

I use the term 'arts-based methods' more specifically to describe the research methods employed in arts-engaged research projects. Arts-based methods employ an element traditionally associated with the arts (often alongside others) as a means of researching a topic. The last 40 years have seen a proliferation of such research methods, drawing upon diverse forms of art practice such as 'creative writing and/or the visual arts: drawing, painting, collage, photography … music, drama, textile arts … and sculpture' (Kara, 2015, loc. 240). Many of these (such as photo-elicitation, collaging, map drawing, video filming and exhibition

---

[4] Within the research methods literature the vocabulary is still relatively unstable and authors vary in their use of such terms.

curation) have been widely used and are now firmly established as part of the accepted repertoire of qualitative research methods.[5]

Sadly, I do not have a definition to offer for art itself. I don't believe there is one. Nor do I understand there to be any ultimate distinction between art and science. This is a point reinforced by Stephen Pattison in his important essay 'Practical Theology: Art or Science' (2007). While rejecting essential differences, Pattison notes the durability of the binary categories in which art and science are conventionally located.[6]

Science	**Art**
Truth	Beauty
Reality	Symbols
Mind/Reason	Body/Passion
Things and events	Feelings and meanings
Objective	Subjective
Explanation	Interpretation
Representation	Construction/Making (up)
Prose	Poetry
Impartial	Partial
Methodological	Intuitive
Evidence/Proof	Insight/Evocation
Useful	Decorative
Logical	Imaginative
Problem-solving; provides answers	Ambiguous; holds mystery
Disciplined	Chaotic
Hard and strong	Soft and woolly
Masculine	Feminine

---

5 Some would see these commonly used methods as simply another means of generating data while others use arts-based methods because they wish to move away from notions of 'data-gathering' altogether and towards projects of cooperative and communal meaning-making.

6 The table here is my adapted and extended version of Richard Brown's categories presented in *A Poetic of Sociology* (1989, p. 26) which are employed by Pattison (2007, p. 261).

Looking at a table such as the one here we would instinctively know in which column to place a particular quality or way of being. However, drawing upon Brown (1989) and Midgley (1989, 2001), Pattison argues strongly against the legitimacy of such divides. There is a historical indivisibility, continuing coalescence and constant dialogue between these spheres. Terms change position as they continually engage with and impact upon one another: 'Scientific endeavour often enriches a sense of wonder and nurtures imagination ... artistic endeavour can enhance the discourse of science, warming up and regenerating frozen metaphors that have come to be regarded as facts and creating new theories' (Pattison, 2007, p. 262).

It is good to be reminded that the art/science binary is a constructed fabulation. However, mobilizing a heuristic distinction between art and science can still remain useful when it enables reclamation of important but devalued sources of insight.

Responsiveness to what is hard to comprehend: embodiment

I shall now begin to explore the responsiveness enabled by arts-engaged research through the example of a field that is notoriously difficult to approach through traditional empirical methods because of its multifaceted and ambiguous nature. I have chosen embodiment for this brief case study.

Bodies are fleshly bounded and discrete yet they are also nodes of relation with other bodies. Our bodies communicate gender, race and age. They often image class and physical ability. In their movements through space, the concealing or revealing of flesh, the wearing of clothing and myriad other signings, they display cultural allegiances, personal capabilities and dis-ease. However, they are also cryptic. They are sites of performance – concealing as well as revealing pain, desire, trauma, histories; they speak in signs we struggle to interpret. They limit our vision by locating us in particular times, spaces and contexts. But they also provide vantage points, epistemological standpoints; they open unique windows on to the world.

Attending to embodiment is therefore complicated, and social researchers thus frequently opt for focusing upon one aspect of embodiment (e.g. disability, gender identity, trauma, fertility, ageing, etc.) and 'abstract' this from the whole. This approach is understandable as it is very difficult to stay with the body in academic work. Phenomenological researchers, for example, while maintaining embodiment is central, often struggle to find means of actually staying with and communicating from 'the flesh'. Theologians face similar challenges complicated by the legacy of somaphobia and a persistent tendency towards analogical thinking that 'reads' the body to pass beyond it.[7] We may start with the body and attempt to remain faithful to both its fascination and appalling contingency, but before we know it we have transubstantiated fleshly confusion into signs and symbols that are much easier to handle. We draw upon bodily metaphors and rhetorically employ bodily terms, but often the body 'itself' is missing.[8]

Artistic engagements do not resolve the difficulties of comprehending the diverse aspects of embodiment. However, they do offer significant means of becoming responsive to embodiment in a variety of ways within research processes. They also draw us back again and again to fleshly matters that we might otherwise seek to transcend.

They do so first by encouraging researchers to attend to their own bodies. Many forms of art are predicated upon bodily responses to materials and contexts. As researchers and co-researchers become familiar with their materials (which might be anything from words to knitting yarn or an urban landscape), they learn to attend to their own embodiment in relation to these other 'bodies'. Embodiment thus ceases to be an 'intrusion' and becomes a research instrument – in the sense of being a site of registering and responding to a range of stimuli. Fully developing modes of embodied responsiveness requires a patient apprenticeship. But even a playful first encounter with artistic practices can be revelatory in terms of what can be brought forth through bodily attentiveness in the creative process – whether this takes place in the (relatively) restrained atmosphere of a creative writing workshop or the exuberant space of a dance studio. Often those engaged will report that they had not attended to some aspect of bodily 'knowledge' before an artistic practice enabled them to do so.

---

7 There are, of course, significant theological exceptions to this tendency that point the way forward for future research (see, for example, Peckruhn, 2017, and Radford, 2023).

8 I served as co-editor of the journal *Theology and Sexuality* for many years and received numerous prospective contributions for consideration that employed sexual images to enquire into the nature of the divine or probe textual traditions and ethical concerns. However, the sex in most of these submissions was symbolic, purged of its sticky traces. There was a deflection away from the body at the same time as its resources were dismembered for discursive construction.

As well as cultivating bodily attentiveness, arts-based methods can enable participants and co-partners in research to communicate their responsiveness in agential ways from the radical specificity of their body-selves. Often when questions are asked in traditional modes of social research, the researcher is seeking to ascertain what people think about something that the researcher has decided is important. The medium of words is adept for the communication of intellectual responses but it takes different skills (and enabling techniques) for people to be able to communicate their embodied responses to situations and issues. Body-talk is not something most people are fluent in. However, creative mediums such as clay, paint and textile threads can be used to enable people to give form to particular experiences that may surprise researchers and co-researchers alike. For example, Penny Stuart (2009) wished to develop an 'embodied ecclesiology' but struggled to gain any meaningful responses when she questioned women about what they found comfortable or discomforting in the bodily experience of going to church. The question did not seem comprehensible. However, when she asked the same women to draw themselves in church and to draw themselves where they felt comfortable, the results were revelatory. The contrast between simple, crude, black and white images they presented of themselves in church and the colourful more complex images they drew of themselves in the bath or in the garden presented a powerful representation of their personal embodied ecclesiologies. This approach allowed women to register embodied responses inaccessible by other means.

Such methods enable those involved in research processes to access, draw upon and communicate things they know in deeply sensate ways. However, artistic approaches also draw upon the ways bodies can create knowledge, in a more active sense, through responsiveness to their environments and their material potentialities. Here the emphasis is not on revealing what is implicit 'within' but on reshaping what is around. Research becomes an embodied making in order to know something not known before. For example, when working in a research project alongside artists, the environmental scientist Leah Gibbs learned from her collaborators how to engage with a living landscape in new and enriching ways. The creatives exemplified and enabled the research team:

[To] use the body and senses to explore and learn, as well as create and communicate ... through various interactions with the site, by gathering, digging, walking, rowing, lugging, listening. We engaged bodily with dirt, documents, river water, the homestead, echoes, cattle, people, weather, cameras, projectors, bird song. (Gibbs, 2014, p. 219)

This is a vivid image of research as a responsive-making that happens *through the body*.

In the above examples of attending, communicating and making, arts-engaged research enables a responsiveness that constructs an accessible bridge between embodiment and knowledge. As Chilton and Leavy argue, it gives epistemological form to 'sensorial experience because, through the arts, we come to *witness and to know* embodied sounds, movements, images, and stories' (2014, p. 403, my emphasis). We might go further and argue that it reminds us all that research is 'embodied creativity ... making things with our bodies' (Ellingson, 2017, p. 191). This encourages us to expand our research imagination and move beyond models of knowledge as abstraction out of life and towards images of embodied responsiveness *in the midst of things*. Ivan Brady describes research as an inquisitive process of rummaging through everyday life to create with the materials it contains: 'centering, decoding, reframing, discovering, and discoursing the clutter of the Made World ... as "embodied" participants and observers, full of touch, smell, taste, hearing, and vision, open to the buzz and the joy and the sweat and the tears – the erotics – of daily life' (Brady, in Ellingson, 2017, p. 82).

To date, it has been those working on the increasingly blurred boundaries of practical theology who have contributed most in terms of theological responsiveness to embodiment. I am thinking here of path-making work undertaken in liberative and constructive modes, much of which it would be difficult to classify exactly: for example, trauma theology, crip theology, queer theology, decolonial and black theology, feminist theology. Some of this employs arts-engaged approaches. I think of Cole Arthur Riley's *This Here Flesh: Spirituality, Liberation, and the Stories that Make Us* – particularly the chapter on 'Body' (2022, pp. 56–68). From a sculptural/visual perspective, Rebekah Pryor's *Motherly* (2022) illustrates the way in which artistic practice generates new forms of embodied witness. Within the sphere of practical theology, if it is more closely defined (although I really don't think it should be!), it is those who have employed creative writing – I include poetry, memoir, autoethnography, creative non-fiction and journalling in this category – as their research methodology who have undertaken some of the most significant responses to embodiment. I would include Melanie May's classic text *A Body Knows* (1995) here alongside Nicola

Slee's embodied poetics (e.g. 2011, 2019) and Campbell's writing on autism and mothering (2021). My own work on infertility would also belong in this place (2015a). Pamela Couture's creative non-fictional work in *We Are Not All Victims* (2016) represents a powerful example of embodied responsiveness in practical theological construction. I treasure her description of being bathed and cared for during a bout of malaria. It is one of the best 'icons' of church I have encountered.

Arts-engaged research not only contributes insights about embodiment to theological reflection. It also enables responsiveness to embodiment to be incorporated into theological construction. As Christian Scharen and Aana Marie Vigen state: '*to do theology and ethics well, scholars need to explore them through visceral ways, within embodied communities*' (Scharen and Vigen, 2011, p. xviii). I would agree with this sentiment but, drawing on Brady, would maybe phrase it a little differently and extend the notion of community that is operative.[9] I aspire towards a theology done in 'erotic' ways within communities of embodiment.

Responsiveness to inaccessible things: affect

In speaking of communities of embodiment I am consciously referring back to the relational ontologies I introduced in Chapter 1. For what I understand by this term are those networks of human and non-human actants, living beings and other entities, that are integrally linked in intra-acting assemblages (see pp. 13–14) in which 'bodies interact with, affect, and are affected *by* nonhuman objects, including inanimate objects (e.g. computers, knives, cars, foods) and the bodies of animals, birds, insects, plants, and other species' (Ellingson, 2017, p. 23, my emphasis). What is particularly important here is that bodily interaction is integrally linked to affect – indeed, *it is* such interactions (in their widest sense) that constitute affect – and which constitute the body itself in this relational frame. This contemporary understanding of affect is rather different to ones that focus upon the psychology of emotions or emotional knowing as a personal interior state. It adapts and extends the terms of reference, but still preserves the defining character of affect – namely, being moved, effected by or acted upon by something that provokes change (affects us). It also reaffirms that affections 'have to

---

9 And echoing the path-making work of James Hopewell who introduced Eros to Congregational Studies (see Walton, 2012).

do with the affected and affecting body ... the sensations and forces our bodies experience as a result of other bodies' (Segarra, Segovia and Sancho-Gil, 2024, p. 145; bodies in this case does not only reference human or living bodies). But 'in this approach, affection would be an invisible force that precedes individuality and places relationality as the ontological axis' (Segovia, Hernández Hernández and Sancho-Gil, 2024, p. 7). In other words, 'affect' is a way of speaking about the mode through which relationality impresses itself and is acutely felt.

The implications of this for research practice is that a concern with affect shifts the focus of attention away from contained phenomena or events and towards networks of relationship in which affects are mobile and transmitted. (Christoffer Kølvraa uses the challenging image of contagion as a way of describing this; 2015, pp. 184–5.) The crucial importance of such networks is something we cannot ignore in these times when political populism, racism and environmental awareness are all high on the agenda of concern. However, networks of affective relations are difficult to imagine within conventional research frameworks as they constitute those modalities or 'forces often ignored in social research ... fundamentally non-representational phenomena that always exceed attempts to categorize them' (Strom and Mills, 2024, p. 664). Furthermore, as Monica Pearl maintains (in relation to queerness), affect can be an outlaw force and attempts to transcribe it in traditional categories may be seeking to 'capture something shifting and subversive and untamed ... naming (and taming) ... harnesses something wild' (2018, p. 201).

Herein lies the significance of the resources art brings to this challenge. It helps us to mark the significance of what lies between us and to draw those invisible lines of connection in the awareness that this is an imaginative and creative process that does not imply mastery. Indeed, the charting of affect through artistic cartography or the creation of mandalas (inspired by spiritual practice) has become a significant means of manifesting affective connections in contemporary research (e.g. Dewing, 2011). However, even such mapping processes are in danger of being too static. A feature of affect is its dynamic nature, registering as the flow of everyday life and as moods, ruptures, shocks and remembrances within bodies personal and social. It has the capacity to move us in powerful ways that are hard to grasp. As Anna Gibbs argues, the 'challenge to apprehend and articulate it' requires an 'affective attunement and resonance' (2015, p. 227). It is a responsiveness that can only be described as a 'poesis', or a making-in-order-to-make-present.

A good example of how such making can happen can be found in Susan Nordstrom's research project which she, very unacademically, describes as 'objects-subjects-events-*a life*-my study-and probably other ideas that I have yet to come across' (2013, p. 245; Nordstrom is deeply influenced here by St. Pierre's post-qualitative research and her advocacy of 'methodless methods', p. 253). In her work she uses household objects, family photographs, ephemera and family genealogies to co-construct with participants a rich and diverse collage of memories, objects, peoples and histories – or 'an ensemble of life' (2013, p. 237). This affective bricolage reveals a great deal more about people in relation than conventional ethnographic methods might achieve.[10]

A more challenging example of research that employs artistic processes of resonance and attunement to explore affect can be found in Elena Trivelli's account of engaging with the disputed history of a crisis in a psychiatric hospital in Gorizia, Italy (2015).[11] Trivelli inquired into this deeply wounded context: engaging with the memories of patients, nursing staff and local leaders, newspaper accounts, personal letters from patients, as well as with the neglected buildings of the institution itself and the artefacts within it. Among these she positioned herself as a conductor or channel, through which the affective archive of something painfully unresolved began to assemble. Trivelli describes the emergence of this archive in terms associated with the processes of art-making. It comes into being through a poesis of resonance and attunement in the same way as an image or poem begins to be formed, and its emergence impacts deeply upon the art-maker themselves. Trivelli's description of the affective intensity of this research process merits quoting at length:

---

10 I am struck by the fact that such research-collaging bears many resemblances to the creative fictions that write affect through entangling characters with objects, contexts, moods, fragments of discourse and wider historical events. Classic examples of this would be Virginia Woolf's *The Waves* (1931) or *Mrs Dalloway* (1925). However, this strategy is one that abounds in women's fictional writing more generally – particularly that which makes its locus in the everyday.

11 Between 1961 and 1968 this facility was led by the radical psychiatrist Franco Basaglia who introduced a new therapeutic regime to the hospital. 'Shock therapies were progressively dismissed, patients became involved in the running of the hospital, individual wards were gradually opened, and patients were allowed to exit the hospital during the day' (Trivelli, 2015, p. 120). While Basaglia's work inspired the formation of a strong collegial team and produced encouraging results, his unconventional approach also generated strong criticism, causing him to resign from his post. He left behind a community riven by conflicting memories of a significant period and hospital buildings transformed by his regime (the bars removed from windows, for example) that quickly began to fall into disrepair.

Monitoring my research progress in a journal, I noted how ... [my] whole body was progressively responding to these voices, entering rooms I had never seen, perceiving people I had never met, whose names were at times illegible, at times incomplete, at times missing ... I began to have insomnia, and I perceived a ghost in the flat in which I was living, whose presence stayed with me in the course of the following months, at times waking me up in a panic in the middle of the night ... my body and my emotions enacting ... an assembled archive of places, narratives, symptoms, and practices, in which ruins and debris, silences and basements emerge ... as voices of a different type, that speak 'when mouths are silent'. (2015, pp. 127–8)

What is striking here is a very frank acknowledgement of the affective woundings that may take place in research such as this. But this account does not just describe the author's experience of being caught up in a difficult situation; it also introduces a literal/literary ghost into the social research machine. I am drawn to the evocation of voices that speak when mouths are silent as a metaphor of affective-artistic responses to situations of damage and loss. As Gibbs argues, writing affect 'effectively' requires affective writing and the consequent opening up to creative 'rhetorical modes ... which enable the staging of passionate engagements' (2015, p. 223) – and also the passing on or transmission of these relational affects to the reader.

To date, attempts to engage with affect in the ways I have described it above are rare in practical theological research – although significant examples do exist. Jonas Ideström and Tone Stangeland Kaufman (2018a) have undertaken one of the few studies to employ Latour's network theory and to draw the lines between people, places and objects in research. Wren Radford's path-making work in theological arts-based research (2022) intertwines people, objects, emotions and histories to create a compelling affective archive to empower political resistance (as I shall explore later). Simon Hallonsten (2024) borrows the techniques of creative non-fiction to present data on online Christian Education as an embodied, affective assemblage of persons, objects, technologies and traditions (2024). Wigg-Stevenson explores what she terms the 'affective structures of faith' in conversation with performance art (2021).

Among these forays into the poesis of affect, Todd Whitmore's *Imitating Christ in Magwi* (2019) is particularly striking. In this he incarnates his understanding of ethnography as a research mode calling upon 'affect and all of the senses at the point of investigation and seeks in writing to, among other things, re-present the field encounter in a way that evokes the senses of the reader' (2019, p. 136). Whitmore aligned his 'life and desires' (2019, p. 25) with that of the community he studied in ways that shockingly confound the realist conventions of ethnographic work in practical theology. For a return to academic life after fieldwork in North Uganda and Southern Sudan, regions experiencing intense and violent conflict for many years, did not mean Whitmore could leave behind his affective involvement with the people, places and events he had encountered. He describes his continued registering of the ongoing presence of Laker, the spirit of a two-year-old murdered Acholi girl he first felt as she pressed herself against his left leg 'with the sensation of the hug around the upper calf/knee area by a small child standing next to you' (2019, p. 202). Laker continues to make such childish demands for attention upon him. This visitation, Whitmore states:

> has required me to reassess – that is, to re-discern – what I think on a wide array of other things; for instance, that rather than what has been called 'magical thinking' being a lack of critical rationality, I have had to reconsider whether critical rationality in many of its modern and postmodern forms is an obstruction to magical thinking. In other words, my pistological conversion (pistis meaning 'faith') has required a radical reworking of other things that I know, involving an epistemological conversion. (2019, p. 203)

Such a conversion implies not only that ways of knowing be reconfigured,[12] but also that creative means must be found to mediate new perspectives that do not constrain its challenge or its impact. The poetics of attunement and resonance that is called for in order to transcribe affect may entail a radical rewriting of practical theology in disturbing and 'magical' ways.

---

12 There is a danger, as stated previously (see pp. 81–2), that we repeat in our ethnographic work the familiar trope of the (dominant/white) outsider learning from their encounter with black and indigenous cultures about a more authentic, simpler or more magical world. There is a fine line between this mode of encounter and the one Ingold describes as learning in the company of others (see p. 8). Noting both the ubiquitous nature of this trope and its presence here does not, in my opinion, negate an appreciation of Whitmore's profound engagement with affect.

Responsiveness through attention and co-creation

In my explorations of embodiment and affect, I have been presenting arts engagement in research as enabling responsiveness: allowing 'us to access and represent aspects of our experience that may otherwise elude recognition and articulation' (Hartley, 2012, p. 265). In this frame, art-making is a critical and rational process that enables the generation of new knowledge. But it is not only the epistemological benefits of arts-engaged research that are foregrounded in the research literature. As Susan Finley asserts: 'At the heart of arts-based inquiry is a radical, politically grounded statement about social justice' (2008, p. 72). It is a means of valuing the insights of people whose contributions are routinely marginalized as arts-based research can not only shift understandings of what knowledge is, but also whose knowledge matters. Crucially, it is also a means of enabling active responses to situations of injustice as people develop transformative visions through art-making practices that foster a sense of political agency among those involved.

There is potential for people from all kinds of backgrounds and contexts to generate transformative insight through engaging in art practices that probe matters of common concern such as mental health, reproductive loss and ageing – all of which present as personal issues, but are undeniably social/political in their construction and impact. However, there is a particular value to employing arts-based methods in contexts in which people have been systematically disempowered. Art offers liberating mechanisms of self-expression to those who have lost trust in the traditional discursive ways of self-representation – having seen these manipulated to become means of stereotyping, pigeon-holing people's experiences and negating the disruptive impact of their testimonies.[13] Furthermore, the art created in such research contexts often possesses the power to speak beyond its initial location to those engaged in wrestling with similar problems or seeking inclusivity in pursuit of the common good.

When these practices are undertaken as research modes in communal contexts, a sense of shared discovery and momentum can develop. As Gioia Chilton and Patricia Leavy affirm, these approaches are 'known for raising critical awareness of injustice and oppression in participatory and action-oriented ways' (2014, p. 407). Because art-making enables

---

13 For a more detailed discussion about how lived experience testimonies can be exploited and abused, as well as how these processes are resisted, see Radford, 2022, pp. 27–51.

people to respond to issues that they had previously been hindered from naming, they not only develop personal awareness but are also able to construct shared responses – or, indeed, hold pain and mark tragic losses together in silent solidarity.

This draws us towards understandings of art that emphasize what Brian Hand (2015) describes as its dialogical, relational and collaborative aspects. Drawing upon movements from surrealism to community arts, he argues that shared art-making is particularly effective in facilitating conscientization processes because the knowledge gained is not alienating but organic to the makers involved (the influence of Paulo Freire is also evident here). Generated within a community engaged in probing their experiences, art becomes 'a process led, rather than a product led, dialogical encounter and participating entails sharing a desire to unveil or discover the power structures of reality with a view to creatively imagining' alternatives (2015). Such processes have the potential to expose the regulatory mechanisms of everyday life, in 'imaginative ways that draw attention to the cruelties and contradictions' (2015), and also offer creative opportunities to lament, memorialize and produce diverse counter-narratives.

In their practical theological research, Wren Radford sought means to enable expression of 'experiences of marginalisation [that] often fall outside of the dominant narratives available for sharing experiences' (2022, p. 32). As they engaged with co-researchers experiencing poverty in multi-faceted, embodied and particular ways, Radford noted the deep weariness that results from the constant questioning people in poverty endure – whether from those authorizing benefit payments, access to medical treatments and social support mechanisms, as well as from those with apparently more benign intentions in relation to local policy-making and social provision. In this context, even those processes that invite participants to 'tell their stories' were understood as having the potential to reinforce 'unequal social power dynamics and exposing those testifying to stigma and judgement, particularly in treating people as a "single issue" … [with the] focus on the ability to provide information or data to be interpreted by those in power' (2022, p. 51). Instead Radford undertook to facilitate collaborative, artistic-making with co-researchers in ways that did not lead to objectification of either the people or the knowledge generated. This enabled the layers of 'creativity, compassion, humour, anger, and courage' (2022, p. 126) that characterize the lives of people struggling with/resisting poverty to be made manifest through powerful creations – such as the 'Fear of the Brown Envelopes' – an artwork that vividly exposes the oppressive nature of the benefits system in the UK.[14] The co-operative art project Radford constructed with co-researchers began in shared processes of personal and communal expression. Its impact rippled outwards through community-exhibiting and other forms of evocative sharing to become a creative political and spiritual intervention.

Responsiveness to indigenous wisdom

In such ways engaging with art in research can function as a means of nurturing agency in knowledge creation among diverse, disenfranchised groups. However, it may also be a means of respectfully honouring established and sophisticated ways of comprehending the world which are expressed in music and dance, myth and story or sacred art. The development of indigenous research methodologies (see Denzin, Lincoln and Smith, 2008) has promoted recognition of the epistemological significance of the communal, creative processes through which traditional wisdom is communicated and creatively reformed in contemporary circumstances. Research in such contexts demands embodied attentive responsiveness; a *deep listening* that does not seek to abstract knowledge out of artistic practices but to encounter it within them.[15] Indigenous research methodologies cherish a holistic vision that does not divide and separate the artistic from the empirical, the sacred from the secular, or the epistemological from the political. In an essay exploring the spaces between indigenous and non-indigenous knowledge systems, Laura

---

14 Radford writes:

In discussing the process of making the piece 'Fear of the Brown Envelope', I noted where the creating-curating group talked about their different experiences around benefits assessments, naming the similar emotions around fear, panic, shame, and dread that became stitched to the envelopes ... In being made from the everyday objects of the brown envelopes that contain these benefits forms, the piece provided a point of connection ... highlighting the particularity of experiences around welfare cuts and assessments. In this way, the significance of the piece resides in its materiality, in making with and re-making the everyday object; recognising the fear and dread this object symbolises for so many people, yet also gesturing to where shared action as a community can be transformative. (Radford, 2022, p. 153)

15 While processes of 'deep listening' often draw upon artistic methodologies, it is important to note that artistic practices themselves do not automatically generate such outcomes.

Brearley and Treahna Hamm outline the principles of deep listening in research as these are articulated and practised by indigenous researchers from the Koori people (Indigenous people from what are now the New South Wales and Victoria areas of Australia). I have summarized these below:

- We invest time in the cultivating of relationships and the building of trust.
- Our comprehension of ways of knowing becomes extended and broadened through patient attention.
- We recognize creativity is embedded in the way we learn and live our lives.
- A quality of care infuses our relationships. We look after one another, collaborating and co-creating within a community of practice.
- Respect underpins our relationships with one another and with the earth.
- We share a sense of service to the community and to future generations.
(Brearley and Hamm, 2009, p. 44, my paraphrase)

A vivid example of the way in which the responsive process of 'deep listening' functions is represented in reflections upon 'yarning' between Australian scholars of diverse heritages concerned to affirm indigenous methodologies in their research work. Yarning is an Australian term for the millennia-old tradition of communal gatherings in which traditional wisdom is performed, explained, examined and passed on:

> [The] centrality of yarning and the need to yarn are driving our work ... For the Indigenous Australian, life is research, but it is through yarning that meaning is made. 'Yarning' ... forms the basis for framing research where questions are not planned, presented to panels of University ethics committees, or known before the work begins. The quality of the encounter rather than mere questioning is the goal of the yarn; the weaving and co-creation of fabrics of meaning emerges through the interweaving of the various yarns. Talking circles where art is concurrently made are so familiar to many Indigenous communities; and it is in the making of the art and the talking of the stories of existence that change occurs. (McKenna and Woods, 2012, p. 7)

Yarning here refers to actual gatherings which become sites of situated, communal research. It also refers to the artistic practices and ways of knowing that the gathered community perform and affirm. Finally, it expresses an approach to research itself as a yarning process.

Responsiveness in 'local practical theological aesthetics'

Research encounters based upon attentive and responsive 'deep listening' in the context of significant cultural practices may be seen as of evident value for researchers within indigenous communities and also members of diasporic groups affirming their heritages in the context of racism. For example, the African American scholars Cynthia Dillard and Charlotte Bell (2011) talk about the necessity of honouring indigenous African knowledges and sacred practices in their vision of 'endarkened feminist' ethnography. Here they make an explicit link between the sacredness of their African inheritance, the need for emancipatory practice, and the necessity of spiritual healing from the effects of the (dominant/white) 'epistemological and methodological tools we've traditionally used to engage research' (2011, p. 338).[16] This healing is presented as 'situated, sacred and spiritual work' (2011, p. 338).

Such approaches constitute a respectful acknowledgement of traditional wisdoms that are rarely presented, or even explicable, in propositional forms but are increasingly recognized as vital political resources – both for the communities involved and as contributions to the shared work of planetary care. However, a creative mode of responsiveness, or deep listening, can be practised in many other contexts because all groups possess cultural and aesthetic practices through which traditions, wisdom and understandings of the sacred are mediated. But my advocacy of learning from indigenous research practices must be tempered by an awareness of the dangers of cultural appropriation.

---

16 In a previous work, Dillard describes three healing methodologies in an endarkened feminist framework:

1. A person must be drawn into and present in a spiritual homeland. 2. A person must be engaged with/in the rituals, people, places in intimate, authentic [and humble] ways. 3. A person must be open to being transformed by all that is encountered and recognize those encounters as purposeful and expansive. Such engagements ... both center the spirit and to shift the epistemological and cultural location of our thought and action in the world. (Dillard, 2008, p. 287)

It would be both inappropriate and ineffective to 'borrow' a tradition or method of artistic communal meaning-making from one context and simply transpose it upon another. What must be worked with are the modes of cultural expression that have a lively presence within the community – although cultures are not hermetically sealed and new practices are always being adopted and 'indigenized'. Goto warns that in relation to its (limited) engagement with art-making and aesthetics, white practical theology has not been sufficiently aware of either the dangers of appropriation or the particular aesthetic 'genius' of specific communities, and has thus practised forms of cultural, racial and ethnic denial (2016, p. 110). Ironically, this denial allows dominant/white onlookers to exercise both a voyeuristic fascination with, and simultaneously discount the significance of, aesthetic self-expression that lies beyond their 'mainstream' concerns. To counter this she advocates the recognition of Local Practical Theological Aesthetics or LPTA (2016, p. 109). This refers to the creative milieu of localized[17] communities of faith in which 'particular cultures, histories, and traditions ... intersect' (2016, p. 110) and which form the aesthetic idiom operative in a particular context. This need not be mono-cultural. The local, as Goto affirms, can be a context of diversity. Engaging with such idioms (which are ubiquitous) and their creative practices can be revelatory in research terms but also as a theological practice 'that precipitates the creative emergence of something of God that needs to be perceived' (2016, p. 3). This generative movement may be described as 'flow', states Goto, referring to an exciting and compelling involvement in something that carries us along and is stimulating, expansive and exuberant.[18] Goto here is drawing attention to the important point: aesthetic engagement generates an irrepressible sense of joy. And joy is a particularly precious political resource in these difficult times.

---

17 Goto has a critical understanding of the term 'local' and critiques the work of Robert Schreiter on local theologies because he does not give attention to 'the complexity of what "local" means for racial/ethnic minority churches in the United States' (Goto, 2016, p. 110).

18 Goto states:

The language of 'flow' that Mihalyi Csikszentmihalyi uses has its own advantages for opening up the notion of revelatory experiencing. Flow 'denotes the wholistic sensation present when we act with total involvement. It is the kind of feeling after which one nostalgically says: "That was fun," or "That was enjoyable."' (in Goto, 2016, p. 7)

In her book on collaborative, arts-engaged research and social justice, Victoria Foster argues that the joy of immersion in the carnivalesque qualities of creativity is one of the most powerful resources available to us:

> The carnival is not able to 'rewrite history, undo the effects of war or alter what is happening on the news'. However, it does offer a 'tantalising promise' of how things might be 'if we altered the conditions that tie us down' ... This is why the 'creative things that make it up ... are so precious: laughter, sex and art' ... Involvement in creative and fun-filled activities spills over into other areas of life. (2016, p. 137)[19]

This insight is echoed by the political theorist William Connolly whose work focuses upon forms of resistance to an apparently all-encompassing neoliberal political regime. While political agency is partly motivated by 'our tacit sense of belonging to a human predicament worthy of embrace', he writes:

> ... grounded too in those uncanny experiences of creativity by means of which something new enters the world ... It ties the sweetness of life to a *vitality* of being, even more than to a preordained end, purpose, or 'fullness' with which it is officially invested. (2012, p. 76)[20]

Goto's celebration of flow, Foster's invitation to the carnival, and Connolly's responsiveness to creative 'sweetness' that reveals a vitality of being, seem to take us a very long way indeed from the traditional territory of qualitative research in practical theology. How do we understand research excellence, or employ terms like validity and rigour, in relation to expressions such as these that seem so very far removed from the familiar categories of assessment we employ to judge the academic merit of our work? Can these be adapted to contain them or will new modes of responsiveness need to be developed on which to base our judgements?

---

19 Foster is drawing here upon Kate Webb's (1994) work on Angela Carter.

20 This is an insight developed by Jane Bennett in her major work *The Enchantment of Modern Life: Attachments, Crossings, and Ethics* (2001), in which she argues that political resistance needs the sustenance of material pleasures in all their creative forms – enjoyed fully in the present moment rather than identified as future goals. It is this taste of beauty that inspires us just as much, or perhaps more, than the restless hunger of lack.

What makes good research?

Unlike some of my other works in practical theology (e.g. Graham, Walton and Ward, 2019; Bennett et al., 2019; Walton, 2014a) this text is not a 'how to' book. It is focused on the 'what and why' of research rather than offering guidance as to how it might be undertaken.[21] However, it is important to (briefly) address some concrete issues relating to validity and rigour at the close of this chapter because they will be of concern to many readers. In so doing I will still try to turn the 'How can I produce good research if I move beyond traditional protocols and practices?' into a different sort of question: 'What is good research anyway?'

There are multiple issues at stake here, not least the fact that qualitative research has never truly broken free of the paradigms established in quantitative research traditions. As Janice Morse writes in a helpful overview of the field:

> The traditional dominance of quantitative research over qualitative research provided qualitative inquiry with a language and a host of habits, particularly in the area of demonstrating reliability and validity, and these elements were adopted in various ways ... On the surface, these practices seemed right, so they were adopted unquestioningly, although subject to periodic modification. (2018, p. 797)

Morse goes on to chart developments that took place over time which sought to provide for qualitative research its own evaluative criteria. She outlines the gradual development of protocols, checklists and procedures intended to ensure that qualitative research could be judged on its own terms and according to agreed standards. This process has entailed considerable soul-searching as to where judgements concerning worthiness and reliability should be located in qualitative projects. Are these to be achieved through the incorporation of some ostensibly 'objective' mechanisms into the research journey (such as computer analysis, triangulation and peer-checking of coding)? Should the internal coherence of research design and processes of the research itself form the basis of judgements concerning its soundness? Or are the opinions of peer reviewers and the wider academic community where authority should lie? More daringly, are the endorsements of participants/co-researchers,

---

21 There are lots of books out there already that address these issues in relation to creative and arts-based research. We just need to read beyond the tribe.

or the active engagement of future 'readers', important criteria by which to judge the worth of a research project?

As will be quite clear from all I have written thus far, I am sceptical concerning what Bochner and Riggs describe as 'correspondence' theories of knowledge (2014). I don't think qualitative research reflects aspects of reality – as if seen in a mirror or when placed under a microscope – however assiduously we engage in the rituals of saturation sampling, audit trails, reflexive attempts to identify bias, peer reviews of coding decisions, etc., etc. Something different is happening in the research process – something much more like creative making. Nevertheless, I have come to respect the sincere attempts to conduct research in as conscientious, careful, open and accountable means as possible, and some of the early attempts to create frameworks for validity and rigour in qualitative research are impressive in their commitment to 'trustworthiness'.

For example, Lincoln and Guba's (1985) advocacy of this quality and their insistence that it must originate in a prolonged relation of profound attention with participants is still a principle of value in all forms of research practice.[22] Furthermore, although I am impatient with the 'host of habits' drawn from quantitative approaches that continue to be endemic in practical theology's qualitative research projects,[23] I do recognize that there are conventions to be acknowledged by researchers who are concerned that their work: receives funding; influences decision-making; is regarded as valid by stakeholders; is accountable to participants/co-researchers; and (less gloriously but crucially) enables researchers themselves to survive within the academy (see p. 75).

When I view efforts to ensure validity and rigour in this pragmatic frame I can recognize that within the internal coherence of any project the insights generated might well be enhanced through approaches such as peer-checking and participant/co-researcher feedback loops, etc., I remain very sceptical concerning the values of triangulation as

---

22 Lincoln and Guba's early work (1985) has been highly influential in the development of ways for evaluating qualitative research. Scholarship in this field has, however, moved on – and they moved with it. It is possible to continue to respect the tone and intent of their endeavours without regarding them as a template for contemporary work.

23 I have served on councils awarding major research funding, have been on scholarship committees making awards for doctoral research, examined numerous doctoral theses, and undertaken research projects myself. These experiences confirm to me that the values of quantitative research are very much alive in contemporary qualitative research practice.

traditionally understood; the insights of one methodological approach are often incommensurate with those drawn from other positions, and thus do not 'secure' the veracity of outcomes in the ways that are frequently suggested. However, when triangulation is radically revisioned as crystallization,[24] the notion that employing different methods within a multifaceted research project may yield deeper, more complex and mutually enriching insights is helpful.

Laurel Richardson, who introduced this now widely adopted paradigm, was careful to point out that crystallization is less a means of developing certainties in research as a way of countering these. She writes, 'Crystallization provides us with a deepened, complex, thoroughly partial, understanding of the topic. Paradoxically, we know more and doubt what we know. Ingeniously, we know there is always more to know' (Richardson, 2000, p. 934). Very significantly, her generative work on this theme was stimulated by the fact that arts-based approaches were beginning to 'break the boundaries' (2000, p. 934) of qualitative research practice and were compelling scholars to consider how the insights they generated might be comprehended and incorporated into mixed-method projects. Clearly, modes of judging rigour and validity still deeply engrained with positivist assumptions inherited from quantitative research would be unworkable in relation to these emerging approaches.

Debates about what kind of knowledge art generates are ongoing, with numerous epistemological and philosophical perspectives in play – some of which are explored in the following chapter. However, in attempting to comprehend this question an important shift in priorities took place which were generated by researchers employing these methods. The ethical and transformative impact of knowledge rather than its reliability, generalizability or status in the academy, began to

---

24 Richardson introduces crystallization in these terms in her landmark essay 'Writing: A Method of Inquiry':

The scholar draws freely on his or her productions from literary, artistic, and scientific genres, often breaking the boundaries of each of those as well. In these productions, the scholar might have different 'takes' on the same topic, what I think of as a postmodernist deconstruction of triangulation ... In postmodernist mixed-genre texts, we do not triangulate, we *crystallize* ... I propose that the central image for 'validity' for postmodern texts is not the triangle – a rigid, fixed, two-dimensional object. Rather, the central imaginary is the crystal, which combines symmetry and substance with an infinite variety of shapes, substances, transmutations, multidimensionalities, and angles of approach. (Richardson, 2000, p. 934)

take centre stage.[25] In the text box below I have summarized two significant attempts to wrestle with the issue of what constitutes excellent research that were generated by influential qualitative researchers who were engaged in writing research creatively and differently.[26]

> **Arthur Bochner and Nicholas Riggs (on narrative inquiry)**
>
> 'The goals of ... narrative inquiry are to keep conversation going (about matters crucial to living well); to activate subjectivity, feeling, and identification in readers or listeners; to raise consciousness; to promote empathy and social justice; and to encourage activism – in short, to show what it can mean to live a good life and create a just society.' In achieving these goals it is recognized that:
>
> 1. The researcher is part of the research data.
> 2. A research text is always composed by a particular somebody in some place; writing and/or performing research is part of the inquiry.
> 3. Research involves the emotionality and subjectivity of both researchers and participants.
> 4. The relationship between researchers and research participants should be democratic.
> 5. Researchers ought to accept an ethical obligation to give something important back to the people they study and write about.
> 6. What researchers write should be written for participants as much as about them; researchers and participants should be accountable to one another, and the researcher's voice should not dominate the voices of participants.
> 7. Research should be about what could be (not just about what has been).
> 8. The reader or audience should be conceived as a co-participant, not as a spectator, and should be given opportunities to think with (not just about) the research story (or findings).
> (Bochner and Riggs, 2014, p. 201)

---

25 Although these qualities are certainly not contradictory!
26 The illustrations given are both from 'text-based' approaches. Clearly, when employing visual and other forms of art differing criteria would be necessary although some overlaps could be expected in values and processes.

> **Norman Denzin (on performative ethnography)**
>
> 'I intend a writing form that moves from interpretation and emotional evocation to praxis, empowerment and social change' (2003, p. 133). Ethnographic texts are valuable that:
>
> 1. Unsettle, criticize and challenge taken-for-granted, repressed meanings.
> 2. Invite moral and ethical dialogue while reflexively clarifying their own moral positions.
> 3. Engender resistance and offer utopian thoughts about how things can be made different.
> 4. Demonstrate they care, that they are kind.
> 5. Show instead of tell using the rule that less is more.
> 6. Exhibit interpretative sufficiency, representational adequacy and authentic adequacy.
> 7. Present political, functional, collective and committed viewpoints.
>
> (Denzin, 2003, pp. 123–4)

It is interesting to notice that a number of qualities overlap in these examples. First, research is set firmly within its political context and researchers assume positions of committed praxis in relation to this. Second, the moral and value-based framework in which research takes place is crucial and results in a co-operative, participatory and egalitarian approach to research processes. Third, instead of the representation being paramount there is an orientation towards transformation; Bochner and Riggs envision good research as being about what could be, rather than what has been, and Denzin highlights the potential to generate utopian visions of how things might be different. Fourth, the 'making of research' as an aesthetic intervention is highlighted – with Bochner and Riggs focusing on the creative work that this entails, and Denzin emphasizing the 'showing' rather than the 'telling' that this implies.

Such approaches to research excellence might appear idealistic or even naïve on first reading. However, even in mainstream contexts they are gaining increasing traction as questions of impact, accountability and engagement are increasingly foregrounded and creative work is being recognized as having transformative potential. In the next chapter

I shall ask what practical theology might discover about its own modes of theological making from attending to artistic practice. However, at the close of this chapter I want to highlight a task as yet unfulfilled that I believe should now rise to the top of our agenda. *When we consider excellence in the engagement between practical theology and qualitative research, where should our priorities lie?* Are the habits of our hearts still formed by inherited sentiments from inappropriate research models that we find difficult to break with? Is there some means of finding a balance between inherited academic conventions and new challenges – or is a new, more radical, approach required? And what would it mean to place committed praxis, moral values, collaborative working, transformative imaginings and creative making at the heart of research practice?[27] Should we 'judge' excellence in research with reference to these values? What kind of theological energy might that shift generate?

---

27 This is currently receiving increased attention within practical theology, which is to be warmly welcomed; see de Roest, 2019.

6

Theology as Art in Our Troubles

In the last chapter I outlined ways in which the employment of creative research methods might offer new resources to practical theology – while making clear that their adoption would not resolve all research difficulties and entails significant challenges. At the forefront of these is the challenge to see ourselves as creative theological makers whose work is responsive not only to the customary requirements of the academy but to our extra-ordinary obligations in these times.

This chapter pursues these themes further by moving from the arena of methodological debates and academic practices into a wider terrain. Here I am concerned not about the adoption of particular research strategies, but rather about ways of understanding the nature and purpose of our theological work more generally. It is my conviction that engaging with some of the ways in which 'art-in-a-context-of-crisis' is currently comprehended will generate insights for practical theological making. I thus offer the invitation to undertake the thought experiment of imagining theology 'as art' in our troubles. That is, I am asking you to view practical theological work as an 'artistic intervention' through the lenses offered below. I shall also note some of the ways in which practical theologians are already engaging in significant ways with the themes I present. Of course, what I present here is not the only way of comprehending the role and significance of theology in the climate disaster. It is simply an opening, a contribution, a making that is offered to continuing conversations in the latent commons.

Staging wreckage and performing ruins

Let us begin not in some art gallery or red-velvet-seated theatre but in a broken and contested place. Maybe it is an abandoned factory. Monumental in scale, it was built to house the enormous heat and light processes and intense human activity of industrial production. It is now empty and polluted by its former use; water drips down one wall. The huge arc lights illuminating the space are powered by humming generators positioned on the cracked concrete floor. Or perhaps we are gathered outside in a conflict zone. There *are* buildings here: houses, libraries, places of worship and schools. Some still appear solid but the roofs and windows are mostly caved in or blown out. It would be more dangerous to shelter inside them than stand out here. On this summer night. As bats dip between the trees and the telegraph polls that are still standing. We should not gather here but we gather anyway. There is a performance going on. We have come to watch, but we are also taking part.

In his book *Performing Ruins* (2020), Simon Murray reflects upon actual performances staged in sites of wreckage, alienation and continuing conflict. While paying close attention to the very differing qualities of these acts (installations, improvisations, collective avant-garde interventions, immersive events or new interpretations of classic works), he also notes a common disposition among those involved in their staging. They had been drawn to perform in ruined sites because of a deeply sensed congruence between the social disintegration their art interrogates and the space in which it is being performed. Murray employs the cultural theorist Raymond Williams's term, 'a structure of feeling' (Williams, in Murray, 2020, p. 4) to describe the shared sense of devastation that is operative here. This has been brought about by diverse factors: climate change, economic uncertainty, racism, fast-paced technological revolutions, terrorism, war, and apparently irresolvable cultural conflicts. The sources are diverse but the 'structure of feeling' is a common one. This mood is heightened and focused when joined together with space, place and bodies in sites of dereliction. He writes: 'Although, of course, it was never articulated as "ontological and epistemological uncertainty", time and again during my fieldwork excursions I would hear artists, performers, activists or curators express *a mood or experience of ruination*' (2020, p. 4, my emphasis).

Murray's work explores how artistic form and body are given to ruination through specific performative actions in specific places. However, he is quite well aware that his project generates a striking image for the role of art more generally in our current cultural climate. Art here 'stages the wreckage'. This evocative term (employed in recent work in performance studies; see the special issue of *Performance Research* edited by Gianna Bouchard and Patrick Duggan (2019) for articles on this theme) refers to the way in which artistic interventions mark, attend to and communicate damage and loss that, lacking such memorializations, could too easily be absorbed into the collective, anaesthetized normality. Staging the wreckage brings into focus what is obscured and denied in order that business can continue as usual. Art can perform this function because it is not a stakeholder in the order of the 'real'. And it is the very structures of 'reality' itself that are overwhelmed when the concealed 'wreckage' of the current order is revealed.

Of course, creative work does not need to be theatrically performed in 'actual' ruins to stage the wreckage, and a wide range of artistic mediums can be employed in order to do so. Similarly, the brokenness might not consist of bricks and mortar, but of broken cultural certainties: visions of humanity, progress, innocence and goodness, or even faith. In relation to these wider scenes of dereliction, two cinematic interventions have been particularly important to me recently. The first is a film on popular release.

The Zone of Interest, directed by Jonathan Glazier, won the Grand Prix at the 2023 Cannes Film Festival and has since garnered many other international awards. It portrays the family life of Rudolph Höss, the commandant of Auschwitz, his wife Hedwig and their five children. The family home is located just outside the camp and Hedwig spends much of her time tending an exquisite garden that lies right beside the boundary wall. We see the family eating together, at play, entertaining guests, and enjoying intimate moments. The horror of the production lies in the fact that the noises of the camp (shouted orders, cries, gunshots and the constant noise of the furnaces) provide the soundtrack to the film just as they must have formed the actual soundtrack to their lives. Similarly, the deep red glow of the blazing ovens shows through the drawn curtains, and soot and ash invade the scrubbed surfaces and green spaces of family life. The film thus portrays the abysmal foundations upon which their 'good life' is maintained. We also witness the destructive toll upon each member of the family as they mobilize their differing devices to obliterate their innate, sensory grasp of what is taking place. The film viscerally returns us to the events of the Holocaust. It engages all our senses to stage what lies beyond description and to reveal the enormous fallacy of inculpability. The body knew. The body always knows. And in staging the wreckage the film goes further. It asks what enormous efforts (personal and social) we are expending to prevent us hearing what Édouard Glissant terms 'the cry of the world' (2020, pp. 7–8) and to avoid seeing the dark red glow in our own skies at night.

The second 'staging of the wreckage' that has affected me is much less well known. It is a filmic representation of ruins that are located close to where I live in Glasgow. St Peters Seminary in Cardross, considered a masterpiece of brutalist architecture, opened for the training of priests in 1966 and closed only 14 years later. The reasons for the closure related to location, vocation and mission; all of which were radically challenged within that short but significant span of years. The Scottish filmmaker Murray Grigor was commissioned to show the seminary at the pinnacle of its short life. *Space and Light* (1972) is filmed in colour and in summer. We follow small groups of young seminarians as they attend lectures, worship, study and relax. We also see shorter sequences of the nuns whose cooking, cleaning and praying sustain the institution. All takes place against a background of luminous, pure forms and clean lines. A second film, *Space and Light Revisited*, was released by Grigor in 2009. It is intended to be shown in parallel alongside the first film.[1] Presented in black and white and filmed in winter it shows the ruins of the seminary. The walls are daubed in graffiti. Broken beams and fallen mortar obstruct the camera views. The chapel roof lies open and the altar is broken. The ruination is complete and this staging of the wreckage could not be more stark. The temple is torn down and the mute question all this brokenness poses to faith is urgent and direct: 'Something is over: what now?'

Artistic stagings of wreckage and performances of ruin have much to contribute to the work of practical theology. We can draw inspiration from, and employ artworks that perform this function, in both our theological reflection and in our research processes themselves. But, more importantly, we can place our core activities within this artistic frame; that is, we can conceive of the things we do and create ourselves (our academic work on faith practices, our research into faith life, and our theological engagements with culture) as performative stagings amid ruins. We can reveal dereliction and allow death to do its important work in every field of our endeavours from religious education to congregational studies.[2]

Work in liturgy, homiletics and ritual has a particularly important role to play here. This may draw upon scriptural traditions that contain many vivid stagings of wreckage. The prophetic writings and the psalms

---

[1] It can be viewed at https://vimeo.com/130985792 (accessed 24.04.2025).

[2] I believe this is what Katherine Turpin achieves in her path-making text on colonial legacies and white racism in the ecclesial and theological contexts (2025). She effectively 'stages the wreckage' that white domination has caused and names this at the heart of the practical theological enterprise.

embody numerous scenes of corporate affliction in which the earth, its creatures and peoples are mutually implicated. And the New Testament writings contain their own dramatic stagings in apocalyptic visions, the passion narratives and early Eucharistic traditions. Marcel Barnard offers a compelling example of how these traditions can be performed today. He combined his practical theological expertise with bold aesthetic wisdom in creating a 'biblical liturgical narrative' (Barnard, 2022, p. 21) that was central to a multi-dimensional artistic/ritual staging held in De Oude Kerk, Amsterdam. Installations (huge black towers) were raised within the historic building itself as symbolic representations of deathly power. Barnard constructed a liturgical framing for the installation that drew upon the apocalyptic visions in Matthew 24 in which the 'earth trembles' along with the people. These are the last tragic/hopeful lines of the litany Barnard created:

Minister: Death everywhere
dead everywhere,
a labyrinth of tombs
a jungle of towering black tombs
as high as the number of deaths underneath
All: The end is still to come. (2022, pp. 22–3)

At the culmination of this staging, a Eucharist was consecrated on an altar where death was manifested in the presence of wilting and dying plant materials alongside the sacramental elements lifted up in God's transforming presence. The example Barnard provides here demonstrates on a broad canvas what might happen in local contexts, on a much smaller scale, as we come to recognize that staging the wreckage is a necessary and important part of (liturgical/ritual) witnessing to faith today. But, as the shape of Barnard's liturgy indicates, death may need to be given space but it does not need to have the last word.

To return again to Grigor's two films of St Peter's seminary. To my mind, the untroubled luminosity of the first film was deeply disturbing. The elegant machine-like austerity of the seminary was too pure, too ordered; too representative of the structures of power that sustained a vision of church that is no longer tenable today. In the space of the ruins, as they exist now, some stirrings of life can be seen. This is apparent not only in the green growing things that are reclaiming the ground but also in the human activities of critique and creativity that the dense graffiti represents. Looking on these ruins (in the brightly coloured photos on my phone – Grigor's black and white is too morbid) I can sometimes be glad that the walls have fallen. Glad that the windows have shattered, that ivy pokes through the hanging frames, and that rank weeds have entirely engulfed the kitchens where the nuns worked. 'Respect existence or expect resistance' reads one piece of graffiti, and a strong image of a young woman has been painted high up in the ruined chapel where she celebrates a Mass of rewilding where once no woman could have presided.

Arranging things differently

The potentiality present within dereliction is a theme that is powerfully manifested in the fictional constructions of W. G. Sebald (a celebrated novelist and critic, Sebald is a major interlocuter in Murray's text). Born in Germany in 1944, Sebald was fixated upon the trajectories of modernity that lead to World War Two, the Holocaust, and associated ongoing atrocities and traumas. His singular preoccupation with these disasters presents as an inconsolable melancholy. However, in contrast to Freudian understanding of melancholia, this is not a 'pathological' response but an artistic commitment. In particular, Sebald maintains, art enables knowledge to be born out of a resolute determination not to turn away from the immensity of loss. Sebald writes:

> Melancholy, the re-thinking of the disaster we are in, shares nothing with the desire for death. It is a form of resistance. And this is emphatically so on the level of art, where its function is far from merely reactive or reactionary. When, with a fixed gaze, melancholy again reconsiders just how things could have gone this far, it becomes clear that the dynamic of inconsolability and of knowledge are identical in function. In the description of the disaster lies the possibility of overcoming it. (Sebald, in Murray, 2020, p. 7)

In her extended essay on art and crisis, Olivia Laing (2020) meditates upon similar themes. To deny the devastation of the contemporary (environmental, social, political) landscape would be appalling. However, she warns against a fatalistic absorption with disaster. When things are broken they are also broken-open. The strewn wreckage provides the material resources for creation. Drawing on the work of Eve Sedgwick, she argues that a work of reparative construction (a re-reading) can begin in such a context. Sedgwick maintains that 'Hope, often a fracturing, even a traumatic thing to experience, is among the energies by which the reparatively positioned reader tries to organize the fragments and part-objects she encounters' (Sedgwick, 2003, p. 46). This reparative reshaping of fragments serves as Laing's model for art and she reflects upon several examples of artwork that embody this process. The fantastical 'Frames' by Joseph Cornell, assembled from objects encountered in his perambulations around New York, bring together residues of enchantment rearranged according to his artistic intuition of their affinity and correlation.[3] Laing is similarly drawn to Robert Rauschenberg's 'combines'. These works are formed out of intercourse between waste and wonder. In his best-known work, 'Bed', Rauschenberg

> requisitioned his own bed clothes, assaulting pillows, sheet and a friend's quilt with gory, libidinal gouts of red, blue, yellow, brown, black paint and stripy toothpaste ... the ecstatic nocturnal residue is ... subversive: a closeted gay man airing filthy laundry in pre-Stonewall public. Making the combines, Rauschenberg felt he was cracking 'the secret language of junk'. (2020, p. 53)

But Laing's most striking and moving analogy for the 'rearranging' that art performs is found in her extended reflections upon the artist, writer and film-maker Derek Jarman's garden at Dungeness on the Kent coast: 'a place unlike anywhere else, a microclimate of extremes, plagued by drought, gales and leaf-scorching salt ... [A] stony desert, overlooked by a looming nuclear power station' (2020, p. 87). Jarman began creating a garden here in 1986 shortly after being diagnosed with HIV. In the stony rubble he arranged driftwood, large rocks and threaded flints together to make sculptural forms. Sea-hardy native plants were arranged alongside their cultivated cousins from domestic gardens – in surprising harmony. His brave work in this extreme space represented an 'energetic, fruitful response to the despair of ... a near-certain death sentence' (2020, p. 88). Pursuing the image of Jarman's creativity further, Laing reflects on how the stories of today's recent migrants (arriving on this same coastline by boat[4]) can be threaded with those of

---

3 He likes objects that have been invested with glamour, mystery, excitement and escape, which although discarded or broken still retain some aura of their former status.

4 These reflections were prompted by a viewing of Sarah Woods's film *Boat People*, which presents narratives of migration in this connected and relational perspective (see Laing, 2020).

countless historical voyagers who have laboured, traded, ventured and sought freedom by setting out on these same seas. Bringing their stories into new shapes and conjunctions, joining them together, is a reparative act. For Laing, it resonates with an image of 'Derek Jarman's hands, stringing ... flints in the bright butter-yellow gorse of his garden at Prospect Cottage in Dungeness' (2020, p. 106). It is a restorative rearranging that sends out a vital message. Fear can give way to hospitality and also to self-recognition. 'We don't have to live like this. There are other ways to conduct yourself, to apprehend the world' (2020, p. 106).

We don't have to live like this and there are other ways to apprehend the world. The themes that Laing is exploring through her engagement with the creativity of Cornell, Rauschenberg and Jarman are ones that have gained philosophical currency through the aesthetic theories of Jacques Rancière and his extensive enquiries into the social functions of art (2006). His key insight is that art may serve to 'redistribute' the accepted order of things so that new possibilities emerge beyond the confines of the dominant cultural imagination. While this is by no means an inevitable process, there is always the potential for radical realignments to occur through encounters with art that confound customary perceptions. 'Art is a work on the distribution of the sensible. Sometimes ... it rearranges the set of perception between what is visible, thinkable, and understandable, and what is not. This is the politics of art' (Rancière, 2015).

That art might play this role, even if only occasionally, is an extravagant claim. However, several months ago I was listening to a lecture by Christopher Smith, Executive Chair of the UK's Arts and Humanities Research Council, and someone who is close to the very heart of the academic system in the UK. It was *sombre* to hear this leading academic insider (someone sitting at the centre of the web) confess the devastating failure of academic research to engage with the huge problems that currently confront us. It was *surprising* to hear him describe this as an aesthetic failure. Systems are maintained, Smith argued, through their imaginative infrastructures (their aesthetic ordering of sense and perception). 'We need to change the ways in which we have imagined the world for the past five hundred years,' he stated, 'and give new meaning to the world around us' (Smith, 2023).

The need for creative interventions that disrupt the ways we perceive and represent reality because things are going horribly wrong is also the predominant theme in Daniel Matthews's book *Earthbound: The Aesthetics of Sovereignty in the Anthropocene* (2021), a work that

Smith drew upon extensively in his talk. In this he argues that the dominant symbolic system, an aesthetic regime through which humans represent themselves to themselves, is based upon notions of separation and bounded discreteness (between persons, peoples, humans and their 'others'). These divisions facilitated the construction of the modern world with its modes of production, knowledge and power. The imaginative structures of modernity still remain in place and retain their strong hold on us – even as it becomes ever clearer that they do not provide the resources we need to flourish within ecosystems based on relational interdependence. It is as if modernity were a play being performed which all involved have become deeply immersed and invested in. The performance is now being continually interrupted (coral whitening, sea rising, species loss, extreme weather) and yet actors, audience and producers keep insisting that the play must go on. Despite their recalcitrance, change is happening. The 'backdrop is moving, scenery and props have come to life,' says Matthews (2021, pp. 33–4). The agency of the manifold beings of earth and the interrelated connections that bind the human to the non-human or the environment are now jolting the performance to such an extent that the old script is finally losing its compelling power.

When Smith and Matthews speak of an aesthetic ordering of perception, their vision extends beyond the realm of what has traditionally been viewed as art. Their 'aesthetics' is operative in the common representations of human being-in-the-world that undergird our legal structures, political systems, extend to our religious practices, and form our understandings of selfhood. Art may serve to sustain these perceptions and, by so doing, contributes to the maintenance of things as they are. However, to return to Rancière, art does not simply trade in mimesis; the imitation/representation of reality. Art is also a sphere in which experiments with what is not presently existing or deemed possible can take place. In this mode it is able to extend, distort, disturb and radically refigure what is commonly understood as 'real'. That is the politics of art.

How far we consider it acceptable, or faithful, to contemplate the rearrangement of our own faith traditions and practices is a topic of perennial debate in practical theology. Since the empirical turn, this debate has been focused upon questions of normativity in relation to research on faith practices. Where does authority lie in encounters between theology and the social sciences? Should the lived experiences, articulated as outcomes of this research, be allowed to provoke changes beyond a restructuring of conventional pastoral approaches? Should they be able to reorder the very structures of belief itself (see p. 47)? Important as these questions may be, they often take place at a comfortable level of abstraction and with a sense that the measured instability we are in the process of considering is something in our power to consent to or control. What contemplating the politics of art in the context of crisis requires is a more radical sense that the 'backdrop' of life itself is moving. It is not simply that old frames of meaning need our careful, expert adjustment. Rather, things we thought were solid and that were loved and trusted are being broken – and we are being broken with them.

Wigg-Stevenson's recent practical theological work engages with Rancière's art-politics in this more challenging frame. She takes as her starting point the power of art 'to rupture and rearrange the very structures by which we perceive reality … in order to transform it' (2021, p. 12). Her work is an interrogation of actual artistic performances that have this shattering impact. She employs these, alongside personal and research narratives, to construct a radical aesthetics. This places contemporary theological work at the site of the deepest, most troubling divine staging:

> I want … to write theology in a way that extends the transgressive power of the cross to rupture, rearrange and thereby transform creation. I'm trying to stand in the shadow of a cross that transforms me. The cross transgresses reality-as-it-is in order to transform it into something new. It is the event that God uses to rupture all of creation so that the brokenness of what was can be rearranged into what could be. (2021, p. 13)

What is important to me here is that the emphasis is placed upon a divine breaking and brokenness that is simply inescapable. We are caught up in it and there is darkness at noon and the graves are open. The challenge for practical theologians is to move into the shadow cast by the cross rather than seek refuge from it – to allow not only our work, but ourselves, to experience this passion. For the divine 'artistic' rearrangement that is being envisioned here is not a replacement of one imperfect system by a readjusted and improved one. Rather, it is a new creation out of brokenness itself.

From ambiguity to mystery

The novelist, art writer and Kierkegaard scholar Siri Hustvedt also maintains that art does not make transformative reconfigurations by exchanging one form of functional, comprehensible reality for another, better, one. She instead argues that the very structures of the sensible itself must be shaken around until defined edges are worn way and everything becomes dangerously mixed or mixed up (2003, p. 91). For Hustvedt views art as emerging from 'boundlessness, brokenness, merging definitions, disjunctions of space and time, and intense emotions' (2012, p. 273). It makes its contribution by breaking down boundaries, allowing multiple forms to interpenetrate, multiple subjectivities to speak in one text,[5] and persistently reveal the utter ambiguity of things (for a fuller discussion of art and ambiguity in Hustvedt's oeuvre, see Walton, 2019b).

As a feminist intellectual, Hustvedt is particularly drawn to the work of women artists in which gendered conventions are jumbled up; anger *and* passivity are presented, both violence and tenderness displayed and in which humour and resistance are combined. This can be seen in Annette Messenger's constructions: 'soft characters and stuffed corpses ... ambiguous beings ... along with their multiple associations and underground narratives that summon carnivals, masquerades, robbers, S&M games, and torture victims' (2012, p. 296). It is similarly revealed in Kiki Smith's work, which invites viewers into a borderland where the 'articulated lines between inside and outside, whole and part, waking and sleeping, human and animal, "I" and "not I" are often in abeyance' (2012, p. 270). Both these artists build upon the monumental achievements of Louise Bourgeois. Bourgeois's work represents for Hustvedt a supreme example of outrageous, unregulated artistic intercourse and miscegenation. The artist draws upon her own body, memories, desires and personal history to present violent, funny and deeply unsettling constructions, such as her immense Maman spiders. Her disturbing 'She Fox' is a mutilated piece; vibrant and powerful but decapitated, and with a huge gash at its throat and possessing not only breasts but also a phallus.

---

5 Hustvedt here is referencing the multiple identities and voices in the work of Søren Kierkegaard. She writes, 'He circled the silence and the wound with torrents of words, with multitongued reflection, and I for one am grateful for those worlds within worlds within worlds ... The meanings proliferate. If we are to read him and his masks well, we must dance with him' (Hustvedt, 2016, p. 36).

> The body of Louise Bourgeois is multiple and potent. It borrows from and transforms the vocabularies of modern art. It is feminine and masculine, terrified and bold, soft and hard. It speaks in the language of space and form and plays with both recognition and strangeness. (2012, p. 252)

In approaching art in this way Hustvedt displays her fascination with the amorphous depths of human subjectivity as explored through psychoanalysis and contemporary neuroscience. But her explorations of the chaotic turmoil *and creativity* of the human psyche lead her beyond these modern disciplines to the ancient categories of mystical theology. She contemplates how art can both bring things into presence and enable encounters with the profound silence and absences at the heart of existence. Those instances in which art performs its 'mixing' between the tangible and the unrepresentable take her breath away. In the face of this 'mystery' Hustvedt reaches for religious language. 'I am alone staring into something alien and incomprehensible ... I am alone with God' (2005, p. 48). This encounter with an absence/presence that exceeds comprehension can be figured as a personal epiphany. However, Hustvedt maintains, we should also regard the revelations of art (or poesis) as a cultural and *communal necessity*. We need to find ways to draw upon the resources of poetics to make visible that which has been obliterated and to enable us to touch that which is unreachable through conventional forms:

> Another mode of expression is required, one that can hold painful contradictions and agonizing ambiguities within it. It becomes necessary to turn to the poetic image, one that splinters into semantic plurality, one that allows us to see, in Celan's words, *'ein Grab in den Lüften'*, 'a grave in the air'. (2016, loc. 845)

Hustvedt's vision of art spans brightly coloured mixings and mixing-ups, the dark greys of the deeply ambiguous and ambivalent and, far beyond both, to the luminous darkness of the ineffable where a grave can be marked 'in the air'. A similar artistic reach is predicated in Timothy Morton's short manifesto *All Art is Ecological* (2021), in which environmental concerns are placed at the centre of their reflections.[6]

---

6 Morton is one of the foremost contributors to debates on materiality through his work on Object Oriented Ontology (OOO). He has consistently addressed this topic through an aesthetic, environmental and queer perspective.

Morton presents art as 'a model for the kind of coexistence ecological ethics and politics wants to achieve between humans and nonhumans' (2021, p. 30). This is because it defies the partition of the things into distinct and separate spheres of being – such as real or imagined, animate or inanimate, agential or inert.[7] Art muddles things up and proliferates multiple connections between them. This, says Morton, represents the nature of encounters with entities that are simultaneously familiar, part of the very fabric of our lives, and yet resolutely foreign to us. For the 'experience of relating to art ... makes it difficult – sometimes impossible – to sustain the valley across which we see other entities as "other"' (2021, p. 94) while *still* allowing for their challenging strangeness to confront us: 'Ethics and politics might be about tolerating, appreciating or accepting strangeness, which boils down to ambiguity: how things can appear to be oscillating between familiar and strange, for example. Doesn't appreciating art have to do with allowing things to be ambiguous?' (2021, p. 94).

The combination of familiarity and strangeness art mediates can generate a sense of unease; a feeling that things are unheimlich or uncanny. But this, Morton maintains, represents an intuition *of how things truly are*. Our current aesthetic order may be still in thrall to a Newtonian imaginary, in which measurable forces act upon defined lumps of stuff, but in Einsteinian symbolics a queer[8] uncanniness prevails. 'Einstein's world', Morton states:

> [I]s a realm of perverse desire, invisible ripples of gravity waves that make up spacetime, the invisible ocean in which the stars float submerged ... [where] time expands and contracts like a polymer. (2021, p. 90)

> There are things within the cosmos that are not only hidden but unknowable. Uncertainty prevails at every level and 'things are mysterious, in a radical and irreducible way'. (2021, p. 11)

It is Morton's thesis that what pertains in this unheimlich and mysterious universe is mirrored within the context of our current planetary

---

7 It was this quality of art that provoked early debates within the new materialisms that drew on the path-making work of Alfred Gell, in *Art and Agency* (1998).

8 Morton is referencing queer identities and queer theory here. This is a significant concern in their writing and political stance.

catastrophe.[9] The myriad uncanny waves of incalculable connections become strikingly apparent when we consider how human actions have impacted upon diverse spheres *and also when we recognize that what goes around comes around.* Changes to entities, objects, neighbourly/ strangers are now insistently making themselves felt within the permeable boundaries of the human. Similarly, the sense of impending disaster has an uncanny quality to it. It combines denial and dread, familiarity and terror and propels us into a weird time zone – that of the now and not yet in which something has happened, is happening, has yet to happen, and yet in which the future remains curiously open. While there is no denying the seriousness of this situation, Morton insists that we should not respond to it in what he regards as a 'Newtonian' mode. In other words, by compiling desperate lists of 'facts', generating fail-safe solutions or seeking to divorce our affective and aesthetic responses to ecological damage from our rational calculations. Instead of accelerating our efforts to a pitch of 'busy, zealous, industrious, "just keep swimming, just keep swimming" intensity (2021: 103)', he advocates adopting a different way of proceeding entirely: that of the 'uncertain' subjunctive mode.

The subjunctive is the form in which we express wishes and desires; it attends to things that have not actually happened but may, might, could, should, would possibly happen. It is the mode of the imagined and it reaches into places that definite, propositional forms cannot access but that are necessary to enter into our current context. However, the sort of meaning-making that the subjunctive makes possible has a fuzzy quality to it. In the subjunctive maybe-sphere things are not either clearly true or false. They have an affective, emotional power that might be described as 'truthy'. 'There is not a sudden point or rigid boundary at which the truthy becomes actually true. Things are always a bit fumbly and stumbly. We are feeling our way around' (2021, p. 6).

So in a world of intricate relations, uncanny conjunctions and environmental change, things 'are connected but in a kinda sorta subjunctive way. There's room for stuff to happen' (2021, p. 21). Morton posits a strong correlation between art and the subjunctive mode, for art is a means of exploring the mights and maybes. It helps us feel our way around a darkened room and it also has the affective power of truthiness that guides us even when we are completely clueless as to where

---

9 Morton presents catastrophe as a 'space of downward turning' that contains more hopeful possibilities within it than disaster (2021, p. 29).

we are ultimately heading. But Morton wishes to claim even more than this and, like Hustvedt, wishes to ascribe a sacred form of agency to art. It acts upon us, it has the power to stun, move and change us. 'Art sprays out charismatic causality despite us' (2021, p. 88). The principal example he uses to describe this is the Rothko Chapel in Houston in which the colours, light and forms not only 'speak' (2021, p. 93) to those present but are incorporated into their very being; 'it is like finding something in me that isn't me' (2021, p. 95). This relation with art, Morton claims, stands for the profligate mixing that lies 'at the basis of being ecological' (2021, p. 96). It also, queerly, represents what love is and can be: an opening up to strangeness and being moved by what we may humbly receive but never control.

I have charted in the work of Hustvedt and Morton 'art lessons' that teach us first to engage with ambiguity and lead us through this to an encounter with mystery. This spiritual epiphany takes place in a context of uncertainty, mixing and strangeness rather than purity, clarity and control. I have also followed Morton in exploring how this learning journey through art might teach us to abide with the unresolvements that constitute life in these times and recognize that we are ourselves mixed-up, 'ecological' manifolds in our beings and becomings.

In terms of practical theology this offers encouragement not to shy away from big questions with uncertain or myriad responses (Pattison, 2007, p. 279),[10] but also to contemplate how spirituality might be reintegrated into our academic endeavours. Ironically, we practical theologians may be far behind the curve here. I cannot help but recall one of the most upsetting moments in my career, which took place at a meeting of the International Academy of Practical Theology in Toronto, 2013. The then President, Claire Wolfteich, gave a generative address on spirituality which blurred the boundaries, made ambiguous, the territories of sacred wisdom and academic research. Like many present, I was shocked by the hostility her approach provoked and the deep discomfort that this mixing aroused.

This response was especially regrettable as spirituality was already being recognized as occupying a very significant place in the landscape of qualitative research methodologies – a development unacknowledged by Wolfteich's critics. I have already referenced Denzin and Lincoln's nomination of the 'eighth moment' in qualitative research as being

---

10 Something I particularly admired in van der Ven's early work was the audacity with which he took on the 'big questions' of life.

characterized by an engagement with sacred epistemologies (see p. 26). This categorization reflected a wider turning towards the spiritual by qualitative researchers that is typified by the influential scholars Yvonna Lincoln and Egon Guba's 'repentance' for the exclusion of sacred knowledges from their previous research paradigms. They write:

> If we had to do it all over again we would make ... axiology (the branch of philosophy dealing with ethics, aesthetics, and religion) a part of the basic foundational philosophical dimensions of paradigm proposal. Doing so would ... contribute to the consideration of and dialogue about the role of spirituality in human inquiry. Arguable, axiology has been 'defined out of' scientific inquiry for no larger reason than it also concerns 'religion'. But defining 'religion' broadly to encompass spirituality would move constructivists closer to participative inquirers and would move critical theorists closer to both (owing to their concern with liberation from oppression and freeing of the human spirit, both profoundly spiritual concerns). (Lincoln and Guba, 2005, p. 200)

This reconsideration of the spiritual in qualitative research was undoubtedly provoked by the work of feminist, black and indigenous researchers who had refused the sacred secular divide for decades. For example, Cynthia Dillard and Charlotte Bell's 'manifesto' for endarkened feminist research places spirituality at the centre of their project:[11]

> [W]e believe that spirituality must be recognized as the center of the thought and discourse for African ascendant people such that we can see our work as both about engagements with Indigenous knowledges and about healing ... Dillard (2008) speaks of healing methodologies as situated, sacred, and spiritual work that happens in multiple spaces and places where African ascendants and other Indigenous peoples find ourselves. (Dillard and Bell, 2011, p. 338)

It is important here to note that thinking about the ways that our approaches to research might be made more sacred is not a departure from endarkened or Black feminist thought, which is deeply embedded

---

[11] It is important to note that spirituality also takes a central place in activist responses and scholarship in relation to the climate crisis. See, just for example, Kimmerer, 2013; Ghosh, 2016; Latour 2024.

with and draws attention to the nature and importance of the spiritual within a Black feminist framework. (Dillard and Bell, 2011, p. 344)

Thankfully, significant steps towards a re-evaluation of the place of spiritual wisdom in our discipline are well underway. There is now much greater acknowledgement that significant knowledge is implicit in spiritual practice and that neglect of this means *'a primary kind of knowing and experience is lost in our epistemologies'* (Cahalan, 2016, p. 318).[12]

Many practical theologians now seek to undertake their academic work in integrally spiritual, 'creative and redemptive ways' (Campbell-Reed and Scharen, 2013, p. 232). The work of theologians of colour/decolonial theologians has been especially important here – as the divisions separating academic epistemologies and spiritual traditions are often breached within their work (see, for example, Riley, 2022; Jennings, 2020; Carvalhaes, 2021; and Liu Wong, 2023). This results in both social/political challenges and disturbing conceptual disruptions. Carvalhaes, for example, argues that in the global environmental crisis we now face, Christians require and should recognize the spiritual resources present in traditional and indigenous wisdom even if these appear strange and require the development of new imaginative capacities:

> They tell us that we need to learn to dream in other ways. To dream the dreams of forests, rivers and animal ... Any discourse or practice related to God must be in flux with the earth. That means a decodification of the theological systems and an entering into a flow of living based on the flying of the birds, the pollination of the bees, the swimming of the dolphins, the pathways under the soil of the worms, the roots of the trees, the lives of the plants. (2021, p. 20)

Encountering the wild

The desperate need for spiritual connections that enable an awakening to 'strangeness' is the major theme in Amitav Ghosh's powerful work, *The Great Derangement: Climate Change and the Unthinkable*

---

12 The practical theologian in the academy, she insists, must become 'grounded in a wisdom epistemology' in which 'the spiritual practice of teachers ... [will] foster the spiritual practice of students' (Cahalan, 2016, p. 321).

(2016). In this he maintains that the cultural and political failure to address the climate emergency is connected to problems inherent in the dominant representative system. It is as if Western cultural conventions were functioning as 'modes of concealment that prevented people from recognising the realities of their plight' (2016, p. 11). The climate emergency appears too extreme, too improbable, too at odds with dominant Western ideals of human singularity, progress and mastery to be accommodated within acceptable cultural repertoires. The reconfigurations it requires appear either excessive or nonsensical. In the light of this 'concealment' he addresses a question to fellow writers and creatives that is also of great significance for practical theologians: is 'the grid of literary forms and conventions' (2016, pp. 6–7) we routinely employ functioning to exclude what lies beyond its frame of intelligibility? In other words, is the power of the credible, the expected and the normal filtering out what is 'not easily accommodated in the deliberately prosaic world' (2016, p. 26)? Are our cautious and careful academic protocols inhibiting our vision?

What the grid of conventions cannot allow to pass through, Ghosh describes as 'the wild'. And an inability to comprehend the wild that, he maintains, has contributed considerably to the great madness we are caught up in:

> Are the currents of global warming too wild to be navigated in the accustomed barques of narration? But … we have entered a time when the wild has become the norm: if certain literary forms are unable to negotiate these torrents, then they will have failed – and their failures will have to be counted as an aspect of the broader imaginative and cultural failure that lies at the heart of the climate crisis. (2016, p. 8)

The wild, as represented by Ghosh, is what we cannot discipline yet at the same time cannot separate ourselves from – no matter how much we strive for distance, discreetness and control. The elemental forces of our planetary system are powerful manifestations of this sphere. However, the wild points beyond tides, air currents and temperature graphs to an unmanageable interrelationality that connects all things in an outrageously fecund spiritual nexus beyond comprehension within 'normal' categories. An encounter with the wild is thus *sublime* in its terrifying and world-shattering senses. Yet Ghosh also believes that this encounter can be revelatory; that within this generative chaos an astonishing, untamed love flames out. For Ghosh, the wild is not only threat but solace. It is the sphere of the sacred. The wild is the place we meet with God.

To locate this vision of the wild more specifically within the concerns of this chapter, Ghosh believes that unarming ourselves and stepping out to meet the wild is the desperate remedy our situation calls for. One of the ways in which we set aside our deranged, defensive strategies is through artistic modes that engage with the fantastic, the mythical, the 'unthinkable'; those mechanisms that loosen our tight grip on a controllable 'reality'. These artistic modes, like fungal threads, intertwine inextricably with the sacred traditions that are the ancient means humanity has employed to explore what lies beyond our control. Ghosh has a profound respect for the power of these spiritual resources and they play an important role in much of his recent writing (e.g. 2021).

In her address to the 2023 meeting of the International Academy of Practical Theology, Elaine Graham drew upon Ghosh's work to construct a generative relation between speculative fiction (particularly cli-fi – that is, climate fiction, fiction rooted in the climate emergency) and scriptural traditions. In this presentation, focused upon the climate emergency, she demonstrated the applicability of his approach to theological reflection (Graham, 2023, pp. 180–1). However, there are other insights Ghosh offers that may become increasingly important as practical theology reorientates itself towards the demands of these times. Of particular importance is his thinking on re-cognition.

One of the problems Ghosh identifies in encountering the wild is that a rupture needs to occur to make this happen. Something needs to break through our sense of secure coherence to make this possible. One of the most important theorists of everyday life, Henri Lefebvre addresses this same issue. Lefebvre argues that although everyday life appears to be the sphere of the banal and the ordinary it is actually the sphere in which the heightened intensities of ecstasy and grief are experienced – in other words, everyday life is *itself* the sphere of sublime disruptions. These streak across it like lightning in the intoxicated joy of the carnival, a moment 'that marvellously overturns structures' (2002, p. 66). They also strike in the utter devastation of tragedy which, Lefebvre maintains, transports us

> ... into a different kingdom which is the kingdom of darkness Daily life has served as a refuge from the tragic ... people seek and find security there. [But to] traverse daily life under the flash of the tragic is

already to transform … So that the irruption of the tragic in everyday life turns it upside down. (2005, pp. 171–2)

Like Lefebvre, Ghosh also insists that events which occur in everyday living have the potential to become passageways into such a kingdom. He writes of his own experience of being caught up in an unexpected weather event and, within the chaos of this, experiencing a moment of sublime encounter; a calm instant in the storm, that was 'strangely like a species of visual contact, of beholding and being beheld' (2016, p. 14). This was a meeting, a revelation, an epiphany. Ghosh calls it 'looking into the tiger's eyes' (2016, p. 29), and once this once mutual beholding had happened it enabled him to return to this point again as a means of comprehending other extremities – particularly that of climate change. Recognition was now possible:

> The most important element of the word recognition thus lies in its first syllable, which harks back to something prior, an already existing awareness that makes possible the passage from ignorance to knowledge: a moment of recognition occurs when a prior awareness flashes before us, effecting an instant change in our understanding of that which is beheld. (2016, p. 4)

This change cannot appear spontaneously, Ghosh argues; it cannot disclose itself except in the flash that represents the presence of its lost other (2016, pp. 4–5). However, artistic work (in Ghosh's case fictional writing) may also be a mode through which people can 'look into the tiger's eyes'. Art can provide a means of rupture that enables us to re-cognize and connect and thus move beyond a presenting experience to embrace wider challenges.

This process, I believe, could also become a focus of practical theological work. Practical theologians are uniquely positioned to enable processes of re-cognition and connection to occur as we root our work in everyday life experiences, but discover, within these, moments or openings through which people might pass through into a different kingdom. As we go about our routine tasks of inquiring into congregational life, exploring a pastoral issue or evaluating educational or missional initiatives, we should always be alert to the intensities within them; the jagged points that can rupture previous understandings and enable us to see ourselves reflected in the tiger's eyes. Instead of simply presenting phenomena to view and leaving others to make meaning from them or, worse still, seeking closure through wrapping them around in trite theological formulae,[13] we should make their discomforting intensity the occasion for theological reflection that will enable further encounters with other extremities.

Such expansive processes can be observed within key works that mark the development of our discipline. I think of Bonnie Miller-McLemore's hugely generative *Also a Mother* (1994) and Todd Whitmore's *Imitating Christ in Magwi* (2019). In both of these works, personal, 'everyday' experience becomes the passageway into a new theological territory and the experience recounted provides the necessary mode of re-cognition that enables this travel to take place. Karen O'Donnell's book *The Dark Womb* (2022) is a recent example of the generativity of this approach. In this she employs autoethnography alongside wider critical analysis to inquire into the experience of pregnancy loss. Her deeply poignant account of the multiple griefs associated with her experiences is a means of both rupturing conventional theological discourse and opening a passage into a spiritual kingdom that is particularly attuned to the griefs of the climate catastrophe.

Making, materials and practice

As I have been exploring the various understandings of art's work above, I have been very aware of a dissident voice sounding increasingly insistent in my ear. Well, two voices and both ears, actually. My father and my daughter, by some quirk of fate or genetics, both found themselves (in different contexts and at different points in life) transformed by encounters with clay. They each became ceramicists; earth workers. Observing their loving absorption in making with clay I have developed a profound respect for the whole muddy, messy process of engaging with this elemental substance; cold when wet, brittle when dry, kiln-shattered (very often) or fire-transformed.

---

13 Tom Beaudoin names this tendency in practical theology 'normative bumpering' and writes:

> Such indicative/imperative rhetoric is common and indicates the inflation of a normative bumper that is a defensive theological strategy, along the lines of 'If Christians are incarnational, then in this circumstance they should live like this,' or 'If God is merciful, then practice should go this way.' The investment in the 'if' is substantial; in a way, it is everything. Practical theology does not commonly see it as its task to substantiate the grounding claims brought in for this normative bumpering. (Beaudoin, 2016, p. 28)

Unfortunately, this visceral appreciation of art-making is missing from what I have written so far. Instead I have presented what is quite a straight and traditional view of art as a sort of product. A 'something' generated by people acknowledged as artists and recognized as such by the legitimating authorities who trade in, display, critique or culturally consume such works. There are (many) other ways of comprehending art than this! And of particular importance to the concerns of this book are those predicated upon the processes of connecting with materials (be these minerals or metaphors), the agency of materials as they give of themselves in creative processes, and the deep embodied knowledge that is required to work with them in this way. These are all issues that would have been foregrounded if my father or daughter had been authoring this work. Or so the voices tell me!

My father would certainly have emphasized the importance of getting things right in the making process. The right spout on the jug, the right handle on the cup. Not just so the pot looks pleasing but also so that it pours well and can be held safely. Form and function in harmony. But there is an internal as well as an external aspect to getting things right. As you place the clay upon the wheel it must be centred correctly and you must be centred also. The balance must be exact so that each particular shaping can take place. My dad's mentor and guide was the craft potter Bernard Leach.[14] Leach insisted that the potter accomplishes two purposes through the same focused act. They are 'making hollow wares ... for the common usage of the home' (1975, p. 47) and participating in a 'never-ending search for perfection of form' (1975, p. 47). Leach held a spiritual view of the creative process, believing that in 'the counterpoint of convex and concave, hard and soft, growth and rest' (1975, p. 48) is to be discerned nothing less than 'the breathing of the universal in the particular' (1975, p. 48). This was a notion my father assented to completely.

My daughter loved and respected her grandfather, but I believe she would see things rather differently to him and likely wish to distance herself from his Leachian worldview. Whereas my father made pots, lovely vessels for use and display, her ceramic art is abstract and

---

14 Leach is widely credited with inspiring the resurgence in craft pottery in the UK during the mid-years of the twentieth century. His spiritual interests and commitments are less well recognized but were a guiding force in his life and work (see Leach, 1973, 1978). Leach fell 'out of fashion' for many years and some critics have interpreted his influence and ideas as regressive (see Britton, 2013). However, there can be no doubt about the significance of his enduring legacy.

challenging – eschewing many of the functional principles that were axiomatic to him, yet her work is resonant with our current cultural context. Emerging from her making are pieces; something like bones, or perhaps fossils, or maybe the scattered fragments of a broken thing; they possess an elegiac quality. Moreover, her creative process does not employ the regular, rhythmic turning of clay and wheel. An unregulated, immediate, tactile responsiveness to materials is foregrounded. My father's pottery is smooth but hers shows the imprints of fingers, hands, arms. It is moulded around her form and yet the clay she works with also retains its own characteristics. This is important to her for she is deeply influenced by new materialist, animist and relational thinking – as are many contemporary creatives. She understands clay as active in the making process and cares about where the clay comes from and its earth connections. The whole material process, from locating clay to engaging with it and from making to showing, is of one continuous piece. Her art is not focused upon the outcome alone.

In many ways, the approaches of both my father and daughter, which place stress upon tacit knowledge in the making process, could be seen as having a closer affinity with the work of practical theologians than some of the examples I reflected upon earlier in this chapter. I think Leach's notion of creating particular things for household use while recognizing that these also connect to 'the universal' would be a vision many of us could own. It sits very well with our concerns to honour everyday faith lives and explore the ways in which these connect to ultimate horizons. In the approaches to making espoused by both my father and daughter great emphasis is placed upon tacit and embodied knowledge; the honed responses embedded in muscle-memory. Similar re-evaluations of practical wisdom have been productive in practical theology in recent years.

In her path-making essay on practical wisdom and the arts of ministry, Miller-McLemore calls for a reassessment of what matters most in practical theology. Arguing that the popular denigration of clerical knowledge (portrayed as implicated in an outmoded 'clerical paradigm' the discipline has advanced beyond) has resulted in neglect of the significant wisdom that is embodied in pastoral practice. The parallel abstraction and complexification of academic theology has similarly divorced its concerns from the challenges of faithful living. 'Theologians in both systematic and practical theology underestimated the intelligence involved in practice and overlooked the limitations of merely academic knowledge' (2007, p. 26). She argues that the recognition that tacit and embodied knowledge is essential to many forms of artistic practice, and this offers an important example to practical theology. It encourages us to revalue the skills that contribute to the arts of ministry and to recognize that these arts themselves replenish and refresh practical theology in myriad creative ways. In relation to the concerns of this chapter, this is self-evidently the case. It would be impossible to imagine practical theology responding to current crises in the ways I have suggested without the wisdom inherent in scriptural literacy, ritual competence, storytelling, spiritual practice, and a habitus of theological reflection.

Miller-McLemore's concern to reappraise practical knowledge is explored in greater depth in the co-authored collection, *Christian Practical Wisdom* (Bass et al., 2016b). In this the authors stress that we 'urgently need the embodied wisdom without which Christianity is just an idea and not a living reality' (Bass et al., 2016a, p. 4). It is this, they claim, that provides the resources needed for *the* 'kind of thinking and action so desperately needed in our deeply troubled global society' (Bass et al., 2016a, p. 4). The authors demonstrate through worked examples various ways in which the wisdom of practice might inform 'imagination, discipline, skill, and body-knowledge fostered wise judgments' (Bass et al., 2016b, p. 329). I was particularly gratified that engagements with various forms of creative practice provided inspiration for their theological reflections on these themes. Particularly significant was the 'interweaving of techne, phronesis, and theoria' (Bass et al., 2016b, p. 329) that the authors witnessed at a pottery studio:

> ... where we drank tea as guests of an internationally admired potter who ... works within traditions learned during his artistic formation in Japan, using clay from local ground, glazes from the ash of local plants, and mixers from recycled machine parts. Under his guidance, apprentices learn how to shape and fire objects that will please the eye, meet human needs, sustain traditions of craft, and (not incidentally) enable them to earn a living. As we talked, they worked at wheels nearby, using tools they had made themselves and asking one another for help as needed. (Bass et al., 2016b, pp. 329–30)

This is a vision of theological making that I can relate to wholeheartedly and which has profound relevance to me. I believe one of the most important art lessons we need to learn right now is not to think differently about things but to 'do' differently about things. Not to focus on what is made only, but what is revealed 'in the making'. This gives us a vision of practical theological research as an ethical sphere of intricate and intimate responsiveness to the world which is as 'alive to us as we are to it' – to echo Ingold again (2018, p. 7). In this, we are immersed in the making of useful things – but also things that provoke and challenge; that bear the imprints of our bodies and surprise us with their resonances.

And more than this. Throughout this work I have been reaching towards a renewal of relationships in practical theology. Often I have considered and imaged this in small domestic terms as a matter of more collegial respect for the difference in 'research preferences'. However, there are other unfortunate divisions in our discipline: particularly between those whose skill and expertise lie in the arts of ministry (liturgy, homiletics, education, missiology, apologetics, social witness, etc.), and those who are concerned with 'empirical' research and the hermeneutics of religious practice. But both of these modes can be regarded as forms of theological making. The first is not simply about skills and professional knowledge but instead about responsiveness to context and reinterpretation of traditions in the light of current challenges. The second, as I have emphasized, is not only about the presentation of neatly presented and preserved slivers of religious life for critical examination. It also reaches through its own poetics to the construction of theological testimony. As it should; as is entirely appropriate and, as I hope, will be increasingly owned by us in the future. Furthermore, these two modes are not distinct. They have always been intertwined and it is precisely in their intertwining that practical theology makes its distinct contribution to the wider theological project.

PART THREE

Makings

In this final part of my work I present three theological makings. These represent, in various forms, my understanding of the vocation of practical theology and the everyday work of practical theologians.

The first chapter is a lightly edited version of my presidential address to the meeting of the International Academy of Practical Theology in Oslo, 2017.[1] It is a 'big deal' indeed to have the opportunity to offer testimony to such a gathering of your peers concerning your understanding of the state of the discipline. It was in contemplating this task that I began to formulate some of the understandings that have now come to fruition in this book. This presentation was also an occasion in which I experimented with poetic forms in the communication of academic concerns, and so it stands as a worked example of this process. In my mind it is a 'performance piece', and whenever I return to it I am vividly reminded of the lecture hall in which it was delivered and the friends and colleagues whose faces I sought out as I spoke.

The second chapter is a personal account of a recent creative encounter that has been surprisingly transformative to me. It narrates my exploration of insights generated through discovering the letters and life history of the twelfth-century intellectual Heloise. Through reflecting upon these, I examine my own vocation as an 'entangled' theologian who is both deeply implicated in the structures of her faith community and also somehow resistant to the comforts of religion. Once again, I am experimenting with rhetorical forms in this writing.

My final 'making' is a short extract from the journal I kept during the COP26 conference on climate change which was held in my home town of Glasgow in 2021. I have been publishing journal extracts throughout my academic career and particularly value journalling as a resource for theological work because it is so capacious. You can fit so many

---

1 This was published in the *International Journal of Practical Theology* as 'A Theopoetics of Practice: Re-forming in Practical Theology' (Walton, 2019a). I have slightly edited that published version for this book but the work remains substantially similar to the text of the speech I delivered at the Oslo conference.

things in. It is personal and political. The body finds entry but so too does the spirit. The emotions can claim a place alongside abstract modes of thinking and they can both rub happily alongside their contraries – all the unthinkings and unsayings. In journalling there is no separation between spheres; they are all jumbled around together. There is a disorderly, syncretistic roominess to the genre that I have come to believe is particularly helpful as a means of comprehending our context and responding to the challenges of our times.

7

Making One: A Theopoetics of Practice

Prologue

The creative moment begins in lack. What is available to work with has all been used before and is no longer in a good state. It would be nice to tidy up the place, sweep the ground, turn over a new leaf, and start again from fresh. But there is no fresh. Only rubble, reworkings and repetition. Dust suspended in darkness. And then what comes is a ray. Not the sun's ray but the damaged and derelict re-forming into a piercing power. That is it. The creative moment.

I think there should be two Holy Weeks. The first, before Easter, could carry on much as before. So we would move through the days of feasting and betrayal, walk the road of sorrows and, in particular, make our journey at a proper pace from Good Friday through Holy Saturday to Easter Day. But we would not stop there. There is so much to experience in the strange season of the empty tomb. Surely it should also be marked by a reverent week of slow pilgrimage in order to focus our attention on what so easily escapes us in the daffodil yellow, egg hatching, grain-rising glory of Easter celebrations. We then could go deeper into that time of absence and loss, wild hope and tender comfort. The season of telling, and telling no one because you are afraid. The time of *noli me tangere*, and plunging your fist into my side; holding my hand, and tracing the wound in my palm with your finger. We need to recognize the loved one – just right at the moment when he is hidden from our sight. We should take breakfast on the beach because we laboured and laboured all night but caught nothing – yet never have our nets been so full.

We need – the Church needs, the world needs – a second holy week. Right now we are living in the strange season of the empty tomb. We inhabit cultures poised between devastation and renewal, populism and participatory inclusiveness, and secularization and enchantment.

We practise a religion sited on the border between hope and loss. This strange season calls for a theopoetics of practice and a re-forming of practical theology, situated in the second holy week.

There is a ray. It does not come from the sun. It comes from the damaged and the derelict re-formed into piercing power.

Consider this image. *Madonna and Singing Angels* was painted by Sandro Botticelli in Florence around 1477. Its clear, luminous beauty characterizes the artist's work and shows the Virgin, holding her child. She wears an expression of sombre contemplation that conveys both blessedness and awareness of impending loss. Around her a choir of angels, in the form of lovely young men holding white lilies, contributes to a scene that combines serene perfection with palpable pity.

Botticelli's work has an arresting presence. It evokes the creative collision of classical and Christian art that shaped this extraordinary Florentine awakening. But there is sadness in its beautiful lines, causing me to remember that, despite its brilliance, Florence would shortly experience the dark days of religious revival led by the millenarian preacher Savaronola. Tradition has it that Botticelli (pupil of Fra Lippi, devotee of Dante, suspected sodomite and painter of too-beautiful images) threw many of his own paintings on the bonfire of the vanities that was the culmination of that particular reign of terror.

The picture has a piercing power. Or so it seemed to a young man who encountered it at the Kaiser Friedrich Museum in Berlin in 1918 while on leave from the terrible conflagration of his own generation in the trenches of World War One. Paul Tillich, weary and shaken in faith, was transfigured by the image:

> Gazing up at it, I felt a state approaching ecstasy. In the beauty of the painting there was Beauty itself. It shone through the colors of the paint as the light of day shines through the stained-glass windows of a medieval church. As I stood there, bathed in the beauty its painter had envisioned so long ago, something of the divine source of all things came through to me. I turned away shaken. That moment has affected my whole life, given me the keys for the interpretation of human existence, brought vital joy and spiritual truth. I compare it with what is usually called revelation in the language of religion. (1989, p. 235)

This first 'shaking of the foundations' that brought a never-to-be forgotten vital joy to Tillich took place in the encounter with this great work.

Later, he explained the religious content of art had not produced this effect. Not the Madonna, the child or the handsome, adolescent angels. No, it was something harder to define. Something closer to what the image evokes than to what it represents: a certain style or substance or manner of being. In fact, for Tillich, as he sought in later years to travel deeper into revelation through art, a very different type of image came to represent what he perceived, rather quaintly, as a Reformation painting *par excellence*. The work that he believed best embodied the qualities of the protesting and re-forming imagination in art was *Guernica*, which Tillich called the most Protestant picture of the modern era (see Price, 1986, p. 496). Pablo Picasso's massive, ugly, disturbing yet sublime work represented for Tillich the great travail of the twentieth century and asked the questions that he believed demanded an answer from any morally speakable theology. In its style and substance he identified the signs of the times.

Guernica was painted in ordinary house paint, matt and flat and black and white. The medium is thought to convey the mundane qualities of news-sheet through which Picasso had first learned of the Spanish civil war outrage. Picasso employs the techniques of late Cubism, offering fragmented, multi-perspectives on its theme. Its visual assemblage recalls the mode of bricolage, pioneered by Picasso himself, that transports everyday objects into art through collage in a manner that simultaneously challenges our views of the objects and our understanding of art itself. In this case, the 'found objects' are the debris of an atrocity and they are painted rather than attached to the picture. The whole is an assemblage of broken bodies, brutalized animals and domestic fragments. The picture is not illuminated by the divine radiance that inspired Botticelli, but rather by the modern hell of the blank electric light that shines in factory, interrogation room and mortuary. Traces of Christian symbols in disordered array are also part of the image. Stigmata on the hands of the dead soldier: place your fingers here. A dove descending, and a little lamp that brings a different kind of light to that of the naked bulb.

In nominating the broken agony of *Guernica* as a revelatory protest, Tillich made a bold move. The theologian of art and imagination David Brown has persuasively argued that if we were to seek our own generation's re-forming spiritual vision in a similar way we should contemplate, for example, the abortion drawings of Tracy Emin or Francis Bacon's triptych imaging the suicide of his lover George Dyer in a hotel toilet (Brown, 2017). Tillich would be adamant that we won't encounter revelation by seeking it first in contemporary religious art, which he regarded as so much kitsch. Of Salvador Dali's *Last Supper* he declared, 'It is sentimental naturalism of the worst kind. Simply junk!' *Time Magazine* gleefully reported Dali's response to this criticism: 'Drunk ... I have been drinking mineral water exclusively for more than ten years' (quoted in Manning, 2009, p. 159).

Approaching theopoetics

It is very early morning on the first day of the week. The faint light gives shapes but not yet colours. What use have we for colours now? We could wait outside until the light is stronger. Instead we bow our heads as we enter the darkened place where the beloved was lain.

Tillich's encounter with art witnesses to the piercing power of theopoetics. It testifies that making, *poesis*, creative work is not merely illustrative – it is epiphanic. Art embodies fundamental questions and, given form, re-formed, they approach us as revelation. This insight should be more explicitly acknowledged by those of us whose work in practical theology draws energy from the dialectical relation between faith and culture.

I remember sitting with the modern re-former of practical theology, Don Browning, in the restaurant. It was my first visit to the USA. I had just read *A Fundamental Practical Theology* (Browning, 1991) and it had caught my imagination. 'I might just become a practical theologian,' I thought. Don acknowledged his debt to Tillich. 'He used to sometimes eat here,' he told me, and he said he liked to sit in that restaurant where Tillich had been. Of course, I know that looking to Tillich is not unproblematic. His relations with women were structured by abuses of sexual and gendered power. And yet I covet for practical theology a similarly passionate, revelatory encounter with creative-making that will transfigure our theological imaginations.

To date, theopoetics, which is shaking foundations elsewhere, has not significantly impacted our discipline. This being the case, to assemble a theopoetics of practice I will look first to constructive theology – why not, since it lies so close to us we can whisper on the same pillow? I shall explore work being undertaken by Catherine Keller who I consider to be our greatest contemporary theologian and whose work is inspired by a theopoetic vision.

Keller's theopoetics looks first to ancient Christian traditions. In the doctrine of *theosis/theopoesis*, cherished by the Eastern Churches, creation and incarnation are part of the same cosmic-making process through which we humans, along with the whole cosmos, are being taken up into the very being of God. Also vitally important for Keller are apophatic mystical traditions that simultaneously find the divine unspeakable and use the most vivid and sparkling resources of language to describe God's piercing darkness.

From more contemporary resources, Keller acknowledges a debt to the heterogeneous forms of theopoetics that emerged with the 'death of God' movement in the 1960s, whose interlocuters debate whether God has been implicated in a fatal metaphysical event or whether the worn-out forms of religious doctrines have killed the sense of God for our culture (for an overview of Keller's theopoetics, see Keefe-Perry, 2014, pp. 78–86). However, in whatever mode, we are presented with the Passion as a radical kenosis: God in flesh entirely abandoning divine power, and this ultimate divine passion demanding a similar kenotic sacrifice from traditional God language, from theology. It too must endure a passion through which it becomes utterly transformed. God's passionate act of worlding requires us to become the poetic makers of new words which create new worlds. God is now formed and re-formed in the active human processes of poesis – of making.

Finally, Keller draws upon the process thinking of Alfred North Whitehead, who famously sought to unite science and religion in a vision of the cosmos coming into being through the lure of God at work in all motions, all life, all force. Her Whiteheadian vision opens a pluriverse of divinely active becoming, a making to be experienced in the pulsing chaosmos bursting with relational intensity, powerfully generative and mysterious. Her vision encompasses the biblical drama of creation out of the depths (2003), contemporary physics from Einstein and beyond with its profound images of relational entanglement (2014), and her beloved apophatic traditions (2007). At the same time, her work remains in urgent conversation with mainstream Christian theology, particularly challenging it to engage with the broken web of creation in our environmental disaster. As she writes:

Theology is not discarded ... Rather it becomes liberated from its world transcending, male divinizing, human-centred habits. (2011, p. 18)

> Each local quantum throb of experience is a node of energies that entangles us in the far reaches of the planet ... into a multiverse whose magnitudes and multiplicities escape all canons of confident knowledge. (2011, p. 22)

> I for one am no longer interested in theology that does not return to the dark brilliance of unknowing. (2011, p. 24)

I love to read Keller's work. I find it dazzling. I read it as an intellectual exercise and as a spiritual discipline. In its theopoesis, in its creative making, are combined an ancient and universal vision of the creator at work in creation with the stark image, raised up and stretching across the cosmos of Christ's Passion and God's self-emptying into the potentiality of human creative-making. These divine acts are brought together in a process-charged, politically engaged, ecologically orientated embrace of mystery illuminated by the dark brilliance of mystical longing. And it all fits together so wonderfully. It is not odd or strange. It hums with power and it speaks a new word. Jeffrey Hocking (2015) describes such new words as something normatively different from the old forms of theology (imaged as enclosed, self-referential, and no longer signifying) in its orientation both to God and the world. Jack Caputo, another 'theopoetician' (2006), albeit in a rather different mode to Keller, describes poetics in this sense as 'a constellation of idioms, strategies, stories, tropes, paradigms and metaphors' (2006, p. 104) that is now enfleshed with revolutionary militancy to bring change. And, reading their work, it is easy to believe theopoetics really does have such significance and momentum.

However, although I admit to being enthralled by the theopoetic murmurings that have crossed my pillow, I am looking for a form of theopoetics that is appropriate to practical theology and touches the ground we walk on. Like Sandro Botticelli's art, I find the forms of theopoetics currently circulating in constructive theology just too 'beautiful', too brilliant – even if this brilliance comes from darkness – for me to absorb. What is my problem?

I retain a distance for four reasons.

First, although I love Keller's exposition of the ancient doctrine of theopoesis, and am comfortable also with the panentheism it inevitably occasions, the notion of creation being raised into the divine risks casting a negative shadow on the material order which can then be seen as iconic rather than incarnational in itself. To be fair, this is far from

Keller's intention as her work elsewhere makes very clear. Yet, while I recognize that there is no absolute divide between theological models, I remain personally more challenged by the messier worldings of God that come through Franciscan theology and which affirm God's radical discharging into the haecceity of matter.

Second, 'death of God' theology tends towards a pure finality; a point that Keller herself has raised in her recent work (2017, p. 7). It offers a kind of closure. God has disclosed God's self to us as pure kenotic self-emptying, and that is it. Breathtaking, beautiful and complete. While this central event does not necessarily preclude the profound experience of absent presence that we narrate in stories of ointment, stones and bandages, it does not really wish to touch wounded hands, or walk a dusty road at dusk. It lacks the taste of salt by the seashore.

Third, process theology seems in danger of becoming too coherent a system. Too much a theory of everything (ecology, philosophy via the hugely influential work of Gilles Deleuze, physics, mysticism). It is a pretty cool theory of everything in its own way (political, relational, intense, throbbing – what's not to love?) but I want to continue to think of God otherwise than through this frame. And I don't quite like the taste of the covert theodicy at play in the thought of God's long-term lure of creation. I don't think God can be caught, not even in the tangled web, or mesh, of process thinking and I am suspicious of *all* forms of theodical accounting. So I can see power and goodness here, and I am inspired by Keller's theopoetics/theopolitics, but I can construct alternative makings out of tradition, theory and imagination. I can imagine cosmos and creator differently ... and then differently again. God always escapes. Theodical equations never balance.

Last, I am temperamentally perverse. When I hear, 'Wow! Now here are words and images that invoke God's glorious passion as an ecstasy made manifest and witnessed in all creation. Now you can both engage with that mystery and name it poetically to create a new theology that does not require the abandonment of reason or, even worse, betrayal of political responsibility. Does that not console you for the fact no one now calls your name softly in the garden?' I reply, 'No. No. I miss that beloved voice.' And, oh, let's be frank, I am a bit too noisy; a bit too fond of a new dress and a glass of red wine; a bit too materially embedded to be properly apophatic. The light that pierces my soul does not emerge from creation's mysterious dark energy but from damaged and derelict material stuff, forming and re-forming itself all around me with a piercing power.

What do I see in the gloom of this place? Nothing holy or majestic. Grave clothes discarded. They remind me of the swaddling bands in which we bind our babies. And so are these too to be left behind now? Outgrown? No longer needed? I reach out and touch them. Softly because they still hold the presence of you. Holding them I am connected to something very small and infinitely tender.

Although, somewhat regretfully, I am not reaching out to embrace its brilliance, I wanted to approach theopoetics through the modes developed in the work of Keller and her companions in order to make something very clear. An engagement with theopoetics reaches far beyond using the resources of poetry to adorn, supplement or even slightly revise our understanding of the divine. I follow Keller when she says theopoetics is not in the business of decorating God's coffin with verse (2013, p. 187). Rather, theopoetics commits us to engage with/participate in theo-making, across all levels: in the heart of God, in the world all around us as it groans in travail and births in glory, in our political and everyday lives. Theo-making is manifest also, but not only, in our faith communities: in our pastoral practices, in our scriptural readings, in our spiritual selves and the accounts we give of faith. The reach is wide and encompasses all that is forming and re-forming around us. Within the context of this much larger vision of theopoetics the creative arts (which theologians frequently lump together as 'poesis') have their very significant role to play with their particular and piercing re-forming, revelatory potential.

And practical theologians have particular insights to bring to reflecting upon this theopoetic process. We may be more able to comprehend, from the habitus of our discipline, the ambivalent, messy, painful, provisional elements that surely characterize theo-making. It is, after all, practice, and practice is our business. However, first, a caveat: we also face temptations of closure in our own world.

If the death of God movement has made the passion into its fixed pole of meaning, perhaps we may be in danger of making Pentecost our own? Much of the very best of contemporary practical theology is ecclesiocentric. A serious reflection upon religious practice keeps many of us focused on theology as it establishes church. Perhaps that is why we often imagine theology as distinct and separate from other discourses – purified by tongues of fire. I am seeking something humbler and less coherent as a theological approach.

Theopoetics from the wisdom of our discipline

Two people walking the road at dusk. Trying to piece together all that has happened in these last few days. But like a cheap clay lamp smashed on the floor, the fragments can't be joined. Dust and tiny pieces. No light here.

In what follows I shall begin to evoke what a theopoetics of practice might look, feel and taste like. But first a genuine and necessary disclaimer. Before progressing further I need to state unequivocally that by engaging with poetics we are not embarking on a new venture. Colleagues from many years ago to the present have been engaged with practical theology from a poetic perspective.[1] Many more of us make an occasional creative turn as we seek spiritual depth in our writing. Some of us understand ourselves as academic practical theologians in the day job, and in another space we are musicians, poets, artists, passionate preachers, liturgists and lovers of lovely things besides. However, to date in practical theology, we have not engaged in great depth *conceptually* with what theopoetics means for us[2] – although a lot of very interesting and important work has been done in the realm of practice.

So, if we were to construct a way of imaging a theopoetics out of the wisdom of our discipline, what would it look like?

Perhaps we could also start with Tillich's protesting image.

Something like *Guernica* indeed.

To recap, it is painted in black and white and in flat house paint – these qualities link it back to the 'everyday' nature of the passion it portrays. And although it does not use found objects as such, it draws upon the technique of assemblage, collage, bricolage, the surreal turning

---

[1] I think of Terry Veling's beautiful, brave and vulnerable oeuvre. Nicola Slee's profound work in poetry and spirituality. Pam Couture's pioneering work in theology and creative non-fiction. Others deeply engaged in exploring various aspects of a life writing include Claire Wolfteich, Jeanne Moessner, Darren Cronshaw, Mary Moschella, and Joyce Mercer. Pete Ward is a theoautoethnographer, Cas Wespener is a novelist, Tom Beaudoin is a musician theologian of postmodernity, and Doug Gay is a singer-songwriter. Michael Stoeber works on spirituality and art. Daniel Louw has advocated new forms of aesthetic reasoning. Bonnie Miller-McLemore has called for a poetics of resistance and has more recently turned her energies to exploring the making of theological writing. This list is illustrative only! I apologize for the very many omissions.

[2] However, Keefe-Perry's *Way to Water* (2014) is a significant text written by a practical theologian that consolidates this field.

of the familiar into the *unheimlich* which marks Picasso's major contributions to modern art. The theopoetics that we might offer the world will have a similar quality – a fragmented wounded making out of the depths of everyday life and practice that draws us into the surprising making and remaking of God.

> *At first the stranger just listened to us talking and then they started to speak. Not to tell a new story but to help us to make sense of ours. An old prophecy here, a new word there, and the scenes started to come together somehow. The picture emerging was not any less painful, I wouldn't say that, but now we could look at it more clearly somehow.*

Bricolage. A word and idea that became important in the theory of art, politics and culture as we passed through the dark portal of World War One to face the great challenges of living in modern times. I point to three intense instances in its development.

I begin with Walter Benjamin's oeuvre. Not with his fabulous 'Theses on the Philosophy of History', with which theology is very familiar (Benjamin, 2015). I turn rather to his unfinished Arcades Project (1999) as a *literary collage* or bricolage, through which he presented a radical alternative history of the nineteenth century and the birth of the modern era. He compiled it through a process of adaptation, pilfering and cunning which, in opposition to the established techniques of historiography that fixated upon big events and great men, craftily redeployed the '"refuse" and "detritus" of history, the half concealed variegated traces of … daily life' (Howard and McLaughlin, 1999, p. ix). Benjamin saw himself proceeding more in the manner of a canny dodger, a magpie collector of common things, or a ragpicker working through cast-offs of culture to create a vivid and revealing assemblage from its discarded scraps. From Benjamin we receive a vision of bricolage that resonates deeply with the ethos of practical theological reflection.

In a different vein, *The Savage Mind*, by Claude Lévi-Strauss (2004), contrasts the way traditional societies generate knowledge through processes of adaptive myth-making with modern scientific forms of understanding. He creates two characters representing these positions: 'the bricoleur' and 'the engineer'.

The bricoleur, the traditional meaning-maker, reworks and recycles existing materials, scraps accumulated over the years, and shapes these to meet needs as they arise. My father was such a bricoleur, keeping in his shed old nails, screws, wires, string, handy bits of wood and leather out of which he fixed our shoes, mended the washing machine, made us toy boats and rabbit hutches. The bricoleur must work with fragments and detritus, having neither resources nor opportunity to enrich or renew their stock. To quote Lévi-Strauss, the bricoleur works 'with whatever is to hand, that is with a set of tools and materials which is always finite and ... heterogeneous because what it contains bears no relation to the current project or indeed to any particular project' (2004, p. 21). The bricoleur is, in this sense, always mired in forms of cultural entanglement – there is no pure or original making.

In contrast, the engineer, representing the modern rationalized disciplines and their technical expertise, uses the correct tools and appropriate materials for the job. Unlike the bricoleur, the engineer can intentionally create a new design, and in this sense at least 'it might be said that the engineer questions the universe, while the "bricoleur" addresses himself to a collection of oddments left over from human endeavours' (2004, p. 19).

So the engineer becomes a systematic theologian and the bricoleur a practical theologian, perhaps? Maybe.

The smell of smoke and cooking fires. Small lights of simple houses. Orange glow in the darkness. We had reached the shelter of the village, our home. The stranger made as if to continue on the road that stretched out to a horizon far beyond us – but we would not allow this. 'Perhaps you might shelter here tonight in this humble place?'

Lévi-Strauss was writing in the days before the challenges of poststructuralism emerged to critique the distinctions previously made between traditional myths and metaphors, on the one hand, and logocentric discourses and grand narratives on the other. Jacques Derrida's riposte to this model – that of course 'the engineer is a myth' (2001, p. 360)[3] – is one that we would now assent to, aware as we now are of the necessity of creative borrowing and crafting from what already lies to hand, even in our most ambitious attempts to question the universe. However, despite our critique of Lévi-Strauss's ethnocentrism and logocentrism, his model presents bricolage as a kind of popular process of making with resources to hand able to sustain a way of life at variance to those envisaged in the totalizing systems of the modern age. As a practical theologian immersed in making within the domestic economy of faith,

---

3 Derrida implies here that the myth might be developed from the imagination of the bricoleur.

I find this evocative and helpful. The mundane location of the bricoleur was particularly important to Michel de Certeau.

De Certeau was to take the concept of bricolage developed by Benjamin, Lévi-Strauss and others and employ it over the full range of topics that are of interest to us here as academic practical theologians. His reflections spanned the nature of disciplinary activity and research, politics under capitalist systems, theology and faith practice. In all of these areas he sought to explore how those who are marginalized and apparently weak are also possessed of powers in practice that enable them to engage in making and shaping, making up and making do, with what is to hand: that is, they employ disregarded, damaged and derelict cultural and spiritual resources. His two major works on practice, *The Practice of Everyday Life* (1984) and *The Mystic Fable* (1995), span the entire stretch between the quotidian and the ecstatic apophatic and so hold the full potential for us to employ them in creation of a theopoetics that authentically touches our hands, our hearts and our souls. However, although his concerns, like ours, are far reaching, they are addressed through a method that creates the opposite of a seamless whole. His dominant paradigm of everyday poesis as bricolage is one that is focused on what he believed was the cultural condition of our time. We don't set off towards the horizon questioning the universe; this is not the way of venturing in the second holy week. We wander around in early morning mists, we walk a dusty road at dusk, we are lost on the seashore. De Certeau's leitmotif was the empty tomb, the road to Emmaus, the disciples fleeing Jerusalem for Galilee, but still enthralled by the lost and beloved other. With de Certeau I am reaching towards a theopoetics that practical theology might recognize and respond to – not one of cosmic coherence and stark beauty, but one of deep and loving attention to what is damaged and derelict, and yet possessed of piercing power.

Poetics of the broken form

> *There are different types of homecoming but this was not the one we would have sought. Not to go back to Galilee, not to go back to the old-time places and the old-time ways. This was no glad return. But it was a return we needed to make. I think we knew that.*

De Certeau was a French theorist, part of the creative intellectual movement that precipitated and reflected upon the Paris 1968 uprisings. He was influenced by Marx's insight that the movements pushing history forward emerge from persons oppressed, marginalized and deviant. He was also *particularly* indebted to the work of Jacques Lacan, who drew upon psychoanalytical theory to create the powerful modernist image of the subject who can only come to selfhood through a process of separation from the full plenitude of maternal connection. The wounds of this separation are felt in a restless desire for what we can never recover. We are lost seekers. We are weary pilgrims who journey towards a sacred presence we will never reach.

And de Certeau was a Jesuit – unorthodox but fundamentally shaped by this tradition that seeks to discover God in all things, that employs a discipline of imaginative contemplation, that enfolds the everyday into the context of God's providential purposes and understands vocation as practice, a means of proceeding, of wandering, of moving about from one place to the next. Practice is a form of embodied witness which was, for de Certeau, also a token of restless desire for the lost beloved.

These diverse influences make de Certeau's work particularly insightful for developing a theopoetics of practice and an understanding of the vocation of the practical theologian as re-former/bricoleur. Fundamental to his oeuvre is the notion that we exist within totalizing systems of disciplinary regulation, of capitalist production, of religious authority, but we are not helplessly and hopelessly fixed and immobile within them. Sensing lack in that which is supposed to secure our satisfaction, we always seek space to move and to make – even in situations where the constraints seem overwhelming. We can engage the 'strategy' (his term) of the system with the 'tactics' (his term) of our imaginative and creative re-forming work – in relation to academic practice, then politics, then faith.

Academic practice

After all the work that has been done to establish practical theology's position within the academy, it feels a little disloyal to bring a hermeneutics of suspicion to this project.[4] However, I am challenged by de Certeau's response to the notion that scientific communities, such as our own, create or advance knowledge by processes of intellectual exploration and mutual critique. You must not forget, he stated, that 'This community is also a factory, its members distributed along assembly lines, subject to

---

4 Particularly when speaking as President of the discipline's learned society.

budgetry pressures, hence dependent on political decisions and bound by the growing constraints of a sophisticated machinery' (1985, p. 204). I know that this description will have resonance for many of us. I am not denying that academic communities have hugely important work to do in this era of knowledge turmoil and culture wars, but we must also recognize the less beneficent, 'knowledge-machine' aspects of our existence. We must become conscious of how in our work we are often tempted to proceed upon regulated and approved paths of knowing in order to show allegiance to the values of a system in which disciplines are given their allotted space to function.

De Certeau's challenge for us, then, is that we should experience discomfort in our apparent belonging. I recognize that this is a hard challenge for those who have spent years resisting the marginalization and exclusion of people like us and a discipline like ours in the academic system. It is yet harder in times that are witnessing the closing of so many established and highly regarded theology departments. But, nevertheless, I am saying that a theopoetics of practical theology might challenge us to embrace a second discomfort, like Paul Ricoeur's second naiveté, and cause us to remember what we knew when we were the vulgar and despised bricoleurs of the theological world. And, further, de Certeau calls upon those who have realized they are not ever completely at home in the academy to become differently productive: first by proceeding not along the fair, broad highways of academic knowledge, signposted by university strategic plans, KPIs and the guidelines of funding councils and grant-making foundations, but along the fault lines, cracks and fissures in our disciplinary endeavours in which these grand designs fragment and begin to creatively re-form. So proceed courageously along the fault lines and become differently productive. And do this, he advises, by using the scraps that the machine-system discards as useless (affective understanding, spirituality, indigenous wisdom, ordinary theology, etc.) as resources in our academic making. In other words, accept that it may be our academic vocation is to be poets of the broken form in theology.

> *It wasn't a bad night to take the boats out but our hands weren't used any more to the handling of oars and the hauling of nets. We had lost the sense of where the shoals were swimming, having been so long away. We worked so hard but caught nothing. We had to be shown. 'SEE! look there, cast there, for the great catch.'*

Politics

De Certeau combines austerity and plenitude in his writing. On the one hand, we are confronted with our human predicament as incomplete, forever hungry, never satisfied and enmeshed within the nets of systems that are beyond our power to break. On the other hand, he presents the everyday world as the sight of marvels, over-abundance, joy and poetic creations of resistance.

We have been through many years of political pessimism and, to be honest, circumstances do appear to justify this deepening depression. However, de Certeau challenges us to recognize forms of resistance to consumer capitalism (and its disastrous consequences) which we may have discounted because our untrained, or perhaps too trained, eyes cannot perceive its hidden ferment in the everyday and also, crucially, because it cuts its fabric from the same stuff the system is woven out of (Walton, 2014a, p. 182).

From his historical studies, de Certeau presents instances of the way in which the indigenous peoples of Latin America responded to the imposed religion of the conquistadors. As religious bricoleurs they transformed symbols and rituals, undertaking a work of theopoesis that enabled these to take on a different meaning than the ones intended in the divine economy of colonialization. In similar ways, he argues, consumers today do not only passively accept the material and cultural economy they have no choice but to receive; they also reimaginatively invent it, whether they are watchers of popular TV programmes, wearers of clothes, users of social media – or whatever. Through their creative work, users *bricolent* 'innumerable and infinitesimal transformations of and within the dominant cultural economy' (de Certeau, 1984, pp. xiii–xiv). He celebrates the creativity of the marvellous 'unrecognized producers, poets of their own acts' (1984, p. xviii).

Such delight and faith in everyday resistance can appear to be an outmoded (belonging to the radical culture of the last century), outrageously optimistic and irresponsibly dangerous approach to politics – particularly in the face of the climate disaster. But the political theorist William Connolly, in his influential work *The Fragility of Things* (2012, see p. 114), encourages a similarly pluralist, relational and spiritual politics of resistance *in relation to the challenges of our times*. He argues that unless we recover faith in human creativity, wonder and joy in the everyday, we will not discover the energy and resources we need to embrace our fragile existence and re-form it. In a passage that bears striking resemblances to de Certeau's writing, he states that sometimes creativity will be manifest in 'surprising moments'; perhaps a political initiative or a social movement could also be:

> ... an artistic innovation, market spontaneity, a language change, a cooking invention, teaching improvisation, a new type of film scene, a musical production, the use of new media, or the invention of a new product. And so on endlessly. Our identification with life ... is grounded ... in ... uncanny experiences of creativity by means of which something new enters the world. (2012, p. 37)

What Connolly is looking for is a bricolage politics rooted in everyday creative practice; a 'positive pluralist assemblage' which draws its energy from creativity and wonder. So in what way does this relate to our project of constructing a theopoetics of practice?

Personally, I am dismayed that many of the theological responses we are making to our political situation, and most particularly the ecological crisis, so often seem to involve a turning away from human creative productivity and our common material existence. So, for example, Sallie McFague, in her book on consumer capitalism, makes a contrast between the grandeur of the natural world of God's creation and the soiled and sullied world of human making (2013). As practical theologians I believe we have to reassert our faith in human practice incorporating both the tragedy and glory of human making. A bricolage indeed. But, Connolly again: 'Existential gratitude ... can go hand in hand with a tragic view of human possibility and can help to render us alert to the fragility of things [even] as we also allow the sweetness of existence to sink into our pores' (2012, p. 181). I believe that our ragged-edged theopoetics must be able to touch the depths of tragedy and go dancing, wait wordless with grief, and wear a red dress and paint her nails.

> *Afterwards we rested on the sands and the sun was warm and the coals were glowing and we were full and sleepy. But, rising above the sound of the sea and the murmur of voices, came the same question again and again. I was not sure if I was being asked, 'Do you love me? Will you follow me once more and leave this harbour and this shelter?' Or 'Do you love me? Then rest here and be comforted. There is a white bird flying. See how the sun shines on the waves and there are small boats upon the water.'*

Faith and the Beloved

My last brief engagement with the work of de Certeau lies in the realm of faith and love. His final great work, *The Mystic Fable*, before his untimely death in 1986, explores the creative flowering of the mystic tradition at the birth of the modern era in the sixteenth and seventeenth centuries: years of rupture, trauma and reformation. His work on mysticism brings together themes I have previously explored. So in one sense mystics are portrayed (like practical theologians) as both at home and not at home in their religious traditions (or disciplines). In this context they will employ the articles of faith as material for construction and reconstruction, just as colonized people employ the materials of their colonizers to construct their own lively and resisting spiritualities. But this does not quite express the deep resonances with which de Certeau speaks of the work of those who dwell within the ruins of faith – people who in times of turmoil seek out the places of debris and dereliction, who even in their emptiness recall the divine other who cannot be contained within them (1995, p. 25). For Philip Sheldrake, this is de Certeau's greatest insight:

> [His] primary symbol of discipleship becomes Christ's empty tomb ... The Church no longer dominates Western culture and strong dogmatic statements will no longer be heeded. Christians are called to journey onwards with no security apart from the story of Christ that is to be (re)enacted rather than authoritatively proclaimed. 'He is not here. He is going ahead of you to Galilee' (Matt. 28:2–7). The Christian vocation for de Certeau is increasingly a question of following the perpetually elusive Christ. (2012, p. 209)

For de Certeau, this is the mysticism of practice.

And this mysticism of practice is both entirely at odds with the way we live now and entirely engaged within it in the manner we explored when discussing the politics of assemblage and the sweetness of life. Always with de Certeau there is difference and engagement, loss and wonder. These mystics who mediate the trauma of their culture by becoming dwellers among ruins, these perpetual seekers and lovers, are not some strange people from another era whose lives we cannot comprehend. They are ourselves, our ordinary selves seeking our beloved. One of the great influences on de Certeau was the Flemish mystic Jan van Ruusbroec who describes the mystic way as the life common to all. This ordinary existence that we craft and create through our own practice is scattered with marvels (de Certeau, Giard and Mayol, 1998, p. 213). In this existence, desire experienced also as piercing joy reaches out to us and reminds us that faith and love can be made here.

And then what comes is a ray. Not the sun's ray but the damaged and derelict re-forming into a piercing power. That is it. The creative moment.

What I have attempted to do here is to explore a theopoetics of practice. I held before you a model in constructive theology that combined the ancient traditions of theosis and apophatic mysticism with radical theology and process thought into a pleasing and coherent whole. And then I said that beautiful as this might be, perhaps practical theology might have a different way of approaching theopoetics. And I held before you an image of God in everyday this-ness that comes out of the Franciscan tradition, finding its way into Duns Scotus and contemporary poetry and philosophy and also into Jesuit practice. Instead of the finality of a kenotic passion, I displayed the ambiguities of divine presence and absence in the second holy week I proposed. Last, I suggested that rather than an encompassing theory of everything providing the motif for our theopoetics, we would probably better proceed as bricoleurs, makers and re-makers. Practical mystics and mystics of practice. Making our poetics out of tragedy and the sweetness of everyday life. Speaking faith and making love out of traditions that are fragmented and yet re-forming. I called upon practical theologians to become poets of the broken form.

But after all this, what exactly have I put before you? Simply a framework that may enable us to begin to imagine a theopoetics of practice? It might appear to have content and structure, but what is it really? The modernist artist and religious poet David Jones described poetry seeking the divine as still 'a made thing with a shape' (Dilworth, 2017, p. 20). To talk about theopoetics is to talk about 'a made thing with a shape', a heuristic frame, a gesture reaching out awkwardly to fashion and form an understanding of what unites God's making and our own creative practice. In that way it is not any different from the rest of theology actually – although tactically we might claim it to be so. But even as a made thing with a shape it has its own fragile life and purpose, and so I place it in your hands.

MAKING ONE: A THEOPOETICS OF PRACTICE

When I was little it was customary in my part of the world for schoolchildren to make Easter Gardens out of everyday scraps and take them home to display during the Easter holidays. I close this chapter with a memory of this practice:

We each had a box. Most children brought a shoe box, but my granddad always took ours to store his flower tubers under the bed over winter. My box was from my dad's new shirt. It was quite big so there was space to work. I took moss, full, cushiony moss of greenest green and laid it over the bottom, forming small hills and valleys. Then I took bare twigs and used glue to stick pink tissue paper flowers on to their small branches. Silver paper made a stream and a small pond. It was so lovely now. Then three flat pebbles and some plasticine shaped a cave. Last of all, two straight sticks tied with string made a cross on the green, green hill.

When I took it home, my moss garden was placed on the centre of the sideboard between Easter eggs and daffodils and I always looked at it every day in the holidays. Outside we didn't have blossom yet and the grass was never so green. I was not too little. I knew that there was sadness in the garden, of course. In my own small, sweet garden, not just on some green hill far away.

But how lovely it was.

8

Making Two: Heloise and Me, or, On Being a (Practical) Theologian

Our work is to make a connection between what is happening, here in this place and now in our lives, with the mystery at the heart of things.

A strange fascination

I have been trying to write a play. It is about Heloise.[1]

I used to make up little dramas when I was a child. I loved doing this. I would imagine the performances as I lay in bed at night, and in the morning cajole and coerce my friends to bring them to life. The self-consciousness of adolescence put an end to these dramatic scenes in the playground, and I never thought I would return to play-making again. I'm glad I did – although it has turned out to be much harder to get my writing to 'speak right' than I ever thought it would. Four years on and the play about Heloise is not finished. To be honest, I don't think it ever will be. But even though my adult construction is never likely to reach a 'stage stage', working on it has been an intense and emotional process.

---

[1] Because what follows draws upon my creative work I have not referenced this text in the usual way. All 'voicings' of Heloise's and Abelard's words are in my own paraphrasing. However, they all reference some actual point in the letters and associated documents. *The Letters and Associated Documents of Heloise and Abelard*, edited by Mary Martin McLaughlin with Bonnie Wheeler (2009), is the translation I used in my research. Specific documents are found as follows: the letters of Heloise and Abelard are to be found on pp. 17–85. Abelard's treatise on women in the religious life is on pp. 99–132; Abelard's rule for nuns is on pp. 133–94; Abelard's letter on the importance of study for nuns lies on pp. 195–207; Heloise's questions on the Bible and Abelard's responses are on pp. 213–70. For Abelard's hymns, see Woods, 1992; and Ruys, 2002. For revisionist histories that credit Heloise with liturgical agency, see David Wulstan, 2003; and Mews, 2002. For general background material, see *Listening to Heloise: the Voice of a Twelfth-century Woman*, ed. Bonnie Wheeler (2000).

MAKING TWO: HELOISE AND ME

You inhabit a character differently when you are seeking to give them a body and a voice. The relationship with Heloise has developed into something hugely important for me.

And it began with a very peculiar sense of calling.

I don't want to sensationalize this. I am not inclined to hear mysterious voices giving me directions no matter how loud they shout. But this was less like an injunction than an intuition. Muffled, formless and persistent. 'There might be something important waiting to encounter you in the person of Heloise. Just perhaps. Maybe. Why don't you look and see?'

Why did I sense this? I honestly don't know! My academic and personal interests tend to be articulated in the present tense. I *do* have an interest in countering women's absences from faith histories, but I *don't* incline towards tales of thwarted romance and retreat from the world. And way back when I started on this journey I knew only of Heloise *with* Abelard. They were the archetypal 'golden couple' – famous French lovers of long ago[2] whose brilliant intellects drew them to each other. Partners whose all-consuming affair was consummated in the birth of a son and (long afterwards) in a secret marriage. Things culminated abruptly and ingloriously with Abelard's castration at the instigation of Heloise's uncle. On Abelard's insistence, Heloise then took religious vows and spent the rest of her life in convent cloisters. Leading to this sad conclusion, I just assumed, lay the familiar forces of ecclesial power, familial coercion and sexual oppression. I did not enquire into the afterlife, or indeed the prequel to this story. I had not read their famous letters and the associated writings penned after their forced separation.

But I was compelled to do so ... and when I began to read I was entranced. My initial delight came from encountering things that I found very funny – although I must remember that my sense of humour is a little idiosyncratic. I found parts of *Das Capital* laugh-out-loud writing! The utter incoherence of capitalist economics, as furiously articulated by Marx, is hilarious. Heloise and Abelard's letters to each other were charged with humour for me in a similar way. They catalogue attempts to reconcile human experience, sexual experience at that, with a cathedral-like cosmological system. It is an ambitious, admirable but fundamentally comical exercise.

This comic sense of dislocation was magnified by the variety of conflicting voices Heloise employs in her writing. She speaks to Abelard with challenging, erotic intimacy as her lover, archly as her husband, and then elegantly and eloquently to her intellectual and spiritual mentor.

---

2 Heloise *c.* 1100–1163. Abelard *c.* 1079–1142.

Each mode of address deconstructs the other, producing fantastic juxtapositions: 'I wish we'd had time for more sex. It's probably easier for you to get over this ... *in the circumstances*. And anyway you are older than me.' 'Dear one, do look after yourself. I worry about you all the time and you mean more than all the world to me – although it might be nice if you asked me how I'm doing from time to time.' And, 'Can you please write me a new religious rule for nuns that enshrines our right to study Greek?' I love this mad mixture. So good.

Of course, I must acknowledge that apart from the vivid letters most of the material we have is in Abelard's voice; it is his writing. Certainly it is. But usually penned as a response to some provocation from Heloise – promptings he could never ignore. And in a collaboration such as theirs the membrane between challenge and response is so permeable that scholars continue to debate who influenced who and where Heloise's trace can be discerned in Abelard's thinking. So this is where I really enter into the story. With a surprise discovery. Everyone knows Abelard was a radical theologian, but Heloise was a theologian too – and not only that. Her way of being a theologian says much to me about the peculiar vocation that has claimed my life but that I have always struggled to embrace. So Heloise meets me here. And as she was way more scholarly, much more radical, and resoundingly more resolute than I am, she challenges me deeply. And she moves me even more.

Heloise the entangled theologian

> Question: Where was Heloise when Abelard underwent his bloody cut?
> Answer: She was visiting the famous convent of Argenteuil for a period of study and of prayer.
> Supplementary Answer: She'd probably taken herself off for a wee while because she was being driven crazy (and was crazy-scared) by the quarrels between her husband and her uncle.
> Qualification to Previous Answers: We'll never know exactly why Heloise had decamped to Argenteuil ... But to use the world-class library seems a likely explanation. In other words – she was probably reading at the time.

Heloise was a brilliant scholar. We know that but tend to place it in a world apart somewhere. Off-stage. It doesn't fit the plot of the love story. But I have let it in now and I am trying to connect it up. I am trying to connect it all up. Some context is necessary.

Heloise lived in a period of intellectual turmoil. Aristotle's writings had been rediscovered in the West (thanks to the work of Muslim scholars) and a whole range of new ideas were conflicting with and confounding the established philosophical/theological schools of France. Abelard was at the centre of this knowledge revolution. At the same time there was a religious revival going on – bigtime. This centred around the leading figure of Bernard of Clairvaux. We can't really use modern terms (re-forming, fundamentalist, fanatical, etc.) to describe this movement, but it nurtured a deep suspicion of the flesh and new fashions of secular learning (particularly those inspired by the pagan Greeks). Established monasteries and convents were already being caught up in this new movement. Established men's and women's institutions, some celebrated for their scholarly excellence, were being re-formed and, in initial phases, the new regimes of austere piety would leave little space for academic explorations and adventures.

So there is Heloise, in the midst of all this, reading by candlelight. Brushing up her Greek perhaps. We think she liked Ovid – who would not like Ovid? We understand she would be familiar with the new philosophical and theological thinking. There is no doubt she knew that scholarly pursuits were becoming a site of deep conflict. We can assume she feared that there might be a time coming when the library doors would be closed to men and locked for women. But she was undaunted as to where her 'scholarly faith' was leading her. 'In an age of stinking religious hypocrisy' (is there any other?) 'it's no big deal to appear pious,' she said in one of her letters. Piety was not the point, but a stance of fierce integrity *in all matters* was a godly thing. And in the disputes, quarrels and confusions in which her life was entangled she was to prove herself no hypocrite but someone possessed of radical views that she was trying to work out as they crossed and connected the different aspects of her life.

So I have introduced the library into the love story and named some of the intellectual and theological passions that are also at play within the romantic fable. The famous 'intercourse', we must remember, took place during the course of Heloise's studies and she opened her arms to much more than desire when she embraced her clerical tutor. Initially she rejected marriage, only agreeing when pressed to distraction by him. She forthrightly declared that sweeter to her 'would be the title of concubine, or whore, rather than wife'.

The reasons for this preference are likely multiple. Unwillingness to conform to the stinking hypocrisy that allowed for all forms of sexual relations for priests like Abelard, provided they remained hidden, but was unwilling to allow those lawfully married and in holy orders to rise to positions of authority within the Church. Perhaps there was also disdain for the hyper-morality of the new religious zealots? Her concerns were also realistic. 'You're a romantic, my dearest darling, but you'd soon rage against being a penniless cleric dwelling in a poor house full of washing and wailing babies.' But, fundamentally, they were matters of principle. Purity of intent is what matters in love rather than outward forms, and thus her compunctions were also theological. Whereas Abelard, after the cut, seems to repent of their wild shenanigans (sex in secret, sex in sacred spaces, sex in Lent) – she holds out. She does not regret. She does not renounce. She is shockingly frank about this. 'Even at holy mass the fervour of our embraces flood my mind.'

I can't but read her refusal of regret as a theological stance, and neither did Abelard. In the end, he can't take any more of it. He instructs, he argues, he commands.

> You must put all *this* behind you, madam. We are no longer what we once were to each other in the flesh. There is a new relationship in faith which requires a different economy of desires. Our new state is more blessed than our old disgrace. Give thanks to God and stop complaining.

And so, it seems, she finally concedes. Humbly, Heloise declares she absolutely will stop going on about sex and is fully determined to act in total submission to Abelard's religious guidance in all matters. And, by the way, she adds, in relation to this please find attached a list of questions about studying the Bible. This (very long) list names many problems that Heloise, and her community of learned women, have encountered in relation to the ancient texts (which they read in Hebrew and Greek of course). It includes the thorny old questions: 'What is the sin against the Holy Spirit?' 'Why do biblical accounts of the same event contradict each other?' and 'Why did Jesus curse the fig tree because it did not have fruit when it was not the season for fruit on a fig tree?' Indeed. It also includes a challenge: 'How come when God's first command to humanity is to have sex, "be fruitful and multiply", has obeying this injunction come to be seen as *so* problematic?' I am paraphrasing, but the question is still there! I like to imagine Heloise and her sisters working on this long, scholarly submission which they devoutly address to Abbot Abelard and thinking, 'Ha! That'll show him.' 'See what he says about this one.' 'We've got him now!' 'How will he get out of that then?' I find this wonderful, reading it as I do, slant-wise, with my feminist hermeneutics and my rather off-beat sense of humour. Well done, Heloise. Keep going. Take your questions and complaints from one sphere to another because all the spheres are connected as we know so well ...

And you are teaching me so much. About being entangled in it all.

Although I must be alert to the dangers of too easy comparisons.

Of course I want to say: 'I too live in a time of changing cosmologies.' The apparently stable categories through which we understood fundamental issues are mutating. It's an age of populisms and fundamentalisms and culture wars. I too encounter stinking religious hypocrisy and condemning zeal. There is a crisis of confidence in established knowledge and an acute sense that it can't now be the same old, same old. Not in philosophy, not in theology, not in this crisis.' There. I have said all that and got it out of my system. But crude correlations aren't really that useful between situations that are so different. And what has helped me so much is not the correspondences between Heloise's context and my own, but the sense I have that she was really trying to engage with all the complicated entanglements of her life with theological persistence and integrity.

My own theological journey began just as second-wave feminism began to speak its challenges to faith. I was involved in disseminating some of the first feminist theological material to be circulated in the UK. Long days (and nights) with sheets of typeset, scalpels and gum; laying out the pages for printing. And afterwards, drinking beer and arguing about new ideas. Pamphlets before books – worship material before doctoral theses. I was 28 years old when I began teaching on the first course in feminist theology to be offered by a UK university. We thought we were doing something new in reclaiming sexuality and the body as sites of theological reflection. How naïve! But I smile when I remember this early passion.

Feminism gave me the scope and permission to mix up theology with embodiment, but comprehending what being an entangled theologian really means came later. With infertility. And those hard years of trying and failing to conceive. While loving my partner. While teaching in the seminary. While being active politically in my community. While being a preacher in my church. While growing as a hungry and curious scholar in the midst of all of these experiences at once. Not untangling one thing from the other. But criss-crossing these modes of registering and reflection. Gradually learning to speak of infertility as an epistemological challenge, a theological location. Discovering how to read the Bible with barrenness as a hermeneutical key and to discover that this reading spoke to people in the spaces and places of my own times who were registering the necessity of bringing grief and loss into the theological sphere. For the times have been hard not only on a personal level. And my own losses and lamentations (like those of some small, belated, female Jeremiah) mirror the losses of the land and people. My entanglement a reality, a location, a parable, a calling.

Heloise the 'locked in' theologian

> Question: What happened to Heloise after Abelard was 'cut off'?
> Answer: She remained in Argenteuil where she had grown up as a convent girl and where she had been nurtured in mind and spirit.
> Supplementary Answer: They locked her in. Consecration was incarceration.
> Qualification to Previous Answers: We are always and already confined.

It is not that Heloise did not believe. She believed in God and in a religious life lived with integrity. But she did not decide on this particular existence for herself. Did not choose this community to which she is now wedded. Nor this role with its ridiculous requirements and soul-restricting conventions. To be sure, some things within and about it are precious. She loves them still. They should be defended and the threats are real. But it is all so heartbreakingly wasteful and wearing and wearisome, and not at all what she wants. What to do? No choice actually. You do what you can.

First, defend what you cherish.

Although you might not always win.

Just a few years on from Heloise's consecration and Argenteuil was under siege. A long dispute concerning the convent's property and land rights was fanned into flame by accusations concerning the immorality of the sisters and their impious occupations. Amid the religious fervour of the times the convent could no longer rely on its reputation or the patronage it had previously received from powerful supporters in the

Church and royal court. The community struggled against the tide but a decision was made to hand over Argenteuil, with its rich resources, to the monks of St Denis. The nuns were to be sent away to other religious houses. This battle was lost. So what happens when defence fails?

Revision and build.

Already a leader, prioress Heloise urgently appealed to Abelard for his support. She requested his help in establishing a new religious community for a group of the exiled sisters in a small oratory he had founded as an isolated place of personal retreat after the trauma of his attack.

The 'Paraclete' (dedicated to the Holy Spirit – the Comforter) had first been a location of quiet solace for Abelard. It became the base from which he began to remount his controversial theological interventions once his intellectual energy returned. It was haphazardly extended when he was joined by many young disciples, but fell into disuse when Abelard moved into new ecclesial roles. It formed an ideal base for the sisters to re-establish their communal lives while discreetly cherishing the particular combination of devotion and scholarship they held dear. Heloise was its inspiration and founding Abbess. Abelard worked closely with her as the community's spiritual guardian. His avowed intention was to place the scholarly work of the sisters in studying religious texts at the heart of their communal life. He had a vision that, 'as learning is all but lost these days in the men's religious houses then it may still be kept alive here; cherished by a group of dedicated and studious women.'

Sadly, we know very little about the ways in which this new form of partnership between Heloise and Abelard developed in the early years of the Paraclete's history. Some details emerge in their later writings preserved in the library of the Paraclete. But historians remind us to be cautious in our interpretation of these texts. What we can be confident of is that the Community of the Paraclete was deeply cherished by its co-founders. It is also very evident that Heloise continually provoked Abelard to respond to challenges she perceived and named in the religious life.

They weren't small ones. 'Abelard – write to me concerning the religious vocation of women and construct me a new rule for the women's community I lead under your direction.' To think seriously about women's vocations and to consider how their life together might properly diverge in some ways from the disciplines of life in monasteries was a huge thing – the significance of which has been long occluded. The first works of Heloise and Abelard I read were in a drastically abridged compilation of their writings. I was only dipping my toes in the water then – not ready to commit at that stage. The editor unapologetically stated they'd cut out Abelard's treatise on women and the religious life as well as his rule for nuns because they were long and boring and, to their mind, not particularly consequential or significant.

How can you say this? To be fair, these texts are quite long and a little boring. If you want the funny bits you need to go to the letters. In these, Heloise's 'helpful' suggestions about the new rule are both practical and hilarious:

'Oh, by the way, I think we should seriously consider whether it would be reasonable to allow nuns a slightly larger wine allowance than is usual for monks? It's well known that women tend to handle drink better.' 'Nuns need to have more clothes than religious men are allowed because our monthly periods mean that our garments need to be washed more often.' And, 'I've been thinking and it's really not a good idea for virgins to lead women's religious houses because they are completely useless in worldly things and, particularly so when it comes to dealing with the powerful men we need to keep sweet. Can you manage to write that in somehow?'

But, such asides aside, Abelard's work here is so significant! Bless him, he is really trying to impress upon a woman who has 'taken the veil', at his express direction, the massive significance of women's place and role in the Christian faith. And he makes a serious stab at this in his treatise; it is not just pious, patronizing drivel. The accompanying 'rule for nuns' is also a sincere effort to construct a holy way of life for women that affirms and acknowledges their intellectual as well as their spiritual inheritance. And it's groundbreaking in many respects – although it has to be admitted Abelard is better at the theory than the practice. Heloise drew up her own rule in time which was a much better work. But still ... something very important is happening here.

Heloise is not sitting in her cell moping; nor is she in the library trying to escape it all by reading. She puts away her books and is with her sisters. She is leading, building, acting, making. Asking how should we be a religious community in this space and place and time (none of which are of my choosing, but here I am anyway)? How can we do it well, properly, what kind of inheritance are we building on and how should this be reformed? It's about those things. It really is about those things.

Of course, I am telling this story my way and highlighting wherein it speaks to me. That's what we all do. But it does not only speak to me, it shouts. It confronts me with my (practical) theological vocation.

I have to be honest here. There was a point, way back, when I was glad, very glad, when they said to me, let us go to the house of the Lord today. I grew up in church and it *was* my glad home. But things have changed. I now find myself in a place whose conventions increasingly constrain me – which is precious and ridiculous all at once; which I frequently wish to escape from but cannot. And what am I called to do here?

Defend what you cherish. Most of the churches I have loved and belonged to in my life have closed. Those still 'hanging on' are struggling with vision, vocation and presence. The mainline denomination I belong to is in freefall decline. There is a struggle going on about training and theology. I am involved in the cajoling and the compromising around this. There is a PowerPoint presentation to prepare and a committee meeting to attend where I will make the case for … and then there is my own congregation. It's not much fun to be sitting for hours in the elders' meeting in the ugly hall on the funny chairs (again) and debating (again) whether to sell the building. It is wearing and wearisome, and it is not at all clear that the things that I have loved and valued will make it through this time of trial. But if I am here, I am part of this. Not a choice.

And alongside this and at the same time there is my wider vocation. Vision and build – not for restoration but for a new time coming. Yes, this is also the work of the practical theologian. To see clearly what is happening and to search for resources that will enable construction in the midst of this. Rediscover a radical tradition and rewrite it. Construct a new rule that is for living in this place and in this time. Not as easy as it sounds because you have to live by it too. And the uneasy sense of confinement always remains. But make, make, make. This is your calling.

Heloise the creative theologian

Question: What happens to great passions in small places?
Answer: They may develop beyond the self. Growing and expanding up to heaven.
Supplementary Answer: They may become crushed into essences, but it's a costly process.
Qualification to Previous Answers: I am sorry, but there are no small places. The cell is a cosmos and the cosmos is a cell.

Heloise is seeking connection. There must be that connection somehow. Between the candle that burns in the chapel through the night and the great fire beyond. Finding this won't make sense of all the mess of things, but it will connect them up. Let me call this connecting worship – although that is an ill-used word. 'We need new litanies. We need new hymns,' Heloise wrote to Abelard. She was writing from a tender and still painful space.

In the early days of their relationship he had composed many love songs for her – works that were sung on every street corner in Paris. The clear intention of these compositions, as Heloise states bluntly, was seduction. 'You have two gifts that open to you the heart of any woman. The beauty of your songs and the sweetness of your singing.' Now she begs him to write songs for her again, and he did. Scholars contend about what exactly he wrote and why. Some think that Abelard used some of his hymnwriting to make a tacit reply to Heloise's laments for their love. That he addressed to her alone a number of *planctus* (songs expressing grief) in his wider corpus. Others think that he was always intending his work for the community of the Paraclete – while recognizing that his hymns would speak to Heloise's heart.

Whatever the case, I find Heloise's request so poignant. She knows she is trading the scents of the bedchamber for the incense of the chapel and that's a bitter bargain for her to make. Yet as ever Heloise is practical. 'We lack liturgies and hymns for some seasons. And we don't always want to be praising holy virgins and martyrs. What we have right now is old-fashioned and stupid. Worse. Much of it requires us to mouth things we don't believe and to do so makes us hypocrites. Give us music that inspires and give us words we can sing honestly.' And so he did. And to my mind this is one of the best (most loving) acts Abelard ever performed. There are litanies and hymns that honour women's voices in the biblical tradition and do not evade even the darkest moments. These are held and hallowed through women's lamentations. The slaughter of the innocents. The lamentation of Rachel weeping for her children. The sacrifice of Jephthah's daughter. Mary mourning her beloved Son. There are works that echo the urgent voices of the separated partners in the Song of Songs and speak of David's lament for Jonathan. The breath of lovers is everywhere in these devotions. They take up and transform conventional observances into the passion of a creation in travail. I am overwhelmed by this.

And I am intrigued by another scholarly suggestion. There are an increasing number of musical historians who believe that Heloise herself was a composer. That she was an audacious dramatist herself and that some of the striking Easter anthems sung and performed at the Paraclete are her compositions. These unite the figure of the dark beloved in the Song of Songs searching for her lover with Mary Magdalene in the garden on Easter morning. They are poetic works of palpable power and, at their breaking heart, a desperate love and longing connect the searcher to the beloved.

I have loved discovering how Abelard and Heloise crafted art out of sorrow and reached out to each other *and to heaven* through worship. For, more and more, I think the point of it all is *worship*. More and more I believe that all I am doing is really about this, and so we need songs for this season. Words *for* our mouths and words *from* our mouths that are not stupid. That don't make us hypocrites when we utter them from the pulpit or say them out loud together. They won't make sense of all this mess of things, but it will sing it out to heaven. And they give form to our grief, to our longing, and bring it before God. It's always worship before theological sense-making in my book. So should practical theologians, then, all become hymnwriters, liturgists and preachers? Go back to the old ways? Well, some of us are rediscovering these roots to tend and revive them, and others have never stopped working in this garden and we need to learn from them. But no, I don't think this. Because worship, as I am framing it, is making that desiring connection and this does not only take place through hymns and liturgies and sermons. And it certainly does not only take place in Christian congregations and communities. Wherever and whenever flame reaches out to flame in stories and gestures, art and actions, this is worship. When the cosmos is transubstantiated in the smallest of cells and the smallest cell becomes a universe – I am calling this worship.

O, Heloise. The Paraclete no longer stands. But wanting to come close to you I have taken myself to medieval convents, climbed their winding steps, looked out of the arched windows that face inwards, and passed through the heavy wooden doors into their chapels. I have shivered as I caught a memory of cold winter nights and women hurrying along stone corridors beneath wooden rafters towards candle-lit altars. To places where, in their warm breath, the pain of all the ages and the longings of every heart of flesh is sung out to the heavens. I have met you there.

Heloise refusing the consolations of religion

> Question: So after all this, did Heloise find comfort at the Paraclete: the place of the Comforter?
> Answer: The community grew and flourished under her direction. She became a well-known and well-loved Abbess who was celebrated for her intelligence, compassion, leadership and practical wisdom.
> Supplementary Answer: There is no happy ending here. Heloise never became reconciled to her fate or to God.
> Qualification to Previous Answers: There is a vocation to refuse the consolations of religion.

In the context of their times, it would have been unthinkable for Heloise or Abelard to have lost faith in God because of what happened to them. Faith just wasn't losable in the way it is now. Abelard appears to have come to some kind of reconciliation that allowed him to view the traumatic end of his physical relationship with Heloise as providential. That is, within the scope of God's loving purposes for him. Perhaps this move was necessary in order to rebuild his life after the public humiliation he had endured. It nevertheless appears to have been sincere, but this acceptance did not render him a pious fool. He continued to pursue a radical theological path and affirm the worth of intellectual questioning despite the continuing persecution he experienced and the charges of heresy it brought upon him. As his production of devotional material indicates, he was also prepared to name intense suffering and loss in the context of faith.

Heloise, however, refused the consolations of religion: 'What happened to us was cruel and I hold God responsible.'

When Abelard attempts to console her by praising her reputation for piety and promising that her dark 'veil of mourning' will be replaced by the golden crowns of honour in heaven, she rejects this comfort. Not only was it 'no big deal' to appear pious, she also maintains that if heaven is a perfect place then no one person is going to enjoy greater dignity there than anyone else. A different economy will operate. Virgins and nuns, monks and martyrs, will be nothing special. Poignantly she states, 'If God lets me into Paradise at all then I'll be happy to sit in a humble corner in a patch of sunlight.'

Behind this fancy lies her continuing refusal to repudiate the sweetness of her human loving or become reconciled to its loss.

Heloise, while you wear the veil, while you kneel at the altar, while you fast, while you bow your head and while you pray ... your eyes remain open: 'I will not be reconciled.'

I know there is a contradiction here. But Heloise was not a hypocrite. She was an unresolvement.

In the context of these times it is belief in God that seems remarkable. In the face of human and planetary travail it is entirely reasonable, and morally justifiable, to reject theism altogether. In all its forms.

I understand this. And yet I am unable to do so.

Like Heloise, I am caught in a net of faith.

Of course, I know all the explanations that are put forward as to why people like me continue to believe against all reason: neurological, genetic, social, cultural, psychological, psychoanalytic. I find them interesting. Coming from the other side, I could also recite the arguments philosophers and theologians continue to make for the plausibility of theism. I find few of these compelling and rarely rehearse them myself. But then I am not primarily an apologist like Abelard. I am a refuser. Like you, Heloise, I am a refuser.

The passion of my theological work, of my theological life, is rooted in loss. I think it always has been. Despite being an early convert to liberation and feminist theologies, I am still (stupidly, I know) proud of the fact that my first published article was titled 'If God is on the side of the poor, why don't they win?' It has always seemed to me that the main theological challenge, the one that opens up all the others, is the ancient and enduring 'question of evil'. How can such agony exist? Why is creation shot through with pain? To me, these are not academic questions requiring justifiable answers. They are a location in which I must dwell. There is a mystery of suffering that must be entered into in order for me to encounter the mystery of God.

So I can keep company with Heloise as she refuses to be comforted. Such a refusal may be the vehicle some people use to escape the sacred altogether. Why linger here? But I don't leave. Heloise had, I have, no choice but to remain – and yet we remain without resolvement.

But is there no love, no tenderness here?

Oh yes, I can say, there is love. There is a touch of unbearable tenderness also.

Weary with the work I do, I often wish to escape the stone cloisters of this old religion. But where else could I take my accusations and laments which are deeper and more fundamental than political protest can articulate – necessary though this clearly is?

I acknowledge a vocation I did not choose. I did not choose this. This calling of God to stand before God and say, I am not reconciled. But in the times when my passion is appeased, when I lack the will to keep my eyes open as I pray, I feel far away from all I know as holy. I sense I have not kept faith. When I stand straight and stubborn in my calling, then something meets me in this dark place. It burns with the same flame that consumes me and we reach towards each other with all the longing that lovers feel when they are separated.

And it is not always cold and dark. There are daytimes too. Sweet ordinary days when I sit happily in a small corner in a patch of sunlight and seek nothing more than this. There is loss, there is longing and there is, incredibly, Paradise. Not as reward, not a restoration, but as the place where those who are tired can sit on the grass and warm themselves in the sunshine. Count the daisies. Listen to the birds.

I wonder if Heloise also experienced this sweetness in her travails. Or was she more resolute than I am? I let myself be very glad in the intensity of small things that seem to me tokens of a consummation that is the other side of loss. Perhaps she found her own places of joy that were *not only* located in the memory of delights denied. I know she laughed sometimes – even if only at the absurdity of it all. Perhaps she mouthed an old love song as the white doves flapped on the pan-tiled roof of the Paraclete on a May morning. Perhaps she let the candle burn long into the night as she struggled to shape the name of God in Hebrew – a word that can be written but not spoken. I hope she experienced pleasure in the paradoxes; in the absurd vocation of the theologian. I hope she did.

9

Making Three: Writings in the Disaster

Monday 1 November

COP26 has begun.[1] The university has returned to Covid lockdown mode. All teaching is being done online because of the disruption to transport systems – the main carriageway into the city from the west is closed. Public transport has been re-routed to take delegates to conference venues, and there are road blocks on many of the streets around the university. The art gallery is surrounded by a 3-metre-high fence to keep protestors out. It has been turned into the world's most exclusive banqueting hall for the world leaders. They will be feasting with the surrealists and impressionists.

Late afternoon I take a walk around the campus area. There are banners on University Avenue welcoming COP delegates. A huge sign over the students' union proclaims hopefully 'It's not too late' but the place is largely deserted. It is a world turned strange. It is as if the catastrophe had already happened and we are living in the aftermath.

As dusk falls I join a small group of protestors outside the art gallery. Big black cars drive past with police escorts. Police vans are hidden in wait down side streets. Helicopters patrol overhead. The rhythmic noise of their blades sets the meter for our chanting. Someone starts drumming. I am outside the fence, on the border, in the loud darkness.

Tuesday 2 November

It seemed a good idea at the time. To respond to COP by organizing a series of video interviews from our Theology and Religious Studies

---

1 COP stands for Conference of the Parties and it is the main decision-making body of the United Nations Framework Convention on Climate Change (UNFCCC). Its members are representatives of the countries that have agreed to be part of the UNFCCC. It usually meets once a year to review progress and agree goals and targets. COP26 was held in my home city of Glasgow.

Department with activists, artists and academics – all speaking about spirituality in the context of climate change. But that meant organizing hours of output with a cast of thousands.[2] Exhausting, stressful, amazing.

So this morning I was recording a conversation between my friend, Israeli poet and literary critic Ariel Zinder, and my colleague, South Asianist Ophira Gamliel. Ariel draws deeply on Hebrew scriptures and Jewish liturgies, Ophira responds with her research on contemporary communities experiencing flooding in Kerala. Their conversation is fascinating: Ariel talking about how the voice of God 'speaks' in Jewish disaster narratives and Ophira talking about the flood ballads produced in Kerala that are jointly owned by Muslim and Hindu communities seeking to comprehend the divine in the midst of a deluge. I am overwhelmed by the poignancy of these poetic works.

Ophira talks as an engaged academic and Ariel as a person of faith. So Ophira says, 'In situations of disaster people seek comfort and gain resilience by turning to their sacred traditions to find meaning.' Ariel is quiet for a while and then he says, 'What happens in the time of crisis is that everything is washed away and, like Job, you stand naked before God with no answers.' I get this. I understand it. Faith is not a comfort here.

Just because it's COP doesn't mean I'm not teaching. My honours class in Theology through Creative Writing was on Zoom. The self-assured students who tend to take this option (piercing, tattoos, wear vintage, migrated from art history or politics) appear more vulnerable when they are sitting in their bedrooms or in shared kitchens with big Minnie Mouse headphones. But it was a good session. We were looking at decolonial literature in the first hour – which seemed right for this season. I gave them time to talk about what was happening. And they ran with the writing exercise based on Édouard Glissant's words 'there is no language for chaos'.

Wednesday 3 November

I go to the University Chapel. It is a place I have come to love over the 20 years I have worked here. So many moments of my life are etched into its soft grey stones. Bill McKibben is speaking. His book *The End of Nature* first introduced the concept of climate change to a popular

---

2 I worked on this initiative alongside my friends Doug Gay and Julie Clague.

audience back in the 1980s. We are posting his talk in our series. Bill is a Methodist layperson whose faith is quietly affirmed. He speaks humbly, naming the dangers, spelling out the overwhelming challenges, and offering no reassurance in his call for struggle. He's been an activist all his life and he's now urging seniors his own age into action. He misquotes Martin Luther King's statement, 'The arc of the moral universe is long but it tends towards justice.' Bill says, 'The arc of the material universe is not as long as you think and it tends towards heat.'

There isn't gonna be an 'arc' for you to find refuge in. Not from this flooding.

I chose an image by Ade Tunge for our publicity and branding. It is of dark doves flying. It evokes the image of the Spirit brooding over the chaos-deep in Genesis and, of course, the story of Noah. But our doves don't fly out and return bringing olive sprigs of hope back to us. They are out there buffeted by the storm and they haven't found a place to rest.

Thursday 4 November

I am in my hiding place. There is a coffee bar just 10 minutes away from the university where hardly anybody goes: because it's just as expensive as other places even though it's less trendy; because it's dark and murky inside; because some of the fabric of the seating is torn and the place could do with a coat of paint; because the coffee is nothing special and neither is the food.

But I like it: because you can always get a seat and some of them have plugs where you can charge your laptop; because the internet connection is fast and efficient; because the woman who works there is very nice and she is called Lily and she calls me Heather; because there is a mezzanine level, and if you sit up there you can't be seen from the street.

I am working on my journal.

I don't keep a journal all the time. Just when I am on holiday (I have more time), and when I am anxious (it helps a bit), or when something important is happening (so I can mark, learn and inwardly digest), also in Lent and Advent (because these are journalling seasons). So quite a lot of the time really.

This feels like one of those 'important times' and I am trying to get things down. But I have problems slowing my thoughts sufficiently to catch them. This happens to me sometimes. Another anxiety symptom.

Everything feels like it is happening very fast inside my head but slow on the outside and I can't match them up.

I shall ask Lily to make me her special tea. It's not on the menu. She only does this for me. The first time was when I asked for a lemon and ginger tea and she said, 'We don't do that ... but I will see what I can do.' She got some fresh ginger from the kitchen and cut it into fine slices and put it in a long glass – not one of their thick, ugly cups. Now sometimes when I come in she says, 'I think we have some ginger in the kitchen, would you like me to make you a tea?' And sometimes I say yes, and other times I say no. I don't want to impose or take her for granted.

But things are a bit much right now. So, praise God, I can hide in here and Lily will make me some hot ginger tea.

Friday 5 November

I had two postgraduate supervisions today. One before lunch and one just after I had finished my egg sandwich. There are two doctoral programmes I work within. The first is in practical theology – a programme for 'researching professionals' who are doing work on aspects of their ministry. The second is our new theology through creative practice programme, in which we have poets, printmakers, film makers and novelists all working on a piece of creative work that has theological significance. So very different.

Today my 'before-lunch' person was a ministry person and my 'after-lunch' person was one of our creatives. However, the issues that came up in supervision were surprisingly similar. And in each case we were moving from the very local and the very practical to the cosmological – in just a matter of minutes. Doesn't matter where you start, I thought ... I think the background of COP helped both of them to make this move. Everything feels interlinked where we are sitting now. And urgent. I love working with these researchers. Love it so much!

It's bonfire night here in Glasgow, and as I walked home I saw fireworks begging to streak the sky and heard the screeching/moaning sound of the rockets rising to explode in stars and fountains.

We've got people arriving tonight for tomorrow's demonstration and it's my turn to cook.

Saturday 6 November

The big march. It is raining. Of course it is raining. In Glasgow it always rains. But how glorious the day is. The labour and trade union movement may not be the force it was, but it still stirs me in my soul when I see the treasured old banners of a thousand campaigns out on the street again. And I love the new banners too: 'Firefighters know an emergency when they see one.' 'It's Capitalism, you idiots!'

The flags of Extinction Rebellion are massed together as the climate activists march in strength. The symbol of an eye sewn on to coats, jackets and hats, printed on flags and painted on faces. 'We are watching.' Glasgow children hold out home-made signs and people from across the globe wave the national flags they carried with them to wave today. At one point on the march I reach the top of a hill. Looking back, the line is endless; looking forward, it goes on for ever. At that very moment a group of young people next to me start singing and people join in all around. The song is 'I Will Survive' and, singing, we move from fear to strength and finish with love; for if we know 'how to love' then we know how to be alive. I am crying. It's raining so who can tell. I myself don't know whether it's joy or the piercing pain in this longing for life that has brought tears to my eyes.

Sunday 7 November

I didn't go to church because I had a houseful of guests. And because we stayed up very late last night talking and drinking wine. And now it's the morning after ...

I love the morning after in a home full of friends. People getting up gradually. Taking a cup of tea back to bed. Reading the weekend papers in the lounge. I love making a huge veggie brunch. We have a very big table that we have had since we got married and it can seat 11 (that's all the seats we have anyway!). I plug in the toaster at one end of the table so people can make more toast as we sit and talk. I always make sure there is marmalade (because I like marmalade and so does my friend Stuart). Reinier puts chillies in the baked beans.

And it is the great feast. And it's the new world coming. And it's everything I could ever wish for. Right here. Right now.

Monday 8 November

Still scheduling some recordings, still dealing with some technical problems, still trying to find people who said they would record for us, but came to COP and then just disappeared in the chaos of it all. But we are nearly there now. Most of the work is done and it's good work, and so varied.

Last week I recorded two sessions in one day. The first was with Catherine Keller. She is wonderful. The most wonderful theologian in the world, I think. Shy, intense, ferociously intelligent, terrifying and tender. She spoke about the sources of her relational theology in ancient theological understandings of theopoesis, the divine presence in all things drawing them into God's very self. In the apophatic mysticism of Nicholas of Cusa who perceived the reconciliation of contradictions (in logical thinking, in relations between peoples, and between the divine and human) within 'the cloud of the impossible'. And also in the contemporary relational ontologies of the philosopher Gilles Deleuze and the physicist Karen Barad. She takes the affinity between subatomic particles as the pattern for a relational universe in which all beings and all things are ultimately entangled. I love this stuff. So good. But heady, difficult, not easy to write on a placard and march beneath it. Complex.

Only a wee break and then a recording with Amitav Ghosh, the novelist and climate activist, my gentle hero, also with two of his friends, the artist Salman Toor and musician Ali Sethi. I was nervous. Very nervous. These are seriously gifted people – oh, but it was lovely. Amitav has been thinking and writing about the power of traditional sacred narratives in communicating the wisdom and imaginative vision we need to combat climate change for many years. He has despaired of traditional realist writing on a subject that is so grave, enormous, unimaginable, that it just defies expression in conventional forms. The work that he has collaborated with Salman and Ali to produce is a folk tale from the Mangrove forests of Bengal. *Jungle Nama* is a homage to the sacred protector of the forest, Bon Bibi. She regulates relations between humans and the devastating powers of floods, wild beasts, and the demonic forces of greed – whose avatar is the devouring tiger. This ballad forms an important part of the life of these precarious coastal communities and it is not written or told – it is performed. Amitav, Salman and Ali shared their 'reperformance' of it in words, art and music. It was enchanting. I am there in the tidelands facing the tiger. I had a long list of serious climate-crisis questions to ask them, but away they all went. I just let the story claim me.

Wednesday 10 November

My mind is racing, I know I'm in a state of adrenaline-fuelled overdrive which is 'not good'. I've been making practical arrangements, demonstrating, attending meetings, reading books and articles at hyper speed so I can interview intelligently. Not sleeping. Crazy tired and manic at the same time – and for what? So much energy over the past months, mine included, has gone into this focused moment when the chance to change appears briefly in our planetary skies. But the news is dismal. Not that I thought it would be good. Not that I expected … not that I ever had faith in the process. Even when I was standing on the top of the hill and looking backwards and forwards at the people, well over 100,000 the BBC says, I knew it was not enough. We were not enough. I can't bear to turn on the television, listen to the radio, check my phone. I just can't bear the blah, blah, blah. Not any more.

I go to the University Chapel for the lunchtime service. We invited some of the brothers from Taizé to visit us for COP and they have brought with them a beautiful Taizé crucifix. Seeing it took me right back to the vivid colours, the incense, the icons and the candles of their abbey where I knelt as a teenager in such a passion of young faith. They also brought with them silence. I had forgotten the power of that silence. Minutes and minutes pass and each one is deeper than the last, and I am drawn down and down into something that is not safety, not comfort, not hopeful and bright, but the space of the impossible, the luminous darkness.

This is where I want to live now. Not in the light but in this place where pain and loss compress into an immense density, into the impossible energy of transfiguration.

Where silence becomes music which gathers and grows and swells into praise.

Epilogue: Not a Conclusion but a Connection

I had thought to end this book where the previous chapter finished. Where God was encountered in both abyss and glory. I considered that was a good place to stop and to stay. But my editor had other thoughts. David Shervington gently suggested that it would be good to include an 'epilogue or conclusion … just to tie things up'.

My initial response to this suggestion was not positive. Did he not get it that the whole purpose of this book was to untie things? To render them less neatly bound up and to unravel some of the knots that hold practical theology in place? However, on reflection I changed my mind. Actually, this book can be seen as an extended exercise in bringing things together, exploring relationship and relationality, making connections and daring to hope these might become transformative. So perhaps it is worth expending just a few more words on where I think these connections might be formed.

First, some connections need to be made in relation to this work itself. It is a peculiar ragbag of a book and it is deeply imprinted with my own character and personality. This has some positive aspects. It is clear I am advocating for certain things, worried about others and want to make some offerings to the field. However, it also betrays my particular take on things. For example, I often approach things in quite a theoretical way (I do love a good theory) and give less attention to specific practices and to alternative ways of being in the world. So when I address the theme of relationality, for example, I do so through the work of 'big white thinkers'. It could have been better addressed, perhaps, through focusing on the visions and actions of people in networks of resistance, or through an engagement with indigenous sacred traditions or contemporary spiritual activism. These may well have been better places for a practical theologian to begin. But they are not the places I inhabit or where I am able to speak from.

EPILOGUE: NOT A CONCLUSION BUT A CONNECTION

While I acknowledge the perspectives I have employed are idiosyncratic, I am nevertheless comforted by Donna Haraway's insistence that the generation of transformative praxis is a communal process (1988). It requires contributions that originate in a wide variety of located and particular contexts. As people committed to change connect up their situated knowledges, our understanding can be expanded, modified and critiqued. It is my hope that my friends and colleagues in practical theology will connect their work to mine and that some of the weaknesses in my writing will be remedied through our conversational work.

So naturally I also hope that this book encourages actual connections between colleagues in practical theology and enables us to talk honestly and generatively about some issues that we may not have addressed communally in the past. I have good reasons for hope here. One of the most encouraging aspects of this writing journey has been the generous support I have received 'along the way' from people whose perspectives differ from my own but who have wished to engage in deeper dialogue about ways of working that matter to us all.

Of particular significance in these conversations has been the 'theological' vocation of practical theology. This concern is central to all my work. I believe that we have a responsibility to bring our empirical, and indeed our creative, research into connection with theological reflection rather than continually offering up insights concerning local practice to ghostly presences somewhere-out-there who we fondly hope will transubstantiate these for us. This will not happen. Theological work is our job to do and there is nobody else who is going to do it on our behalf. But perhaps we need to widen our affinity circles as we embark on this task.

I discern a growing sense among us that discrete boundaries between the theological disciplines have outlived their usefulness.[1] I am very glad of that. Not least because the space allotted to practical theology was one of domestic utility in which practical theologians were not really expected to conceptualize or create. We made this space our own, found many ways to contribute from within it. What we have learned here about the significance of practice for theology will remain our particular charism. However, we need to forge deeper connections with construc-

---

[1] It is hard to place some of today's most creative theologians in one 'camp' or another. I think, for example, of Karen O'Donnell, Shelly Rambo, Cláudio Carvalhaes, Willie Jenkins, Callid Keefe-Perry and many others whose work defies such demarcations.

tive and systematic theologians as we share the resources we need for theological existence today. It's time to leave the house and join the conversations taking place outside. Nor should our conversations be with theologians alone.

Anna Tsing's description of a latent commons emerging on the unkempt verges of the current order has been a guiding image throughout this work. This imagined space is one in which 'mutualist and nonantagonistic entanglements [are] found within the play of this confusion' (2015, p. 55). This vision of sharing, surviving and growing together 'in the commons' contrasts with some of the forms of theological separatism that have developed within practical theology over the years. These have stressed the importance of nurturing our own domain rather than mingling in the confusion of open and unregulated spaces. This does not mean I cannot appreciate why van der Ven advocated for intradisciplinary processes in research or sympathize with what lay behind Frei and Lindbeck's visions of a coherent discursive community in contemporary Babel. I register the radical appeal of notions of an alternative, countercultural Ecclesia offering generous hospitality while preserving its own distinctive character, and feel within myself the theological anxieties that notions of merging and mixing provoke.

But in this crisis time I do not think the preservation of theological discreteness should predominate. Connections are what matter now. Not just because when the tides rise the islands are flooded first. Nor because making connections gifts us with the resilient wisdom that others can offer. It is not even that there is a missional imperative to incarnate God's presence through being alongside others in the troubles. Although all of those things are true and important there is something else to register here.

The reason why relations, relationality and connection matter so much is that a huge shift is taking place in the way human beings perceive themselves and their place in the world. As I have discussed, this 'cosmological' change may be communicated using metaphors from the sciences that refer to the associative properties of particles or the intertwined processes of fungal life. It can also be traced in symbols drawn from the imaginaries of philosophy, the social sciences, indigenous religions and the animisms of new materialism. All of these illuminate in their diverse ways the interwoven threads that form the tapestry of existence. They reveal an astounding interconnectedness as the very fabric of the universe and they have erupted into prominence because they address our current context in which 'the whole world is finding itself tipped into a new cosmological situation and confronted with precarity' (Latour, 2024, p. 8).

It is the crises we are facing that have proliferated images of connection out of which a new cosmology is being born. By attending to their contemporary cultural manifestations we are reading the signs of these times. We are also discerning revelations of the living God. I believe that we are being powerfully addressed and must respond at all levels – spiritually, politically and theologically.

Previously established theological frameworks have separated out rather than connected up; dividing immanence from transcendence, earth from heaven, and people from the kin creatures of this planet and the material web of life. However, we have within our sacred traditions resources that enable us to imagine faithfully in other ways. As Latour bluntly puts it in an address to Christian theologians, and to practical theologians in particular, we have the resources in incarnational theology to mark, renew and address our relations with one another, with the earth and with God. To preach a new word. 'There are, fortunately, possibilities in incarnation,' he writes. 'It's up to the theologians to find them' (Latour, 2024, p. 11).

These weighty concerns seem a long way from issues relating to research methodologies that have consumed a lot of my time and energy over the past years. However, this book has been an exercise in connecting up, and this includes connecting the micro-processes of research that occupy us on a day-to-day level with the bigger issues confronting us. I have argued that the developments in research methods and methodologies I have explored correlate with the cosmological shifts we are currently experiencing. This does not mean that I am implying that any specific new (or old) approach has a special authority or status. At their most basic level, research methods are simply flawed and imperfect ways of constructing images that help us address some aspect of existence. They continually mutate and develop. But creatively engaging with them can help us see things differently, become more responsive, and thus more deeply connected to the enormous challenges before us.

I think I have done enough connecting-up-the-connections now. And it is time to finish.

I began this book by recalling the words of a prayer I say every time I step into the pulpit to preach. On each occasion I bow my head and commit my meditations to God who is my rock and my redeemer. A God who spans the contraries of eternal stability and mortal flesh.

In conclusion, I repeat the gesture I perform each time I draw an act of worship to its close. I ask for the blessings of God upon what has been gathered and shared and upon those who have come together for work and praise. I ask for the blessing of God who counters all divisions and has spoken peace to earth.

I call upon God,
Who is never one or two but always more,
Who leaks, pours, and floods into flesh and form.

I call upon God,
Who begins with what is broken,
Who enters into hell.
Who dawns in death's garden; song among the stones.

I call upon God,
Who does not refuse weak words, small actions, little lives,
Who brings all-each safe home.

I ask God's blessing on this work.

Suggested Reading in Creative Research Methods

Barone, Tom, and Eisner, Elliot W., 2011, *Arts Based Research*, Thousand Oaks, CA: Sage Publications.
Barrett, Estelle, and Bolt, Barbara (eds), 2010, *Practice as Research: Approaches to Creative Arts Inquiry*, London and New York: I. B. Tauris.
Bennett, Zoë et al., 2018, *Invitation to Research in Practical Theology*, London: Routledge.
Chilton, Gioia, and Leavy, Patricia, 2020, 'Arts-based Research Practice: Merging Social Research and the Creative Arts' in Patricia Leavy (ed.), *The Oxford Handbook of Qualitative Research*, 2nd edn, Oxford: Oxford University Press, pp. 601–32.
Cole, Arthur Riley, 2022, *This Here Flesh: Spirituality, Liberation and the Stories that Make Us*, London: Hodder and Stoughton.
Denzin, Norman, Lincoln, Yvonna, and Smith, Linda Tuhiwai (eds), 2008, *Handbook of Critical and Indigenous Methodologies*, Thousand Oaks, CA: Sage Publications.
Ellingson, Laura, 2017, *Embodiment in Qualitative Research*, New York: Routledge.
Foster, Victoria, 2016, *Collaborative Arts-based Research for Social Justice*, London: Routledge.
Goto, Courtney, 2016, *The Grace of Playing: Pedagogies for Leaning into God's New Creation*, Eugene, OR: Pickwick Publications.
Goto, Courtney, 2016, 'Reflecting Theologically by Creating Art: Giving Form to More than We Can Say', *Reflective Practice: Formation and Supervision in Ministry*, 36, pp. 78–92.
Grierson, Elizabeth, and Brearley, Laura (eds), 2009, *Creative Arts Research*, Rotterdam: Sense Publishers.
Higgs, Joyce et al. (eds), 2011, *Creative Spaces for Qualitative Researching*, Rotterdam: Sense Publishers.
Holman-Jones, Stacy (ed.), 2013, *Handbook of Autoethnography*, London and New York: Routledge.
Jennings, Willie James, 2020, *After Whiteness: An Education in Belonging*, Grand Rapids, MI: Eerdmans.
Kara, Helen, 2015, *Creative Research Methods in the Social Sciences*, Bristol: Policy Press.

Knowles, J. Gary, and Cole, Ardra L. (eds), 2008, *Handbook of the Arts in Qualitative Research*, Thousand Oaks, CA: Sage Publications.
Knudsen, Britta Timm, and Stage, Carsten, 2015, *Affective Methodologies: Developing Cultural Research Strategies for the Study of Affect*, Basingstoke: Palgrave Macmillan.
Leavy, Patricia, 2015, *Method Meets Art: Arts-based Research Practice*, 2nd edn, New York and London: The Guilford Press.
Leavy, Patricia (ed.), 2018, *Handbook of Arts-based Research*, New York and London: The Guilford Press.
Mannay, Dawn, 2015, *Visual, Narrative and Creative Research Methods*, London: Routledge.
Nelson, Robin (ed.), 2015, *Practice as Research in the Arts*, Basingstoke: Palgrave Macmillan.
Pattison, Stephen, 2007, 'Practical Theology: Art or Science?' in Stephen Pattison, *The Challenge of Practical Theology: Selected Essays*, London: Jessica Kingsley Publishers, pp. 261–89.
Peckruhn, Heike, 2017, *Meaning in Our Bodies: Sensory Experience as Constructive Theological Imagination*, Oxford: Oxford University Press.
Radford, C. L. Wren, 2021, 'Creative Arts-based Research Methods in Practical Theology: Constructing New Theologies of Practice' in Andrew P. Rodgers and Nicola Slee (eds), *Celebrating the Past, Present and Future of British and Irish Practical Theology*, London: Routledge, pp. 59–74.
Radford, C. L. Wren, 2022, *Lived Experiences and Social Transformations: Poetics, Politics and Power Relations in Practical Theology*, Leiden: Brill.
Savin-Baden, Maggie, and Wimpenny, Katherine, 2014, *A Practical Guide to Arts-related Research*, Rotterdam: Sense Publishers.
Smartt Gullion, Jessica, 2018, *Diffractive Ethnography: Social Sciences and the Ontological Turn*, New York: Routledge.
Tsing, Anna, 2015, *The Mushroom at the End of the World: On the Possibility of Life in Capitalist Ruins*, Princeton, NJ: Princeton University Press.
Walton, Heather, various articles and publications available at: https://www.gla.ac.uk/schools/critical/staff/heatherwalton/#publications,articles (accessed 02.04.2025).
Wigg-Stevenson, Natalie, 2021, *Transgressive Devotion: Theology as Performance Art*, London: SCM Press.

Bibliography

Aist, Rodney, 2017, 'Pilgrimage in the Celtic Christian Tradition', *Perichoresis*, 15(1), pp. 3–19.
Anderson, Linda, 2004, *Autobiography*, London and New York: Routledge.
Auerbach, Erich, 1953, *Mimesis: The Representation of Reality in Western Literature*, Princeton, NJ: Princeton University Press.
Banner, Michael, 2016, *The Ethics of Everyday Life: Moral Theology, Social Anthropology, and the Imagination of the Human*, Oxford: Oxford University Press.
Barad, Karen, 2014, 'Diffracting Diffraction: Cutting Together-Apart', *Parallax*, 20(3), pp. 168–87.
Barnard, Marcel, 2022, 'Aesthetics and Religion' in Birgit Weyel et al. (eds), *The International Handbook of Practical Theology: A Global Approach*, Berlin: De Gruyter, pp. 13–27.
Bass, Dorothy et al., 2016a, 'Framing: Engaging the Intelligence of Practice' in Dorothy Bass et al., *Christian Practical Wisdom: What It Is, Why It Matters*, Grand Rapids, MI: Eerdmans, pp. 1–20.
Bass, Dorothy et al., 2016b, 'Collaborating: An Invitation to Experiment, an Expression of Thanks' in Dorothy Bass et al., *Christian Practical Wisdom: What It Is, Why It Matters*, Grand Rapids, MI: Eerdmans, pp. 325–33.
Beaudoin, Tom, 2016, 'Why Does Practice Matter Theologically?' in Bonnie J. Miller-McLemore and Joyce Ann Mercer (eds), *Conundrums in Practical Theology*, Leiden: Brill, pp. 8–32.
Behar, Ruth, 1995, 'Introduction: Out of Exile' in Ruth Behar and Deborah A. Gordon (eds), *Women Writing Culture: A Reader in Feminist Ethnography*, Berkeley, CA: University of California Press, pp. 1–32.
Behar, Ruth, 2003, 'Ethnography and the Book that was Lost', *Ethnography*, 4(1), pp. 15–39.
Benjamin, Walter, 1999, *The Arcades Project*, trans. Eiland Howard and Kevin McLaughlin, Cambridge, MA: Harvard University Press.
Benjamin, Walter, 2015, *Illuminations*, trans. Harry Zorn, London: The Bodley Head.
Bennett, Jane, 2001, *The Enchantment of Modern Life: Attachments, Crossings and Ethics*, Princeton, NJ: Princeton University Press.
Bennett, Jane, 2004, 'The Force of Things: Steps Toward an Ecology of Matter', *Political Theory*, 32, pp. 347–72.
Bennett, Zoë et al., 2018, *Invitation to Research in Practical Theology*, London: Routledge.

Bialecki, Jon, 2018, 'Anthropology and Theology in Parallax', *Anthropology of This Century*, 22 (no page numbers: online only), http://aotcpress.com/articles/anthropology-theology-parallax/ (accessed 22.12.2024).
Bielo, James S., 2018a, 'Anthropology, Theology, Critique', *Critical Research on Religion*, 6(1), pp. 28–34.
Bielo, James S., 2018b, 'An Anthropologist is Listening' in Derrick Lemons (ed.), *Theologically Engaged Anthropology*, Oxford: Oxford University Press, pp. 140–55.
Blake, William, 1970, *Songs of Innocence and Experience: Shewing the Two Contrary States of the Human Soul*, Oxford: Oxford University Press.
Bochner, Arthur, and Riggs, Nicholas, 2014, 'Practicing Narrative Inquiry' in Patricia Leavy (ed.), *The Oxford Handbook of Qualitative Research*, Oxford: Oxford University Press, pp. 195–222.
Bons-Storm, Riet, n.d., 'The Birth of the IAPT, a Personal Impression', https://www.ia-practicaltheology.org/history/ (accessed 03.09.2024).
Bouchard, Gianna, and Duggan, Patrick (eds), 2019, *Performance Research Special Edition*, 24(5).
Brady, Ivan, 2004, 'In Defense of the Sensual: Meaning Construction in Ethnography and Poetics', *Qualitative Inquiry*, 10, pp. 622–44, doi: 10.1177/1077800404265719.
Brearley, Laura, and Hamm, Treahna, 2009, 'Ways of Looking and Listening: Stories from the Spaces Between Indigenous and Non-indigenous Knowledge Systems' in Elizabeth Grierson and Laura Brearley (eds), *Creative Arts Research: Narratives of Methodologies and Practices*, Rotterdam: Sense Publishers.
Britton, Alison, 2013, 'Overthrowing Tradition' in Jo Dahn and Jeffrey Jones (eds), *Interpreting Ceramics: Selected Essays*, Bath: Wunderkamer Press, pp. 36–43.
Brown, D., 2017, *Divine Generosity and Human Creativity: Theology through Symbol, Painting and Architecture*, London: Routledge.
Brown, D., Davaney, S. G., and Tanner, K. (eds), 2001, *Converging on Culture: Theologians in Dialogue with Cultural Analysis and Criticism*, Oxford: Oxford University Press, pp. 56–70.
Brown, Richard, 1989, *A Poetic for Sociology: Towards a Logic of Discovery for the Human Sciences*, Chicago, IL: Chicago University Press.
Browning, Don S., 1991, *A Fundamental Practical Theology: Descriptive and Strategic Proposals*, Minneapolis, MN: Fortress Press.
Cahalan, Kathleen A., 2016, 'Unknowing: Spiritual Practices and the Search for a Wisdom Epistemology' in Dorothy Bass et al., *Christian Practical Wisdom: What It Is, Why It Matters*, Grand Rapids, MI: Eerdmans, pp. 273–323.
Cameron, Helen et al., 2010, *Talking About God in Practice: Theological Action Research and Practical Theology*, London: SCM Press.
Campbell, Eilidh, 2021, *Motherhood and Autism: An Embodied Theology of Mothering and Disability*, London: SCM Press.
Campbell-Reed, Eileen R., and Scharen, Christian, 2013, 'Ethnography on Holy Ground: How Qualitative Interviewing is Practical Theological Work', *International Journal of Practical Theology*, 17(2), pp. 232–59.
Caputo, John, 2006, *The Weakness of God: A Theology of the Event*, Bloomington, IN: Indiana University Press.

Carvalhaes, Cláudio, 2021, 'Decoloniality: Theory and Methodology' in Valburga Schmiedt Streck, Júlio Cézar Adam, and Cláudio Carvalhaes (eds), *(De)coloniality and Religious Practices: Liberating Hope*, Tübingen: Index Theologicus, pp. 13–22.

Childers, Sara, 2014, 'Promiscuous Analysis in Qualitative Research', *Qualitative Inquiry*, 20(6), pp. 819–26.

Chilton, Gioia, and Leavy, Patricia, 2014, 'Arts-based Research Practice: Merging Social Research and the Creative Arts' in Patricia Leavy (ed.), *The Oxford Handbook of Qualitative Research*, Oxford: Oxford University Press, pp. 601–24.

Chopp, R., 2001, 'Theology and the Poetics of Testimony' in D. Brown, S. G. Davaney and K. Tanner (eds), *Converging on Culture: Theologians in Dialogue with Cultural Analysis and Criticism*, Oxford: Oxford University Press, pp. 56–70.

Coakley, Sarah, and Robbins, Joel, 2018, 'Anthropological and Theological Responses to Theologically Engaged Anthropology' in J. Derrick Lemons (ed.), *Theologically Engaged Anthropology*, Oxford: Oxford University Press, pp. 355–76.

Cole, Arthur Riley, 2022, *This Here Flesh: Spirituality, Liberation and the Stories that Make Us*, London: Hodder and Stoughton.

Connolly, William, 2012, *The Fragility of Things*, Durham, NC: Duke University Press.

Couture, Pamela, 2016, *We Are Not All Victims: Local Peacebuilding in the People's Republic of Congo*, Münster: LIT Verlag.

Dawney, Leila, 2020, 'Decommissioned Places: Ruins, Endurance and Care at the End of the First Nuclear Age', *Transactions of the Institute of British Geographers*, pp. 45, 33–49.

de Certeau, Michel, 1984, *The Practice of Everyday Life*, trans. Steven Rendall, Berkeley, CA: University of California Press.

de Certeau, Michel, 1985, *Heterologies: Discourse on the Other*, trans. Brian Massumi, Minneapolis, MN: Minnesota University Press.

de Certeau, Michel, 1995, *The Mystic Fable, Volume One, The Sixteenth and Seventeenth Centuries*, trans. Michael Smith, Chicago, IL: University of Chicago Press.

de Certeau, Michel, Giard, Luce, and Mayol, Pierre, 1998, *The Practice of Everyday Life, vol. 2: Living and Cooking*, Minneapolis, MN: University of Minnesota Press.

de Freitas, Elizabeth, 2016, 'The New Empiricism of the Fractal Fold: Rethinking Monadology in Digital Times', *Cultural Studies ↔ Critical Methodologies*, 16(2), pp. 224–34.

de Roest, Henk, 2019, *Collaborative Practical Theology: Engaging Practitioners in Research on Christian Practice*, Berlin: Brill.

Deleuze, Gilles, 1993, *The Fold: Leibniz and the Baroque*, trans. Tom Conley, Minneapolis, MN: University of Minnesota Press.

Deleuze, Gilles, and Guattari, Felix, 1987, *A Thousand Plateaus: Capitalism and Schizophrenia*, Minneapolis, MN: University of Minnesota Press.

Denzin, Norman, 2003, *Performance Ethnography: Critical Pedagogy and the Politics of Culture*, Thousand Oaks, CA and London: Sage Publications.
Denzin, Norman, Lincoln, Yvonna, and Smith, Linda Tuhiwai (eds), 2008, *Handbook of Critical and Indigenous Methodologies*, Thousand Oaks, CA: Sage Publications.
Denzin, Norman, and Lincoln, Yvonna (eds), 2018, *The Sage Handbook of Qualitative Research*, 5th edn, Thousand Oaks, CA and London: Sage Publications.
Denzin, Norman, and Salvo, James, 2020, *New Directions in Theorizing Qualitative Research: Performance as Resistance*, Gorham, ME: Myers Education Press.
Derrida, Jacques, 2001, *Writing and Difference*, trans. Alan Bass, 2nd rev. edn, New York and London: Routledge.
Dewing, Jan, 2011, 'Bringing Merleau Ponty's Inspirations to the Doing of Research' in Joy Higgs et al. (eds), *Creative Spaces for Qualitative Researching*, Rotterdam: Sense Publishers, pp. 65–76.
Dillard, Cynthia B., 2008, 'When the Ground is Black, the Ground is Fertile: Exploring Endarkened Feminist Epistemology and Healing Methodologies in the Spirit' in Norman K. Denzin, Yvonna S. Lincoln, and Linda Tuhiwai Smith (eds), *Handbook of Critical and Indigenous Methodologies*, Thousand Oaks, CA: Sage Publications.
Dillard, Cynthia, and Bell, Charlotte, 2011, 'Endarkened Feminism and Sacred Praxis: Troubling (Auto)Ethnography through Critical Engagements with African Indigenous Knowledges' in George J. Sefa Dei (ed.), *Indigenous Philosophies and Critical Education: A Reader*, Lausanne: Peter Lang, pp. 337–49.
Dilworth, Thomas, 2017, *David Jones, Engraver, Soldier, Painter, Poet*, London: Jonathan Cape.
Driscoll, Christopher, and Miller, Monica, 2018, *Method as Identity: Manufacturing Distance in the Academic Study of Religion*, Lanham, MD: Lexington Books.
Dudley, Carl (ed.), 1983, *Building Effective Ministry: Theory and Practice in the Local Church*, San Francisco, CA: Harper & Row.
Dulles, Avery, 1974, *Models of the Church*, New York: Image Books.
Ellingson, Laura, 2017, *Embodiment in Qualitative Research*, New York: Routledge.
Ellingson, Laura, and Sotirin, Patty, 2020, *Making Data in Qualitative Research: Engagements, Ethics, and Entanglements*, New York: Routledge.
Essén, Anna, and Värlander, Sara Winterstorm, 2012, 'The Mutual Constitution of Sensuous and Discursive Understanding in Scientific Practice: An Autoethnographic Lens on Academic Writing', *Management Learning*, 44(4), pp. 395–423.
Evans, Alice, and Evans, Robert, 1983, 'The Case of Wiltshire Church: A Narrative' in Carl Dudley (ed.), *Building Effective Ministry: Theory and Practice in the Local Church*, San Francisco, CA: Harper & Row, pp. 4–20.
Fassin, Didier (ed.), 2012, *A Companion to Moral Anthropology*, Oxford: Wiley-Blackwell.
Fassin, Didier, 2014, 'The Ethical Turn in Anthropology: Promises and Uncertainties', *HAU: Journal of Ethnographic Theory*, 4(1), pp. 429–35.

Finley, Susan, 2008, 'Arts-based Research' in J. Gary Knowles and Arda L. Cole (eds), *Handbook of the Arts in Qualitative Research: Perspectives, Methodologies, Examples, and Issues*, Thousand Oaks, CA: Sage Publications, pp. 71–82.

Foster, Victoria, 2016, *Collaborative Arts-based Research for Social Justice*, London: Routledge.

Fountain, Philip, and Lau, Sin Wen, 2013, 'Anthropological Theologies: Engagements and Encounters', *The Australian Journal of Anthropology*, 24(3), pp. 227–34.

Fournier, Matt, 2014, 'Lines of Flight', *TSQ: Transgender Studies Quarterly*, 1(1–2) (double edn), pp. 121–2.

Frei, Hans, 1993, *Theology and Narrative: Selected Essays* in George Hunsinger and William C. Placher (eds), New York and Oxford: Oxford University Press.

Ganzevoort, Ruard, 2004, 'Van der Ven's Empirical/Practical Theology and the Theological Encyclopaedia' in Chris Hermans and Mary Elizabeth Moore (eds), *Hermeneutics and Empirical Research in Practical Theology: The Contribution of Empirical Theology by Johannes A. van der Ven*, Leiden: Brill, pp. 53–74.

Gell, Alfred, 1998, *Art and Agency: An Anthropological Theory*, Oxford: Clarendon Press.

Ghosh, Amitav, 2016, *The Great Derangement: Climate Change and the Unthinkable*, Chicago, IL: University of Chicago Press.

Ghosh, Amitav, 2021, *Jungle Nama*, London: John Murray Press.

Gibbs, Anna, 2015, 'Writing as Method: Attunement, Resonance, and Rhythm' in Britta Timm Knudsen and Carsten Stage, *Affective Methodologies: Developing Cultural Research Strategies for the Study of Affect*, Basingstoke: Palgrave Macmillan, pp. 222–36.

Gibbs, Leah, 2014, 'Arts–Science Collaboration, Embodied Research Methods, and the Politics of Belonging: Site Works and the Shoalhaven River, Australia', *Cultural Geographies*, 21(2), pp. 207–27.

Glissant, Édouard, 2020, *Treatise on the Whole-World*, trans. Celia Britton, Liverpool: Liverpool University Press.

Goto, Courtney, 2016, *The Grace of Playing: Pedagogies for Leaning into God's New Creation*, Eugene, OR: Wipf and Stock Publishers.

Goto, Courtney, 2018, *Taking on Practical Theology: The Idolization of Context and the Hope of Community*, Leiden: Brill.

Graham, Elaine, 2013a, *Between a Rock and a Hard Place: Public Theology in a Post-Secular Age*, London: SCM Press.

Graham, Elaine, 2013b, 'Is Practical Theology a form of Action Research?', *International Journal of Practical Theology*, 17(1), pp. 148–78.

Graham, Elaine, 2017a, *Apologetics without Apology: Speaking of God in a World Troubled by Religion*, Eugene, OR: Cascade Books.

Graham, Elaine, 2017b, 'On Becoming a Practical Theologian: Past, Present and Future Tenses', *HTS Teologiese Studies/Theological Studies*, 73(4), a4634, https://doi.org/10.4102/hts.v73i4.4634.

Graham, Elaine, 2023, '"Another World?": Practical Wisdom for the End-Times', *International Journal of Practical Theology*, 27(2), pp. 179–96.

Graham, Elaine, Walton, Heather, and Ward, Frances, 2019, *Theological Reflection Methods*, 2nd edn, London: SCM Press.

Hallonsten, Simon, 2024, *Online Small Groups as Sites of Teaching: An Action Research Dissertation into Christian Religious Education in the Church of Sweden*, Stockholm: Enskilda Högskolan.

Hammersley, Martyn, 2010, 'Research, Art, or Politics: Which Is It To Be?', *International Review of Qualitative Research*, 3(1), pp. 5–9.

Hand, Brian, 2015, 'A Struggle at the Roots of the Mind', *Imma Magazine*, 11 November, https://imma.ie/magazine/a-struggle-at-the-roots-of-the-mind-service-and-solidarity-in-dialogical-relational-and-collaborative-perspectives-within-contemporary-art/ (accessed 12.12.2024).

Haraway, Donna, 1988, 'Situated Knowledges: The Science Question in Feminism and the Privilege of Partial Perspective', *Feminist Studies*, 14(3), pp. 575–99.

Haraway, Donna, 2016, *Staying with the Trouble: Making Kin in the Chthulucene*, Durham, NC: Duke University Press.

Harding, Sandra, 1991, *Whose Science? Whose Knowledge? Thinking from Women's Lives*, Ithaca, NY: Cornell University Press.

Hartley, N., 2012, 'Spirituality and the Arts: Discovering what Really Matters' in M. Cobb et al. (eds), *Oxford Textbook of Spirituality in Healthcare*, Oxford: Oxford University Press, pp. 265–71.

Hauerwas, S., 1978, 'Jesus, the Story of the Kingdom', *Theology Digest*, 26(4) (Winter 1978), pp. 3–24.

Hauerwas, S., 1981, *A Community of Character: Toward a Constructive Christian Social Ethic*, Notre Dame, IN: University of Notre Dame Press.

Hocking, Jeffrey S., 2015, 'Risking Idolatry? Theopoetics and the Promise of Embodiment', *Theopoetics: A Journal of Theological Imagination, Literature, Embodiment, and Aesthetics*, 1(2), pp. 17–42.

Hopewell, James, 1988, *Congregation: Stories and Structures*, London: SCM Press.

Howard, Eiland, and McLaughlin, Kevin, 1999, 'Translators' Foreword' in Walter Benjamin, *The Arcades Project*, Cambridge, MA: Harvard University Press.

Hustvedt, Siri, 2003, *What I Loved*, London: Sceptre.

Hustvedt, Siri, 2005, *Mysteries of the Rectangle: Essays on Painting*, New York: Princeton Architectural Press.

Hustvedt, Siri, 2012, *Living, Thinking, Looking*, London: Sceptre.

Hustvedt, Siri, 2016, *A Woman Looking at Men Looking at Women: Essays on Art, Sex, and the Mind*, London: Hodder & Stoughton, Kindle edn.

Ideström, Jonas, and Kaufman, Tone Stangeland, 2018a, 'Why Matter Matters in Theological Action Research: Attending to the Voices of Tradition', *International Journal of Practical Theology*, 22(1), pp. 84–102.

Ideström, Jonas, and Kaufman, Tone Stangeland, 2018b, *What Really Matters: Scandinavian Perspectives on Ecclesiology and Ethnography*, Eugene, OR: Pickwick Publications.

Ideström, Jonas, and Kaufman, Tone Stangeland, 2018c, 'The Researcher as Gamemaker: Response' in Jonas Ideström and Tone Stangeland Kaufman, *What Really Matters: Scandinavian Perspectives on Ecclesiology and Ethnography*, Eugene, OR: Pickwick Publications, pp. 173–81.

Ingold, Tim, 2017, 'Anthropology Contra Ethnography', *HAU: Journal of Ethnographic Theory*, 7(1), pp. 21–6.

Ingold, Tim, 2018, 'Art and Anthropology for a Living World', https://chaire-arts-sciences.org/wp-content/uploads/2018/05/Art-and-Anthropology-for-a-Living-World-DEF.pdf, pp. 1–10 (accessed 10.12.2024).
Ingold, Tim, 2020, *Correspondences*, Cambridge: Polity Press.
Inhorn, Marcia, and Birenbaum-Carmeli, Daphna, 2008, 'Assisted Reproductive Technologies and Culture Change', *Annual Review of Anthropology*, 37, pp. 177–96.
Jardine, Alice, 1985, *Gynesis: Configurations of Women and Modernity*, Ithaca, NY: Cornell University Press.
Jennings, Willie James, 2020, *After Whiteness: An Education in Belonging*, Grand Rapids, MI: Eerdmans.
Jordan, Mark, 2013, 'Writing the Truth', *Practical Matters*, 6, pp. 1–5.
Kaufman, Tone Stangeland, 2016, 'From the Outside, Within or In Between? Normativity at Work in Empirical Practical Theology' in Joyce Mercer and Bonnie Miller-McLemore (eds), *Conundrums in Practical Theology*, Leiden: Brill, pp. 134–62.
Keefe-Perry, L. Callid, 2014, *Way to Water: A Theopoetics Primer*, Eugene, OR: Cascade Books.
Keller, Catherine, 2003, *The Face of the Deep: A Theology of Becoming*, New York: Routledge.
Keller, Catherine, 2007, *On the Mystery: Discerning Divinity in Process*, Minneapolis, MN: Fortress Press.
Keller, Catherine, 2011, 'The Energy We Are: A Meditation in Seven Pulsations' in Donna Bowman and Clayton Crockett (eds), *Cosmology, Ecology and the Energy of God*, New York: Fordham University Press, pp. 11–25.
Keller, Catherine, 2013, 'Theopoetics and the Pluriverse' in Roland Faber and Jeremy Fackenthal (eds), *Theopoetic Folds: Philosophizing Multifariousness*, New York: Fordham University Press, pp. 180–95.
Keller, Catherine, 2014, *Cloud of the Impossible: Negative Theology and Planetary Entanglement*, New York: Columbia University Press.
Keller, Catherine, 2017, *Intercarnations: Exercises in Theological Possibility*, New York: Fordham University Press.
Keller, Catherine, and Schneider, Laurel, 2011, 'Introduction' in Catherine Keller and Laurel Schneider (eds), *Polydoxy: Theology of Multiplicity and Relation*, New York: Routledge, pp. 1–16.
Kimmerer, Robin Wall, 2013, *Braiding Sweetgrass: Indigenous Wisdom, Scientific Knowledge, and the Teachings of Plants*, London: Penguin Books.
Kirmayer, Laurence, 1996, 'Landscapes of Memory: Trauma, Narrative and Disassociation' in P. Antze and M. Lambek (eds), *Tense Past: Cultural Essays in Trauma and Memory*, London: Routledge, pp. 173–98.
Kleinman, Adam, 2012, 'Intra-actions: An Interview with Karen Barad', *Mousse Magazine*, 34 (Summer), pp. 76–81.
Kølvraa, Christopher, 2015, 'Affect, Provocation, and Far Right Rhetoric' in Britta Timm Knudsen and Carsten Stage (eds), *Affective Methodologies: Developing Cultural Research Strategies for the Study of Affect*, Basingstoke: Palgrave Macmillan, pp. 183–200.

Krabbe, Silas C., 2016, *A Beautiful Bricolage: Theopoetics as God-Talk for Our Time*, Eugene, OR: Wipf and Stock.
Laing, Olivia, 2020, *Funny Weather: Art in an Emergency*, Basingstoke: Pan Macmillan.
Larson, Timothy, 2014, *The Slain God: Anthropologists and the Christian Faith*, Oxford: Oxford University Press.
Lather, Patti, 2016, 'Top Ten+ List: (Re)Thinking Ontology in (Post)Qualitative Research', *Cultural Studies ↔ Critical Methodologies*, 16(2), pp. 125–31.
Latour, Bruno, 1993, *We Have Never Been Modern*, trans. Catherine Porter, Cambridge, MA: Harvard University Press.
Latour, Bruno, 2024, *If We Lose the Earth We Lose Our Souls*, Cambridge: Polity Press.
Law, John, 2007, 'Making a Mess with Method' in W. Outhwaite and S. P. Turner (eds), *The Sage Handbook of Social Science Methodology*, London: Sage Publications, pp. 595–606.
Leach, Bernard, 1973, *Drawings, Verse and Belief*, London: Jupiter Books.
Leach, Bernard, 1975, *The Potter's Challenge*, New York: E. P. Dutton.
Leach, Bernard, 1978, *Beyond East and West: Memoirs, Portraits and Essays*, London: Faber and Faber.
Lefebvre, Henri, 1991, *A Critique of Everyday Life, Vol. 1*, trans. John Moore, London: Verso.
Lefebvre, Henri, 2002, *A Critique of Everyday Life, Vol. 2, Foundations for a Sociology of the Everyday*, trans. John Moore, London: Verso.
Lefebvre, Henri, 2005, *A Critique of Everyday Life, Vol. 3, From Modernity to Modernism*, trans. Gregory Elliott, London: Verso.
Lemons, Derrick, 2016, 'The Slain Resurrected God: A Reconsideration of Anthropologists and the Christian Faith', *The Cambridge Journal of Anthropology*, 34(2), pp. 141–3.
Lemons, Derrick (ed.), 2018a, *Theologically Engaged Anthropology*, Oxford: Oxford University Press.
Lemons, Derrick, 2018b, 'An Afterword: Conversations Among Theology, Anthropology, and History', *St Mark's Review*, 244, pp. 114–23.
Lévi-Strauss, Claude, 2004, *The Savage Mind*, Oxford: Oxford University Press.
Lincoln, Yvonna, and Guba, Egon, 1985, *Naturalistic Inquiry*, Thousand Oaks, CA: Sage Publications.
Lincoln, Yvonna, and Guba, Egon, 2005, 'Paradigmatic Controversies, Contradictions and Emerging Confluences' in Norman Denzin and Yvonna Lincoln (eds), *Sage Handbook of Qualitative Research*, 3rd edn, Thousand Oaks, CA: Sage Publications, pp. 193–205.
Lincoln, Yvonna, Lynham, Susan, and Guba, Egon, 2018, 'Paradigmatic Controversies, Contradictions and Emerging Confluences Revisited' in Norman Denzin and Yvonna Lincoln (eds), *Sage Handbook of Qualitative Research*, Vol. 5, pp. 108–50.
Lindbeck, George, 1984, *The Nature of Doctrine: Religion and Theology in a Postliberal Age*, Louisville, KY: Westminster John Knox Press.
Liu Wong, Maria, 2023, *On Becoming Wise Together: Learning and Leading in the City*, Grand Rapids, MI: Eerdmans.

Lovelace, Richard, 1642, 'To Althea from Prison', *Poetry Foundation*, https://www.poetryfoundation.org/poems/44657/to-althea-from-prison (accessed 22.12.2024).
MacIntyre, Alasdair, 1981, *After Virtue: A Study in Moral Theory*, Notre Dame, IN: Notre Dame Press.
McClintock Fulkerson, Mary, 2007, *Places of Redemption: Theology for a Worldly Church*, Oxford: Oxford University Press.
McFague, Sallie, 2013, *Blessed Are the Consumers: Climate Change and the Practice of Restraint*, Minneapolis, MN: Fortress Press.
McKenna, Tarquam, and Woods, Davina, 2012, 'An Indigenous Conversation: Artful Ethnography: A Pre-Colonised Collaborative Research Method?', Victoria University, https://vuir.vu.edu.au/22800/ (accessed 13.12.2024).
McLaughlin, Mary Martin, with Wheeler, Bonnie (eds), 2009, *The Letters and Associated Documents of Heloise and Abelard*, New York: Palgrave Macmillan.
Manning, Russell, 2005, *Theology at the End of Culture: Paul Tillich's Theology of Culture and Art*, Leuven: Peeters Publishers.
Manning, Russell, 2009, 'Tillich's Theology of Art' in Russell Manning (ed.), *The Cambridge Companion to Paul Tillich*, Cambridge: Cambridge University Press.
Marcus, George E., 1986, 'Problems of Ethnography in the Modern World System' in James Clifford and George Marcus (eds), *Writing Culture: The Poetics and Politics of Ethnography*, Oakland, CA: University of California Press, pp. 165–93.
Marcus, George E., and Cushman, Dick, 1982, 'Ethnographies as Texts', *Annual Review of Anthropology*, 11, pp. 25–69.
Matthews, Daniel, 2021, *Earthbound: The Aesthetics of Sovereignty in the Anthropocene*, Edinburgh: Edinburgh University Press.
May, Melanie A., 1995, *A Body Knows: A Theopoetics of Death and Resurrection*, New York: Continuum.
Mercer, Joyce Ann, and Miller-McLemore, Bonnie (eds), 2016, *Conundrums in Practical Theology*, Leiden: Brill.
Merz, Johannes, and Merz, Sharon, 2015, 'Secular and Religious Symbiosis: Strengthening Postsecular Anthropology through Commitments to Faith', pp. 1–16, https://www.academia.edu/12735521/Secular_and_Religious_Symbiosis_Strengthening_Postsecular_Anthropology_through_Commitments_to_Faith (accessed 02.09.2024).
Mews, Constant, 2002, 'Heloise and Liturgical Experience at the Paraclete', *Plainsong and Medieval Music*, 11(1), pp. 25–35.
Midgley, Mary, 1989, *Wisdom, Information and Wonder*, London: Routledge.
Midgley, Mary, 2001, *Science and Poetry*, London: Routledge.
Milbank, John, 1993, *Theology and Social Theory: Beyond Secular Reason*, Oxford: Basil Blackwell.
Miller-McLemore, Bonnie J., 1994, *Also a Mother: Work and Family as Theological Dilemmas*, Nashville, TN: Abingdon Press.
Miller-McLemore, Bonnie J., 2007, 'The Clerical Paradigm: A Fallacy of Misplaced Concreteness?', *International Journal of Practical Theology*, 11(1), pp. 19–38.

Miller-McLemore, Bonnie J., 2012a, 'Five Misunderstandings about Practical Theology', *International Journal of Practical Theology*, 16(1), pp. 5–26.

Miller-McLemore, Bonnie J. (ed.), 2012b, *The Wiley Blackwell Companion to Practical Theology*, Oxford: Wiley-Blackwell.

Miller-McLemore, Bonnie J., 2017, 'A Tale of Two Cities: The Evolution of the International Academy of Practical Theology', *HTS Teologiese Studies/Theological Studies*, 73(4), pp. 1–11.

Mockler, N., 2011, 'Being Me: In Search of Authenticity' in Joyce Higgs et al. (eds), *Creative Spaces for Qualitative Researching*, Rotterdam and Boston: Sense Publishers, pp. 159–68.

Moraga, Cherríe, and Anzaldúa, Gloria (eds), 1981, *This Bridge Called My Back: Writings by Radical Women of Color*, Watertown, MA: Persephone Press.

Morse, Janice, 2018, 'Reframing Rigour in Qualitative Inquiry' in Norman Denzin and Yvonna Lincoln (eds), *The Sage Handbook of Qualitative Research*, 5th edn, Thousand Oaks, CA and London: Sage Publications, pp. 797–819.

Morton, Timothy, 2021, *All Art Is Ecological*, London: Penguin Books.

Moschella, Mary Clark, and Willhauck, Susan (eds), 2018, *Qualitative Research in Theological Education: Pedagogy in Practice*, London: SCM Press.

Murray, Simon, 2020, *Performing Ruins*, Basingstoke: Palgrave Macmillan.

Niebuhr, Helmut Richard, 1951, *Christ and Culture*, New York: Harper and Brothers.

Nordstrom, Susan, 2013, 'Object-Interviews: Folding, Unfolding, and Refolding Perceptions of Objects', *International Journal of Qualitative Methods*, 12, pp. 237–57.

O'Donnell, Karen, 2022, *The Dark Womb: Reconceiving Theology through Reproductive Loss*, London: SCM Press.

O'Donnell Gandolfo, Elizabeth, 2018, 'Encountering God and Being Human "Where the Wild Things Are": Maternal Experiences as an Eco-feminist Source for Theological Anthropology', *Louvain Studies*, 41(3), pp. 298–316.

Orye, Lieve, 2018, 'Weaving Theological Anthropology into Life: Editorial Conclusions in Correspondence with Tim Ingold', *Louvain Studies*, 41(3), pp. 328–55.

Papailias, Penelope, 2021, 'Data-Stories for Post-Ethnography', *Entanglements*, 4(1), pp. 176–98.

Pattison, Stephen, 2007, 'Practical Theology: Art or Science?' in Stephen Pattison, *The Challenge of Practical Theology: Selected Essays*, pp. 261–89.

Pearl, Monica, 2018, 'Theory and the Everyday', *Angelaki*, 23(1), pp. 199–203.

Peckruhn, Heike, 2017, *Meaning in Our Bodies: Sensory Experience as Constructive Theological Imagination*, Oxford: Oxford University Press.

Pillow, Wanda S., 2003, 'Confession, Catharsis, or Cure? Rethinking the Uses of Reflexivity as Methodological Power in Qualitative Research', *International Journal of Qualitative Studies in Education*, 16(2), pp. 175–96.

Pratt, Mary Louise, 1986, 'Fieldwork in Common Places' in James Clifford and George Marcus (eds), *Writing Culture: The Poetics and Politics of Ethnography*, Berkeley, CA: University of California Press, pp. 27–50.

Price, Joseph L., 1986, 'Expressionism and Ultimate Reality: Paul Tillich's Theology of Art', *Soundings: An Interdisciplinary Journal*, 69(4), pp. 479–98.

Pryor, Rebekah, 2022, *Motherly: Reimagining the Maternal Body in Feminist Theology and Contemporary Art*, London: SCM Press.
Radford, C. L. Wren, 2021, 'Creative Arts-based Research Methods in Practical Theology: Constructing New Theologies of Practice' in Andrew P. Rogers and Nicola Slee (eds), *Celebrating the Past, Present and Future of British and Irish Practical Theology*, London: Routledge, pp. 59–74.
Radford, C. L. Wren, 2022, *Lived Experiences and Social Transformations: Poetics, Politics and Power Relations in Practical Theology*, Leiden: Brill.
Radford, C. L. Wren, 2023, '"My Body Is Where I Exist": Poverty, Disability, and Embodied Resistance as a Theology of Practice', *International Journal of Practical Theology*, 27(1), pp. 62–79.
Radford, C. L. Wren, 2024, Private correspondence by email with the author, 9.10.2024.
Ragoné, Helena, 1996, 'Chasing the Blood Tie: Surrogate Mothers, Adoptive Mothers and Fathers', *American Ethnologist*, 23(2), pp. 352–65.
Rambo, Shelly, 2010, *Spirit and Trauma: A Theology of Remaining*, Louisville, KY: Westminster John Knox Press.
Rambo, Shelly, 2017, *Resurrecting Wounds: Living in the Aftermath of Trauma*, Waco, TX: Baylor University Press.
Rancière, Jacques, 2006, *The Politics of Aesthetics: The Distribution of the Sensible*, trans. Gabriel Rockhill, New York: Continuum.
Rancière, Jacques, 2015, 'The Politics of Art: An Interview with Jacques Rancière', *Verso*, https://www.versobooks.com/en-gb/blogs/news/2320-the-politics-of-art-an-interview-with-jacques-ranciere (accessed 12.12.2024).
Rawlins, William K., 2007, 'Living Scholarship: A Field Report', *Communication Methods and Measures*, 1(1), pp. 55–63.
Reda, Nevin, 2018, 'Muslim Studies at Emmanuel College: The Opportunities and Challenges of Intercultural Pedagogies and Emerging Epistemologies', *The Muslim World*, 108(2), pp. 218–37.
Rich, Adrienne, 1978, *The Dream of a Common Language*, New York: W. W. Norton.
Richardson, Laurel, 2000, 'Writing: A Method of Inquiry' in Norman Denzin and Yvonna Lincoln (eds), *Handbook of Qualitative Research*, 2nd edn, Thousand Oaks, CA: Sage Publications, pp. 923–48.
Ricoeur, Paul, 1985, *Time and Narrative, Volume Two*, Chicago, IL: University of Chicago Press.
Riley, Cole Arthur, 2022, *This Here Flesh: Spirituality, Liberation, and the Stories That Make Us*, New York: Penguin Random House.
Rivera, Mayra, 2007, *The Touch of Transcendence: A Postcolonial Theology of God*, Louisville, KY: Westminster John Knox Press.
Robbins, Joel, 2006, 'Anthropology and Theology: An Awkward Relationship?', *Anthropological Quarterly*, 79(2), pp. 285–94.
Robbins, Joel, 2020, *Theology and the Anthropology of Christian Life*, Oxford: Oxford University Press.
Ruys, Juanita Feros, 2002, 'Planctus magis quam cantici: The generic significance of Abelard's planctus', *Plainsong and Medieval Music*, 11(1), pp. 37–44.

St. Pierre, Elizabeth A., 2016, 'The Empirical and the New Empiricisms', *Cultural Studies ↔ Critical Methodologies*, 16(2), pp. 111–24.
St. Pierre, Elizabeth A., 2020, 'Post Qualitative Inquiry, the Refusal of Method and the Risk of the New' in Norman Denzin and Michael D. Giardina (eds), *Qualitative Inquiry and the Politics of Resistance: Possibilities, Performances and Praxis*, New York: Routledge, pp. 12–23.
St. Pierre, Elizabeth A., Jackson, Alecia Y., and Mazzei, Lisa A., 2016, 'New Empiricisms and New Materialisms: Conditions for New Inquiry', *Cultural Studies ↔ Critical Methodologies*, 16(2), pp. 99–110.
Sedgwick, Eve K., 2003, 'Paranoid Reading and Reparative Reading; Or, You're So Paranoid, You Probably Think This Essay Is About You' in Eve Sedgwick, *Touching Feeling: Affect, Pedagogy, Performativity*, Durham, NC: Duke University Press, pp. 123–52.
Segarra, Judit Onsès, Segovia, Sara Victoria Carrasco, and Sancho-Gil, Juana María, 2024, 'Secondary School Teachers' Learning Cartographies as Experiences of Being Affected' in Sara Victoria Carrasco Segovia, Fernando Hernández Hernández, and Juana María Sancho-Gil (eds), *Affective Cartographies: Affinities and Affects in Arts, Research, and Pedagogies*, Cham: Palgrave Macmillan, pp. 137–56.
Segovia, Sara Victoria Carrasco, Hernández Hernández, Fernando, and Sancho-Gil, Juana María, 2024, 'Exploring Relationships Between Affects and Different Cartographical Conceptions in Various Contexts and Educational Research Settings' in Sara Victoria Carrasco Segovia, Fernando Hernández Hernández, and Juana María Sancho-Gil (eds), *Affective Cartographies: Affinities and Affects in Arts, Research, and Pedagogies*, Cham: Palgrave Macmillan, pp. 1–15.
Sheldrake, Philip, 2012, 'Michel de Certeau: Spirituality and the Practice of Everyday Life', *Spiritus: A Journal of Christian Spirituality*, 12(2), pp. 207–16.
Slee, Nicola, 2011, *Seeking the Risen Christa*, London: SPCK.
Slee, Nicola, 2017, 'Poetry as Feminist Research Methodology in the Study of Female Faith', in Nicola Slee, Fran Porter, and Anne Phillips (eds), *Researching Female Faith: Qualitative Methods*, London: Routledge, pp. 37–53.
Slee, Nicola, 2019, *Sabbath: The Hidden Heartbeat of our Lives*, London: DLT.
Slee, Nicola, 2020, *Fragments for Fractured Times: What Feminist Practical Theology Brings to the Table*, London: SCM Press.
Smartt Gullion, Jessica, 2018, *Diffractive Ethnography: Social Sciences and the Ontological Turn*, New York: Routledge.
Smith, Christopher, 2023, '"The Darkness Thinking the Light": Imagination Infrastructure for the Present Day', unpublished lecture, University of Glasgow, delivered 7 June 2023.
Spry, Tami, 2011, *Body, Paper, Stage: Writing and Performing Autoethnography*, Left Coast Press, CA: Walnut Creek.
Staude, John-Raphael, 2005, 'Autobiography as a Spiritual Practice', *Journal of Gerontological Social Work*, 45(3), pp. 249–69.
Strom, Kathryn, and Mills, Tammy, 2024, 'Enacting Affirmative Ethics through Autotheory: Sense-making with Affect during COVID-19', *International Journal of Qualitative Studies in Education*, 37(3), pp. 660–75.

Stuart, Penelope, 2009, 'A Search for Sacred Bodies', *Practical Theology*, 2(1), pp. 75–91.
Swinton, John, 2012, 'Where Is Your Church? Moving Towards a Hospitable and Sanctified Ethnography' in Pete Ward (ed.), *Perspectives on Ecclesiology and Ethnography*, Grand Rapids, MI: Eerdmans, pp. 71–94.
Tanner, Kathryn, 1994, 'The Difference Theological Anthropology Makes', *Theology Today*, 50(4), pp. 567–79.
Tanner, Kathryn, 1997, *Theories of Culture: A New Agenda for Theology*, Minneapolis, MN: Fortress Press.
Tillich, Paul, 1966, *The Shaking of the Foundations*, London: Pelican.
Tillich, Paul, 1989, *On Art and Architecture*, ed. John Dillenberger and Jane Dillenberger, New York: Crossroad.
Trivelli, Elena, 2015, 'Exploring a "Remembering Crisis": "Affective Attuning" and "Assemblaged Archive" as Theoretical Frameworks and Research Methodologies' in Britta Timm Knudsen and Carsten Stage (eds), *Affective Methodologies: Developing Cultural Research Strategies for the Study of Affect*, Basingstoke: Palgrave Macmillan, pp. 119–39.
Tsing, Anna, 2015, *The Mushroom at the End of the World: On the Possibility of Life in Capitalist Ruins*, Princeton, NJ: Princeton University Press.
Tsing, Anna, and Ebron, Paulla, 1995, 'In Dialogue: Reading Across Minority Discourses' in Ruth Behar and Deborah Gordon (eds), *Women Writing Culture: A Reader in Feminist Ethnography*, Oakland, CA: University of California Press, pp. 390–411.
Turpin, Katherine, 2025, *Questioning Our Faith in Practice: Unlearning White Supremacy in Practical Theology*, Leiden: Brill.
Tveitereid, Knut, 2018, 'Making Data Speak – The Shortage of Theory for the Analysis of Qualitative Data in Practical Theology' in Jonas Ideström and Tone Stangeland Kaufman (eds), *What Really Matters: Scandinavian Perspectives on Ecclesiology and Ethnography*, Eugene, OR: Pickwick Publications, pp. 41–57.
van Deusen Hunsinger, Deborah, 1995, *Theology and Pastoral Counseling: A New Interdisciplinary Approach*, Grand Rapids, MI: Eerdmans.
van Maanen, John, 1988, *Tales from the Field*, Chicago, IL: University of Chicago Press.
van der Ven, Johannes, 1988, 'Practical Theology: From Applied to Empirical Theology', *Journal of Empirical Theology*, 1(1), pp. 7–27.
van der Ven, Johannes, 1993, *Practical Theology: An Empirical Approach*, Kampen: Kok Pharos.
van der Ven, Johannes, 1998, *God Reinvented: A Theological Search in Texts and Tables*, Leiden: Brill.
Vigen, Aana Marie and Scharen, Christian (eds), 2011, *Ethnography as Christian Theology and Ethics*, London: Continuum.
Walton, Heather, 2011, 'When Love is not True: Literature and Theology After Romance' in Heather Walton (ed.), *Literature and Theology: New Interdisciplinary Spaces*, Aldershot: Ashgate, pp. 37–54.
Walton, Heather, 2012, 'Poetics' in Bonnie Miller-McLemore (ed.), *The Wiley-Blackwell Companion to Practical Theology*, Oxford: Wiley Blackwell, pp. 183–92.

Walton, Heather, 2013, 'Desiring Things: Practical Theology and the New Materialisms' in Reinder Ruard Ganzevoort, Rein Brouwer, and Bonnie J. Miller-McLemore (eds), *City of Desires – A Place for God: Practical Theological Perspectives*, Berlin: LIT Verlag, pp. 131–40.

Walton, Heather, 2014a, *Writing Methods in Theological Reflection*, London: SCM Press.

Walton Heather, 2014b, 'Seeking Wisdom in Practical Theology', *Practical Theology*, 7(1), pp. 5–18.

Walton, Heather, 2015a, *Not Eden: Spiritual Life Writing for This World*, London: SCM Press.

Walton, Heather, 2015b, 'The Consolation of Everyday Things', *LIR Journal*, 4, pp. 138–53.

Walton, Heather, 2019a, 'A Theopoetics of Practice: Reform-ing in Practical Theology', *International Journal of Practical Theology*, 23(1), pp. 1–21.

Walton, Heather, 2019b, 'Creativity at the Edge of Chaos: Theopoetics in *A Blazing World*', *Literature & Theology*, 33(3), pp. 336–56.

Ward, Pete (ed.), 2012a, *Perspectives on Ecclesiology and Ethnography*, Grand Rapids, MI: Eerdmans.

Ward, Pete, 2012b, 'Introduction' in Pete Ward (ed.), *Perspectives on Ecclesiology and Ethnography*, Grand Rapids, MI: Eerdmans, pp. 1–11.

Ward, Pete, 2018, 'Is Theology What Really Matters?' in Jonas Idestrőm and Tone Stangeland Kaufman (eds), *What Really Matters: Scandinavian Perspectives on Ecclesiology and Ethnography*, Eugene, OR: Pickwick Publications, pp. 157–72.

Ward, Pete, 2022, 'Theology and Qualitative Research: An Uneasy Relationship' in Pete Ward and Knut Tveitereid (eds), *The Wiley Blackwell Companion to Theology and Qualitative Research*, Oxford: Wiley-Blackwell, pp. 7–15.

Ward, Pete, and Tveitereid, Knut (eds), 2022, *The Wiley Blackwell Companion to Theology and Qualitative Research*, Oxford: Wiley-Blackwell.

Watkins, Clare, 2015, 'Reflections on Particularity and Unity' in Sune Fahlgren and Jonas Idestrőm (eds), *Ecclesiology in the Trenches: Theory and Method Under Construction*, Cambridge: The Lutterworth Press, pp. 139–54.

Webb, Kate, 1994, 'Seriously Funny' in Lorna Sage (ed.), *Flesh and the Mirror: Essays on the Art of Angela Carter*, London: Virago Press, pp. 297–307.

Weyel, Birgit et al. (eds), 2022, *The International Handbook of Practical Theology: A Global Approach*, Berlin: De Gruyter.

Wheeler, Bonnie (ed.), 2000, *Listening to Heloise: The Voice of a Twelfth-century Woman*, New York: St. Martin's Press.

Whitmore, Todd D., 2019, *Imitating Christ in Magwi: An Anthropological Theology*, London: T&T Clark.

Wigg-Stevenson, Natalie, 2015, 'From Proclamation to Conversation: Ethnographic Disruptions to Theological Normativity', *Palgrave Communications*, 1, pp. 1–9, https://www.nature.com/articles/palcomms201524#citeas (accessed 04.09.2024).

Wigg-Stevenson, Natalie, 2017, '"You Don't Look Like a Baptist Minister": An Autoethnographic Retrieval of "Women's Experience" as an Analytic Category for Feminist Theology', *Feminist Theology*, 25(2), pp. 182–97.

Wigg-Stevenson, Natalie, 2018a, 'What's Really Going on: Ethnographic Theology and the Production of Theological Knowledge', *Cultural Studies ↔ Critical Methodologies*, 18(6), pp. 423–9.
Wigg-Stevenson, Natalie, 2018b, 'Trying to Tell the Truth About a Life: The Problem of Representation for Ethnographic Theology' in Jonas Ideström and Tone Stangeland Kaufman (eds), *What Really Matters: Scandinavian Perspectives on Ecclesiology and Ethnography*, Eugene, OR: Pickwick Publications, pp. 183–99.
Wigg-Stevenson, Natalie, 2021, *Transgressive Devotion: Theology as Performance Art*, London: SCM Press.
Wigg-Stevenson, Natalie, 2022, 'Luring the Divine: Affect, Esthetics, and Future Directions for Ethnographic Theology's Contribution to the Christian Traditions' in Pete Ward and Knut Tveitereid (eds), *The Wiley Blackwell Companion to Theology and Qualitative Research*, Oxford: Wiley-Blackwell, pp. 49–57.
Williams, Rowan, 2000, *On Christian Theology*, Oxford: Blackwell Publishing.
Woods, Patricia, 1992, 'The Festival Hymns of Peter Abelard: A Translation and Commentary of the "Hymnarius Paraclitensis Libellus II"', PhD thesis, University of Glasgow, https://theses.gla.ac.uk/74829/ (accessed 12.12.2024).
Woolf, Virginia, 1925, *Mrs Dalloway*, London: Hogarth Press.
Woolf, Virginia, 1931, *The Waves*, London: Hogarth Press.
Wulstan, David, 2003, 'Heloise at Argenteuil and the Paraclete' in Marc Stewart and David Wulstan (eds), *The Poetic and Musical Legacy of Heloise and Abelard*, Ottawa: The Institute of Mediaeval Music.
Wyman, Jason, 2017, *Constructing Constructive Theology: An Introductory Sketch*, Minneapolis, MN: Fortress Press.
Zaidi, Saiyyidah, 2023, 'Exploring the Expansion of British Practical Theology: An Enquiry using c/Critical i/Intersubjectivity, Conversation, and Autoethnography as a Methodological Approach', *Practical Theology*, 16(6), pp. 693–706.
Zaidi, Saiyyidah, and Stoddart, Eric, 2024, 'The Messy Art of Conversation in Practical Theology: Explorations and Reflections', *Practical Theology*, 17(4), pp. 282–94.

Other media

Callaghan, Karen, Marojevic, Leah and Kennedy, Samir, 2019, *Latent Commons* (video/performance), https://sam-w.com/work/latent-commons (accessed 05.06.2025).

Index of Names and Subjects

Abelard, Peter 168n1, 175–6, 178, 180
  and Heloise 169–72, 175–8
abstinence, experiential 74–6, 78–9
abstract knowledge 10, 102 *see also* theory
academic research 97, 128–9, 135
academy *see* International Academy of Practical Theology
accountability 13, 20, 74, 119
actants 14, 103
action research 44, 48, 76
Actor Network Theory (ANT) 13–14, 106
aesthetics 22, 26, 112–13, 119, 125, 128–30, 133–4, 136, 137n1
affectivity 78, 97, 104–7 105n10, 134
African
  knowledges and sacred practices 112
  people and spirituality 136
agency 14, 52, 56, 58, 79n8, 108, 110, 129, 142
agendas 16, 41, 44, 46, 104, 120
allegiances 3, 34, 162
allegory 89–91, 90n15
ambiguity 23, 57, 62, 91, 99, 131–3, 135, 166
ambivalence 24, 85–6, 90, 96n3, 132, 156
American Academy of Religion 44
Anderson, Linda 83n11
anger 109, 131
Anthropocene 7
anthropology 4, 8–9, 24, 38–9, 48–50, 52, 52n29, 53–4, 55, 57–8, 57n35, 59, 61, 69
  engagement with theology 50–4
anxiety 5, 7, 47, 52n29, 62, 185, 192

apocalypse 5, 6, 125
apophatism 153, 160, 166
appropriation 8, 85, 112–13
art 15, 67, 104, 109, 117, 127, 130–3, 135, 140, 150
artistic engagement 96, 100
artistic intervention 121–3, 128
artistic methods 32, 110n15, 123
artistic modes 95, 139
artistic practice 9, 28, 100, 102, 110, 112, 120, 143–4
arts-based methods 67, 97, 101, 108
arts-based research 32, 95, 96n2, 106, 108
arts-engaged research 97, 99, 101–3, 108, 110, 114
artworks 110, 124, 127
assemblage 14n6, 106, 151, 157–8, 165
attentiveness 5, 9, 20, 22, 83–4, 100–1, 110, 112
attunement 15, 22–3, 104–5, 107, 141
Auerbach, Eric 92n18
Augustine 82–3
austerity 77–9, 163
Australian life 111
authority 47, 57n35, 72, 76–7, 84, 115–16, 129, 161
autoethnography 32, 79n8, 102, 141
axiology 136

Banner, Michael 49, 55–6, 55n32, 55n33, 57n35, 58
Baptist Union 45, 76n7
Barad, Karen 12–14, 22, 188
Barnard, Marcel 125
Barth, Karl 43
Basaglia, Franco 105n10

Beaudoin, Tom 141n13
Behar, Ruth 71–2, 79, 84–6, 197
beliefs 43–4, 52n29, 61, 89
Bell, Charlotte 112, 136
Benjamin, Walter 158, 202
Bennett, Jane 13–14, 114
bias 21–2, 116
Bible 92n18, 172, 174
Bielo, James 52, 52n30, 57n35
binaries 17, 70, 98, 99
black church 81
black feminist thought 136–7
black theology 102
blood tie 56–7, 56n34
Bochner, Arthur 118
bodies 7, 32, 58, 63, 100–4, 106, 123, 131, 132, 145
Boisen, Anton 38
Bons-Storm, Riet 42
borrowed tools 41, 45–7, 49–50, 55, 62
Botticelli, Sandro 150
boundaries 3, 12, 17, 18, 22–3, 26, 28, 44–5, 53–4, 64, 79n8, 102, 131, 134, 191
Bourgeois, Louise 131–2
Brady, Ivan 102–3
Brearley, Laura 111
bricolage 25, 105, 151, 157–9, 160, 163–4, 166
brokenness 121–4, 126, 130–1, 151, 160–2
Brown, Richard 98
Browning, Don 15, 38, 41–2, 41n7, 46, 81, 82n10, 152
budgets 76, 162
Bunyan, John 83n11

Cameron, Helen 45, 76
Campbell-Reed, Eileen 83
capitalism 161, 163–4, 169, 187
Carvalhaes, Cláudio 137, 191
catastrophe 15, 134n9
categorization 21, 24, 24n4, 30–1, 104, 136
Catholicism 34, 40, 44, 50n25
causality 13, 135
Celan, Paul 132
Chalcedonian paradigm 46

challenges 1, 11, 16, 26, 34–5, 37, 44–7, 54, 70
change 35–6, 47, 55, 58, 63, 129
chaos 83, 86, 132, 138, 140, 153, 184
charity, acts of 53
child abuse 54
Childers, Sarah 33
childlessness 56 *see also* infertility
Chilton, Gioia 102, 108
Chopp, Rebecca 93
Christian anthropology 50
Christian art 150
Christian communities 43–4, 47, 63, 92n18
Christian distinctiveness 43
Christian interventions 38n1
Christian theology 58, 153
Christian traditions 149, 153, 167, 178
Christianity 52–4, 56, 64, 82, 137, 144, 165, 177
Christ's empty tomb 165
church, the 14, 43, 90–1, 92n18, 113n17, 156, 165
clay, encounters with 101, 141–4
Clifford, James 24, 89
climate activism 187–9
climate change 6, 7, 13, 27, 63, 121, 136n11, 138, 140, 141, 147, 188
climate fiction 139
closure 74, 141, 155
Coakley, Sarah 53–4, 53n31, 59
coherence 83, 86, 92–4, 115–16, 139, 155–6, 160, 166
co-living 17, 35, 64
collaboration 14, 52, 52n30
collage 105, 151, 157, 158
collegiality 1, 36, 44, 105n11, 145
colonial gaze 23, 27–8
colonialism 8, 23, 25, 51, 67, 70, 81–2, 85, 90, 90n15, 124, 163
colour, use of 35, 44, 79, 124, 132, 135, 189
commons 62–4 *see also* latent commons
communal expression 108, 110
communal life 14, 43, 89, 91
communication 101, 110, 147 *see also* stories

INDEX OF NAMES AND SUBJECTS

communities 4, 27–8, 63, 91, 103, 107, 109–10, 111, 172, 175, 180
  ecclesial 42–3
confession 57n35, 76
conflicts 33, 122
confusion, discovery within 6, 61, 85–6
congregational studies 27, 41, 81–2, 87–8
congregations 4, 41–3, 87n14, 88–90, 92
connections 6, 9, 14, 17, 23, 29, 31, 37, 104, 133, 134, 177–8, 179, 190, 191, 192
Connolly, William 114, 163–4
consciousness 3, 14, 118
constructive theology 16, 34, 53n31, 136, 152, 166, 191–2
contagion 104
contemporary anthropology 4, 57n35
contemporary theology 51, 130, 152
contemporary theory 1, 9, 14, 16, 45
contestation phase of research 26
contexts 14, 34–5, 38, 55, 57, 108, 145
continuity 12, 58
contributions 36, 50, 52, 102, 131, 145
conventions 8, 24, 73, 94, 138
convents 171, 174, 179
conversations 38–9, 38n1, 50, 53, 70–1, 118, 184, 192
conversion 58, 107
conviviality 6, 17, 35, 55
COP26 conference 147, 183–4, 183n1
Cornell, Joseph 127
correlation 15, 127, 173
correspondence 9, 59, 86, 116
cosmology 2, 186, 192
cosmos 133, 153
counterculture 43, 92n18, 192
counter-perspectives, descriptions of diverse cultures 89
Couture, Pamela 103
craft pottery 141–4, 142n14
creation 153
creative arts 15, 156
creative borrowing 159
creative non-fiction 26, 102, 106

creative practice 123, 142–4, 166, 168n1, 186
creative theology 121, 177, 191
creative turn 96, 157
creativity 46, 107, 114, 163–4
credibility, academic 75n5, 76–7
credible, power of the 138
crip theology 102
crisis 34, 37, 54, 105, 121, 126, 130, 144, 184, 193
crisis of representation 18, 25–7, 70, 80
critical distance 71–2, 76
critical theory 51, 136
cross, power of the 130
crystallization 117, 117n24
Csikszentmihalyi, Mihalyi 113
cultural
  appropriation 112–13
  change 54, 58, 86
  diversity 89
  expression 113
  forms 13, 15
  imagination 83n11, 128
  theory 67, 122
  understandings 23, 55
  wisdom, focus on 97
Cushman, Dick 74

d'Argenteuil, Heloise see Heloise
data 7, 9, 17, 20, 26, 31, 71, 98, 106
de Certeau, Michel 50, 160–5
de Freitas, Elizabeth 12
death 124–5
death of God movement 153, 155
decision-making, ensuring influence of research 116
decolonial theology 102, 137
decolonial theory 4
deep listening 110–12
Deleuze, Gilles 11–12, 14–15, 155
Denzin, Norman 25–7, 30–1, 119, 135
dereliction 122–4, 126, 165
Derrida, Jacques 159
dialogue 38–40, 49–51, 52n30, 59, 61, 99, 109, 119, 136, 191
diaspora 112
difference 17, 33–4, 46, 52n30, 56, 61, 63–4, 89, 91, 98, 145, 165

Dillard, Cynthia 112, 136
disaster 15, 31, 63, 121, 126, 134, 153, 163, 184
discipline 33, 34, 42, 44n12, 46, 50, 54, 74, 89, 137, 141, 162, 192
disciplines 10, 11, 25, 38–9, 39n3, 46, 49–50, 51, 53, 55, 61–2, 64, 143, 145, 161
discomfort 33, 58, 101, 162
discordant elements 78
discourses 10, 14, 19, 22–3, 35, 37, 59, 69–70, 72, 72n2, 78–9, 94, 102, 136–7, 141, 159
discovery 9, 80, 108
discursiveness 72–3, 82, 94, 108
disruption 15, 78, 94, 128, 137, 139
distinction/distinctiveness 12–15, 17, 26–7, 43, 45, 53, 62, 87n14, 92n18, 98–9, 133, 145, 156, 159, 192
divergence 47, 51, 96n3
diversity 1, 17, 26, 30, 44–5, 64, 113
divisions 73n3, 75n5, 88, 129, 137, 145
doctrine 16, 34, 43–4, 46, 53–4, 91, 92n18
dogmatic theology 34, 49
dominant/white
  epistemological tools theory 112
  groups 35, 107n12
  voyeurism 113
Douglas, Mary 50
dreams 137
Driscoll, Christopher 74
Duns Scotus 166

Easter 149, 167
Eastern Churches 153
ecclesiology 44–5, 64, 92, 92n18, 101, 156
echo-chamber, working in 48
ecological issues 5, 6, 26, 129, 132–4, 154, 164
ecology 10, 14, 20, 71
economics 4n2, 13, 38, 169
Einstein, Albert 15, 133
elites, theology 59
Ellingson, Laura 32, 71
embodied
  ecclesiology 101
  humans 14, 57

manifestation 32
practices 53
research 32
responsiveness 100–3, 110
wisdom, need for 143–4
embodiment 17, 26, 70, 90–1, 97, 99–103, 173
emergence 4, 5, 13, 15, 37, 47, 105
Emin, Tracy 151
emotion 32, 62, 72, 84.103, 106, 110n14, 118, 131, 134, 148
empirical theology 19, 40, 41n6, 42, 42n9, 44, 75
empirical turn 1, 3, 4, 38, 40, 42, 129
empiricism 3, 18–21, 33–4, 41–3, 46, 49, 95, 145
encounters 4–6, 8, 38, 49–50, 61, 64, 78–82, 107, 111–12, 132–3, 141–3, 147, 150–2, 169
endarkened feminism 112, 112n16, 136
engagement 38, 38n1, 51–3, 64, 95–6, 109, 128, 136, 141, 144
entanglement 5–6, 12–13, 54, 61, 63–4, 67, 147, 153–4, 159, 173–4, 192
entities 13, 14, 19, 103, 132–4
entry, feature of ethnographic writing 81–2
environment 2, 11, 37, 61, 63, 129, 132–4, 137, 153
epiphany 132, 135, 140, 152
epistemology 10, 13, 15–17, 20, 28–9, 31, 61, 74, 95, 96, 102, 107, 110, 136–7, 137n12
epochs 4, 15
eschatological theologies 58
ethics 22, 49, 56, 58–9, 118, 133
ethnicity 27, 113
ethnographic theology 47, 90
ethnography 1, 4–5, 7–8, 17, 23–8, 42, 47–50, 50n25, 55n32, 57n35, 61, 67, 69–70, 79–90, 94, 106–7, 119
Eucharist 125
Europe 40, 42, 80
evaluation 28, 72n2, 115–16, 116n22, 137, 140, 143
Evans, Alice 87–8
Evans, Robert 87–8

INDEX OF NAMES AND SUBJECTS

Evans-Pritchard, E. E. 50
everyday life 41–2, 53, 102, 104, 109–10, 139, 140, 166
everyday practice 34, 44, 54
evidence 3, 19, 34, 72, 75–7
existence 9, 20, 132, 161–2, 193
experiences 1, 8, 20, 93, 109–10, 141, 149
experiential abstinence 74–6, 78–9
experimentation 26, 33–5, 38, 48, 79n8, 129, 147
exploration 52n30, 62, 72, 76, 80, 108, 132, 147, 161, 171
expression 10–11, 20, 28–30, 108, 109–10, 113, 114, 132, 188

faith 16, 19, 27, 36, 40, 42, 44–5, 47, 64, 64n38, 84, 89, 106, 124, 129, 181, 184
faith communities 42, 91, 113, 156
familiarity and strangeness 133
fault lines 33, 35, 162
Fear of the Brown Envelopes 109–10, 110n14
feminism 4, 24, 112, 112n16, 136–7
feminist research 33, 83–4, 136–7
feminist theologies 33, 38, 38n1, 42, 102, 173, 181
fiction 22, 86, 126, 139 *see also* realist fiction
film 123–5
Finley, Susan 108
first-person narratives 24, 80
flow 104, 113–14, 113n18, 137
fluidity, need for 1
fold, the 11–12
Foster, Victoria 114
Fountain, Philip 51
fragility 5, 61, 90–1, 163–4, 166
fragments 92n18, 105n10, 127, 143, 151, 157–9
frameworks 3n1, 16, 23, 74, 83, 96n1, 104, 112n16, 116, 119, 137, 166, 193
Francis, Leslie 40
Franciscan tradition 166
Frei, Hans 43, 92
funding 42, 76–7, 116, 116n23
fungal life 5, 7, 192

threads 139
future relationships 193

Geertz, Clifford 42–3, 53, 70
gender 33, 54, 131, 152
genealogies 43, 45, 50, 82, 105
generalizations 13–14, 34, 117
generativity 45, 63, 71, 91, 113, 117, 135, 138, 139
genres 24, 25, 55n32, 57, 57n35, 71–2, 75, 80, 86–7, 91, 93, 117n24, 148
Ghosh, Amitav 137–40, 188
Gibbs, Leah 101, 106
gift giving 50, 55, 59–60, 62
Glazier, Jonathan 123
Glissant, Édouard 64–5
global injustices 11
God 37, 58, 62, 84, 91, 93, 130, 139, 153, 155, 161, 166, 180, 181
good life 118, 123
Good Samaritan Church 91
Goto, Courtney 21, 27–9, 113–14, 113n17
Graham, Elaine 38, 64, 76, 76n7, 139
grid of conventions 138
grief 56, 139, 141, 164, 174, 178–9
Grigor, Murray 124–6
grounded theory analyses 32
Guattari, Félix 14
Guba, Egon 116n22, 136
Guernica (Pablo Picasso) 151, 157
guidelines for research 31–2

Hamm, Treahna 111
Hammersley, Martyn 74, 76
Hand, Brian 109
Haraway, Donna 6
Hauerwas, Stanley 43, 45, 92n18
healing methodologies 112, 112n16, 136
heaven 179–80
Heloise
and Abelard 169–70, 171–2, 175–8
as a composer 178–9
cruelty of religion 180–1
establishment of a new community 175
exploration of insights 147
her life in a period of turmoil 171

incarceration 174-5
  a play about 168-9
  practical leadership 176
  theological questions 172-3
Heloise and Abelard *see* Abelard, Peter; Heloise
hermeneutics 25, 92, 145, 161, 172, 174
hero stories 48-9, 54, 83n11
heurism 8n5, 40, 54, 61n37, 99, 166
hierarchy 24, 28, 34
Hiltner, Seward 15, 38
historical conversations 38n1
histories, entanglement with 13
holism 20, 78, 110
Holocaust 93, 123
holy week 149-50, 160, 166
homiletics 124, 145
Hopewell, James 90-1
hostility 135
humanity 14, 17, 55, 61, 123, 139
humans 5, 6, 9, 14, 17, 24, 52, 55, 89, 125, 129, 132-3, 163-4, 192
humour 109, 131-2, 135, 169, 173, 182
Hustvedt, Siri 131-2
hyper-reflexivity 28-9

identity 3, 3n1, 7, 12, 22-3, 42-4, 53, 56-7, 63, 75, 89, 93, 131n5, 133n8
ideology 56, 74, 77
Ideström, Jonas 106
ignorance 82, 140
images of diversity 11-16
imaginaries 24, 192
imagination 8, 12, 19, 62, 79, 96, 102, 104, 109, 128, 137, 161, 188
immorality 174
impartiality 19, 24, 98
impractical theology 49
inanimate beings 14, 103, 133
inclusive agenda 44
indigenous people 26, 107, 110-12, 136-7, 163
individuation 12
infertility 56-7, 173-4
Ingold, Tim 4, 8-9, 62, 85, 145, 206
injustice 11, 17, 30, 108
inquiry 7, 9, 16-17, 25-7, 29, 31, 108, 115, 117n24, 118, 136

insights 32, 34, 50-1, 54-5, 75, 78-9, 103, 108
integrity 24, 171, 173-4
interconnectedness 5, 13, 192
interdisciplinary aspects 2, 17, 38-9, 54, 55, 61-2, 69
interior assent 52n29
International Academy of Practical Theology 3, 28, 30, 34, 42, 42n9, 116, 117, 121, 135, 139, 147, 161-2
international conversation 42
interpretation 20, 26, 30, 32, 73, 76, 92, 95, 98, 119, 150
intervention 10, 29, 38n1, 70, 73n5, 75n5, 77, 110, 119, 121-3, 128, 175
intra-action 13, 20
intraconnections 16
intradisciplinary aspects 41, 54, 63, 192
invisible lines 86, 104
Italy 105

Jardine, Alice 51n28
Jarman, Derek 127-8
Jesuit practice 161, 166
Jones, David 166
journal extracts 147-8, 185
journey 48, 79, 83-5, 83n11, 149, 161, 165, 191
joy 6, 84n12, 91, 113-14, 150, 163, 182, 187
judgement 3, 22, 47, 55, 58, 77, 90, 109, 114-15
justice 1, 4n2, 9, 26, 27, 36, 108, 118

Kay, Peter 40
Keller, Catherine 13, 16, 152-4, 156, 188, 203
Kierkegaard, Søren 131n5
Kingdom of darkness 139-40
Kirmayer, Laurence 93
knowing 13, 24, 28, 61, 62, 74, 97, 107, 111-12, 117, 137, 162
knowledge 7-8, 10, 13, 57, 74, 96n1, 102, 108, 110, 116-17, 126, 137, 142-4, 173
Koori people 111

INDEX OF NAMES AND SUBJECTS

Laing, Olivia 126–8
landscapes 4–7, 9–10, 14, 35, 61, 71, 101, 126, 135
language 24, 115, 132
Last Supper (Salvador Dali) 152
latent commons 5, 6, 61, 61n37, 63–4, 121, 192
Lather, Patti 33, 35–6
Latin America 163
Latour, Bruno 13–15, 50, 62–3, 106, 193
Laurel Schneider 16, 203
Law, John 87
Leach, Bernard 142–3, 142n14
learning 6, 62, 107, 112, 175
Leavy, Patricia 102, 108
Lefebvre, Henri 139–40
legitimacy 26, 47, 72n2, 142
Leibniz, Gottfried 11–12
Lemons, Derrick 50
Lévi-Strauss, Claude 158–9
liberation 84, 101, 108, 136
liberation theology 4n2, 38, 38n1, 153, 181
Lincoln, Yvonna 25–7, 31, 116, 135–6
Lindbeck, George 43, 92, 192
lingua franca 76–7
listening 8, 57, 84, 110–12
literary forms 79–82, 86–7, 91–3, 138
literature 19, 35, 48, 83, 87, 184
liturgy 96n2, 124–5, 157, 168n1, 178, 179, 184
lived
 beliefs, Christianity 52
 experiences 20, 53, 108n13, 129–30
 practice 92
 religion 53–4
local, use of term 113, 113n17
local practical theological aesthetics (LPTA) 113
locations, gendered 26
logical priority 46–7
Lovelace, Richard 14

MacIntyre, Alasdair 43
Madonna and Singing Angels (Sandro Botticelli) 150
magical thinking 107
magisterial theology 34, 47

making 104–5
makings 147, 155
manifold beings 129, 135
Marcus, George 74
marginalization 30, 85, 108–9, 160
Marx, Karl, influence on de Certeau 161
materialism 13–14, 132n6, 142–3, 163, 192–3
material/s 34–5, 58n36, 71, 100, 102, 154–5, 158–9, 163–5, 173, 185
matter 12–13
Matthews, Daniel 128–9
McClintock Fulkerson, Mary 81–2, 90–1
McFague, Sallie 164
McKibben, Bill 184–5
melancholy 126
Meland, Bernard 19
memories 105, 131
men, challenging their conventions 24
mental health 29, 108
Merz, Johannes 61
Merz, Sharon 61
Messenger, Annette 131
metaphors 16, 27, 55, 72, 192
methodological approaches 2, 32–3, 74–5, 116–17
methodological tools 39–42
methodologies 1, 9, 25, 27, 31, 35, 37, 47–8, 67
methods, methodless 105
micro level aspects 9, 12, 96
migrants, stories 127–8
Milbank, John 59
Miller, Monica 74
Miller-McLemore, Bonnie 38, 46, 141, 143–4, 157n1, 203, 209
ministry 143–5
minoritized people 27, 113n17
misrepresentation 21–2, 97
missional
 engagement, and qualitative research 44
 imperative 192
 initiatives 140
 practice 77
mixed-method approach 32, 117
models 24, 30, 38–40, 64, 67, 90, 101, 120, 155, 166

modernist phase of research 25
modernity 126, 129
modes 2, 54, 57, 62, 70, 72–6, 77–8, 86–7, 107, 113, 129, 134, 145
moments in qualitative research 25–7
monadological thinking 11–12
moral aspects 26, 90, 119, 120
moral theology 49, 55, 197
Morse, Janice 115
Morton, Timothy 132–3, 132n6, 134n9, 135
motifs 83n11, 86
movements 4, 4n2, 19, 25, 32, 40–2, 44, 53, 99, 109, 161, 164
multi-species mixing 5, 61
multiverse 154
Murray, Simon 122, 126
musical theology 157
Muslim scholars 64
mystical theology 132
mysticism 83, 153, 155, 165, 188
myths 60, 67, 71n2, 72, 83n11, 92n18, 139, 158, 159, 159n3

naïve scientific model 78
narratives 11, 32–3, 38, 43, 59, 72, 77, 80–2, 83n11, 84–5, 87–9, 91–3, 92n18, 93n19, 109, 118, 125, 153, 188
narrator role 73, 79, 80, 86, 88
networks 13–14, 31, 44, 57, 76, 92, 103–4, 106, 190
neutrality 7, 26
new research methods 30, 34–6, 40, 95
New Testament writings 125
new theology 54, 141, 155, 186
Newtonian
 imaginary 133
 mode 134
Nicholas of Cusa 188
Niebuhr, Reinhold 38
Nordstrom, Susan 105
normalizing of realist stories 93
normativity 34, 40, 42, 47, 47n19, 78–9, 90, 129, 141n13
norms 47, 52, 52n29, 71, 89, 138
North America 4

Object Oriented Ontology (OOO) 132, 132n6
objectification 80, 85, 89, 109
objectivity 3, 7, 25, 74, 79–80, 89
objects 13, 103, 105, 106, 127, 141–4, 151
observation 13, 15, 17, 19–20, 24, 57n35, 72, 73–4
O'Donnell, Karen 141
O'Donnell Gandolfo, Elizabeth 62
older people 108, 185
ontological
 inseparability 13
 penumbra 61–2
 turn 51–2
ontologies 1, 8–9, 11, 15, 16, 31, 52
openness 1, 10, 55, 62
oppression 23, 26, 28, 52–4, 64, 89, 108–9, 136, 161
order 16, 46, 78, 128
Orye, Leive 62
othering 3n1, 23, 81n9
outcomes 14, 30, 31, 32, 58n36, 59, 76, 76n6, 97, 110n15, 117, 129

painting 15, 150–1
Papailias, Penelope 70
Paraclete 175, 178–80
paradigms 14, 25, 31–2, 35, 46, 58, 97, 115–17, 136, 143, 154, 160
participants 8n4, 20, 24, 26, 27, 28, 48, 52, 82, 109, 116, 118
participatory
 approach to research 34, 76
 inclusiveness 149
 research into women in ministry 45
particles 12, 188, 192
past, danger of looking back 50
pastoral
 practices 143, 156
 theology 40, 46
path-making 50n26, 61–2, 93, 96n2, 102, 106, 124n2, 133n7, 143
pathways 17, 57, 137
Pattison, Stephen 72, 99
Pearl, Monica 104
pedagogical practice 28, 89
peers, addressing 147
Pentecost 156
people of colour 26, 30

INDEX OF NAMES AND SUBJECTS

perception 9–10, 128, 129
performance 28, 32, 43, 48, 61, 82, 86, 99, 106, 122, 124, 129–30, 147, 188
performatism 43, 70, 77, 119, 122, 124
personhood 58, 60
perspectives 4n2, 10, 11, 20, 37–8, 57, 62, 63, 64, 78, 107, 157, 157n1
pessimism 163
phenomena 10, 13, 16, 20, 72n2, 78, 104, 140–1
phenomenology 20, 25, 99–100
philosophy 37, 41, 51, 55, 57, 117, 128, 136, 192
physics 12, 153
Picasso, Pablo 151
piety 171, 180
pilgrimage 83, 85, 149
Pilgrim's Progress (John Bunyan) 83, 85
Pillow, Wanda 21
pistological conversion 107
Places of Redemption (Mary McLintock Fulkerson) 27, 81, 82n9, 90, 91
planet, the 6, 9, 31, 112, 133–4, 138
pluriverse 153
poesis 104–6, 152, 156, 160
poetics 27, 45, 67, 69–71, 87, 93–4, 107, 132, 147, 157, 166
poetry 15, 28, 166
policy-makers, appealing to 76
politics 13, 24, 71, 162–4
populist politics, threats of 31
positionality 22, 76
positivism 19, 22, 25, 30, 32, 117
postcolonialism 23
postliberal theology 43, 45, 53, 92–3
postmodern thinking 26, 43, 107, 117n24
post-qualitative research 105
postsecular anthropology 62
poststructuralism 23, 32, 32n7, 51n27, 159
poverty 109
power 7, 18, 20, 21, 23, 24, 27–8, 95, 109, 125, 130, 134, 138, 139, 150, 152
practice 26, 44, 47, 52, 89, 161

pragmatism 32–3, 47, 77, 116
prayer 37, 53, 83–4, 170, 182, 193
preconceptions 4, 31
pregnancy loss 141
presidential address 147, 147n1
privilege 18, 21, 26, 27, 28n6, 29, 81
process theology 155
processes 11–12, 19, 21, 24, 41, 63, 64, 71, 109, 115, 142, 147
professional advancement 77 *see also* funding
Project Violet 45, 76n7
Protestant model 52n29
Pryor, Rebekah 102
psychology 4n2, 38, 38n1, 41, 46, 55, 103
public policy, Christian approaches 4n2, 38n1
public theology 38, 38n1

qualitative inquiry 17, 25, 115
qualitative research 1, 4–5, 7–9, 16, 17, 19–23, 25–7, 30–3, 37, 44–9, 63, 69–71, 73–6, 83, 85, 97–8, 105, 114–16, 116n22, 135–6
quantitative research 4, 17, 26–7, 31, 33, 42, 73, 75, 115, 116
quantum thinking 12–13, 15, 154
queer aspects 44, 56, 102, 133n8

race 26, 99
racism 24, 54, 89
Radford, Wren 95–6, 96n2, 96n3, 106, 109, 110n14
radical theology 166, 170, 180
Rahner, Karl 40
Rambo, Shelly 86, 93, 191
Rancière, Jacques 128, 130
Rauschenberg, Robert 127
Rawlins, William, K. 75
readers 28–9, 79–80, 118
realignments 31, 128
realism 55n32, 87, 91–2, 93
realist fiction 86–8, 91–2
rearrangement 127–30
reason 19
reciprocity 50, 55
re-cognition 139–41
recognition, academic 33–4
reconciliation 16, 180–1, 188

redemption 83-6, 84, 91, 137
re-evaluations 137, 143
reflection 38-9, 38n1, 44n15, 51, 56, 58-9, 61, 90, 94, 111, 127, 131n5, 132, 156, 160 see also theological reflection
reflexivity 1, 9, 20-3, 26, 28-9, 59, 62, 76, 79n8, 82, 116, 119
relatedness 31
relational ontologies 1, 11, 16, 17, 30, 37, 71, 103
relational theology 188
relational turn 16-17, 19-20, 22, 33
relationality 1, 11-13, 15-17, 20, 26, 30, 32-3, 36, 37, 63-4, 103-4, 106, 129, 153, 188
relationships 14, 28, 33, 48-9, 56, 62, 82, 104, 111, 145
  Heloise and Abelard 169-70, 179
reliability 24, 34, 73-4, 115
religion 4, 10, 38, 40, 41, 52, 132, 136, 145, 172-3, 181-2
religious turn 50-1, 51n28
reparative reshaping 126-7, 128
representation 21-2, 23-7, 28, 33, 35, 70, 89, 138
reproductive loss 108
research 20, 24, 25-8, 30-2, 36, 41, 44, 70, 71, 73, 74, 76, 76n7, 79n8, 81, 84, 84n12, 85, 86, 96, 102, 105, 105n10, 106, 108, 110, 111-12, 115, 118-19, 120, 128, 136, 145, 193
research excellence 1, 31, 95, 104, 118-20
research funding 33, 116
research methods 2-4, 9, 25, 26, 30-2, 34, 45, 48, 97n4, 102, 193 see also arts-based methods
research processes 20-3, 25, 41, 42, 71, 100
research projects 30, 41, 71, 116 see also arts-engaged research
research tools 45-8, 95
researchers 9, 10, 16-17, 20, 21-3, 24, 27-8, 30, 33, 75n5, 85-6, 100, 118
resilience 5, 6, 36, 184, 192
resistance 114, 114n20, 119, 131, 163

resonance 16, 104-5, 107, 145
responsibility 13, 19, 74, 155, 180, 191
responsiveness 67, 96-7, 96n3, 99, 101-4, 110, 112, 145
revelation 16, 21, 43, 62, 82, 100-1, 113, 113n18, 132, 138, 140, 150-2, 156, 193
revising practices 17
Richardson, Laurel 117n24
Ricoeur, Paul 87
Riggs, Nicholas 118
rigour 25, 67, 78, 114-17
Riley, Cole Arthur 102
rituals 29, 53, 73, 124, 144, 163
Robbins, Joel 49, 50n25, 55, 55n32, 58-9
ruination 5, 122-4, 165
rupturing 89, 141
rush of stories 7

sacred 26, 45, 61, 69, 96n2, 110, 112, 135-6, 139, 181, 184, 188, 190, 193
Saint Paul 51
Scharen, Christian 83, 103
Schmitt, Carl 51
Schneider, Laurel 16
science 12, 15, 19, 31, 37, 153
scientific writing 72-9, 73n2, 75n5
scientism 72, 76, 94
Scripture 16, 91, 92n18, 124-5, 139, 156
Sebald, W. G. 126
secular thought 3, 26, 45, 48, 50, 61, 69, 84, 92n18, 136, 171
Sedgwick, Eve 126-7
seeing 27-8, 63, 94, 96n3
self-determination 26
self-expression 28, 108, 113
selfhood 83, 129, 161
self-recognition 128
self-reflexivity 22, 28
semantic plurality 132
semblance 87-8
senses 6-7, 101-2, 106-7, 123
separation 12, 20, 63, 129, 192
sex 100, 114, 170-2
sexual images 100n8
sexuality 54, 173

INDEX OF NAMES AND SUBJECTS

shaping, ability of marginalized groups 160
shared symbolic system, theory as 11
Sheldrake, Philip 165
shifts 10, 35, 36, 91, 108
silence 132, 189
Slee, Nicola 45, 83–4, 84n12
Smartt Gullion, Jessica 11, 16
Smith, Christopher 128–9
Smith, Kiki 131
social
  challenges, response to 1
  change 27, 119
  disintegration 122
  inquiry 7, 16
  justice 27, 108, 118
  movements 164
social research 1–2, 9, 19, 25, 26, 30–1, 34, 38, 69, 99, 101, 104, 106
social sciences 3–4, 8, 9, 11, 13–14, 15, 29, 38, 38n1, 40–1, 43, 46–7, 50, 61, 73
social theory 4n2, 38, 38n1, 51
social/cultural aspects 11, 43, 72
sociology 1, 4, 38, 69
solidarity 2, 27, 33, 36, 109
somaphobia 100
Sotirin, Patty 71
space 28, 62, 110–11, 122, 161, 191, 192
speculative fiction 139
spiritual practice 83, 137n12
spirituality 5, 10, 16, 26, 45, 56, 82–3, 86, 90–1, 107, 135–9, 136n11, 151, 154
St Peter's seminary 124, 125
St. Pierre, Elizabeth 11, 19, 32n7, 105
staging 122–5, 130
stakeholders, appealing to 76–7, 116
Stangeland Kaufman, Tone 106
stereotyping 108
stories 2, 7, 39–40, 48–9, 60, 80–2, 83n11, 84, 85, 89, 92, 92n18, 109, 127–8, 188
strange season 149
strangeness 132–3, 135, 137
structures 13–14, 21, 106, 109, 123, 125, 129–31, 147
subjectivity 74, 80, 118, 131, 132
subjunctive, and art 134–5

sublime, the 138–40
sweetness 114, 164, 166, 178, 180, 182
Swinton, John 45–6
symbols 11, 15–16, 24, 50, 59, 72, 98, 100, 110n14, 125, 129, 151, 163, 165, 187, 191, 192
systematic theology 38, 41, 46, 49, 53n31, 54, 143, 159, 191–2

tacit knowledge 143
tactics 161
tangled lines 86
Tanner, Katherine 34–5
TARN *see* Theological Action Research Network (TARN)
tension 62, 80, 85–6
territories 10, 33, 50, 51n27, 53, 61, 64, 80, 83n11, 114, 135, 141
terror, climate emergency 7, 134
The Letters and Associated Documents of Heloise and Abelard (Mary Martin McLaughlin) 168n1
theologians of colour 137
Theological Action Research Network (TARN) 44, 76–7
theological allegiance, type of research practice 34
theological reflection 4, 16, 19, 21, 40–2, 46, 53, 54, 86, 93, 103, 124, 139, 141, 144, 158, 191
theological work 43, 121, 140, 181, 191
theopoesis 154
theopoetics 16, 147n1, 150, 152–8, 160–2, 164, 166
theoretical aspects 1, 9–10, 14, 37, 51n27, 52
theoretical turn 11, 16
theory 10–11, 15, 32, 50–1, 139, 155, 190
theosis 166
thick descriptions 42
thinking, reorienting 32n7
Tillich, Paul 15–16, 38, 150–1, 205
Tracey, David 15
tradition 25, 67, 110–12, 145
tragedy 19, 139, 164, 166
transcendence 16, 153, 193
transformation 8, 16, 36, 37, 42, 50,

53, 63, 77, 82, 108, 119, 131, 147, 191
trauma 93, 93n19, 99, 165
trauma theology 102
travel writing 80, 82, 86
trials 81–2, 83n11, 177
triangulation 116–17
Trivelli, Elena 105
tropes 24, 67, 77, 79, 81, 81n9, 85, 87, 107
troubled times 54, 57, 67, 85, 93, 144, 192
trust, qualitative research 116
truth 15, 43, 57, 134
Tsing, Anna 1, 4–9, 24–5, 60–1, 64, 85, 192
Turner, Edith 50
Turner Victor 50
Turpin, Katherine 21, 23, 29, 124
typologies 31, 38

uncertainty 7, 10, 62, 64, 78, 122, 133–5
understandings 3n1, 5, 9–11, 13–16, 18, 23–4, 54–5, 57n35, 58, 67, 71, 85, 108–9, 112, 129, 140, 141, 147, 151, 188
unfamiliar 51, 59, 79, 93
unfoldings 12, 89
unheimlich 85, 133, 158
United States of America 19, 38, 38n1, 41, 41n6
universe 12, 14–15, 72, 133–4, 159, 179, 185, 188
unknowing 154

validation 22, 25, 73, 97
validity 3, 9, 19–20, 22, 25–6, 117
van der Ven, Johannes 3, 19, 40, 46, 50
van Deusen Hunsinger, Deborah 46
van Maanen, John 73, 80
van Ruusbroec, Jan 165
Vigen, Aana Marie 103

vitality 19, 46, 92, 114
vocation 67, 78, 95–6, 147, 161, 165, 170, 175–7, 181–2
voices 29, 32, 80, 84, 106

Ward, Pete 43, 46, 63
ways of knowing 94, 107, 111–12
ways of life 43, 61, 87, 90, 176
weather events 140
West, the 52, 85, 90, 138
Western liberal humanism 89
what and why 115
white issues 21–2, 23–5, 29, 82, 107, 112, 124, 190
Whitehead, Alfred North 153
Whitmore, Todd 83, 106–7, 141
Wigg-Stevenson, Natalie 3, 45, 47, 90, 106, 130
wild, the 138–9
William Blake 85n13
Williams, Raymond 122
Williams, Rowan 10, 78–9
wisdom 34, 43, 54, 58–60, 84–5, 97, 110–12, 125, 135, 137, 137n12, 143–4, 157, 179, 188
witnesses 28, 102
Wolfteich, Claire 135, 157
women 24, 44–5, 56–7, 76n17, 83, 105n10, 131, 169 *see also* Heloise
world, the 11, 15, 30, 37, 58, 61, 86, 87, 99, 110, 128, 164, 192–3
worldly church 90–1
worlds, taking the reader into 79–80
worldviews 9, 33, 37, 45, 51, 70, 90, 96
worship 173, 179
wreckage 122–6
writing 24, 26, 28, 29, 69, 70–1, 73, 76–7, 76n6, 79n8, 94, 106, 147–8, 163, 168–70, 184
Wyman, Jason 34

Yale University 43–4, 91–2
yarning 111–12

www.ingramcontent.com/pod-product-compliance
Lightning Source LLC
Chambersburg PA
CBHW032336300426
44109CB00041B/1059